EIDOS | Studies in Classical Kinds

Thomas G. Rosenmeyer, General Editor

The Idea of EPIC

The Idea of
EPIC

J. B. Hainsworth

University of California Press

Berkeley • Los Angeles • Oxford

University of California Press
Berkeley and Los Angeles, California

University of California Press, Ltd.
Oxford, England

© 1991 by
The Regents of the University of California

Library of Congress Cataloging-in-Publication Data
Hainsworth, J. B. (John Bryan)
    The idea of epic / J.B. Hainsworth.
        p.   cm.—(Eidos)
    Includes bibliographical references.
    ISBN 0-520-06814-9 (alk. paper)
    1. Epic poetry, Classical—History and criticism. I. Title.
II. Series: Eidos (University of California Press)
PA3022.E6H25 1991
883'.0109—dc20   90-10956
                                                                                    CIP

Printed in the United States of America

1   2   3   4   5   6   7   8   9

The paper used in this publication meets the minimum requirements of
American National Standard for Information Sciences—Permanence of
Paper for Printed Library Materials, ANSI Z39.48–1984. ⊚™

Contents

Preface

The exciting turmoils of three decades of revolution in criticism have left the classic texts much as they were: the canonical exemplars that continue to organize our Western concepts of literature. The idea of a literary form presupposes such exemplars, and for that reason for students of the literatures inspired by Graeco-Roman culture the exemplars continue to be worth examining. Of no genre is this truer than of the epic. Whatever else it may be—and to be successful it must be something besides—an epic has a certain form. To ask why a lyric poet sings may seem a silly question, but to ask why an epic poet chose to express his thought in thousands of verses is to pose a question that can only be answered from literary history. In these pages I have tried to describe the aspects of the classical epic that seemed to me to shape the literary thought of modern exponents of the genre. To read *Paradise Lost* is to realize how self-conscious epic poetry is. There is no epic poem that does not confront its predecessors; the themes that recur in the epic—heroism, the nation, the faith—are evolving ideas; and the idea itself is cumulative, though to the end the Homeric foundation was never obscured. I have begun, therefore, at the beginning; Homer, Virgil, and Lucan are, naturally, the foci of attention, but other figures held in less regard deserve and have been given consideration. What their modern successors made of the Homeric and Virgilian legacy is the subject of another book, and for a scholar with a greater expertise than mine. It is no more than hinted at here. Nor can I do more than speculate why the genre died.

The reading of the great epics is a lesson in humility, in the face of their critics as well as the poets. The ideas of many colleagues are acknowledged in the notes; many others, such is the corpus of current scholarship, are unacknowledged since, I hope, they have become part of common thinking. This is especially true where valuable criticism is published in languages other than English or may otherwise be inaccessible to many students. I have been greatly assisted by the officers and referees of the University of California Press, especially where I had written *urbi* rather than *orbi;* and I owe particular thanks to Professor Thomas G. Rosenmeyer of the University of California, Berkeley. These are not easy times for classical studies in British universities, and its devotees have had to shoulder extra burdens and spend to their distraction much effort in the arena of politics. Professor Rosenmeyer's editorial patience has been inexhaustible. He changed my estimate of Apollonius, he read several drafts, and his ever-helpful advice and readiness to exchange ideas have been a great encouragement to me. Where my chapters fall short of his standards, the fault, I need not say, is mine.

Oxford   J. B. H.
October 1989

I

What Is an Epic?

> There is nothing in nature more irksome than
> general discourses, especially when they turn
> chiefly upon words.
>
> Addison

A limerick, it may be said, is defined by its form, a satire by its
spirit, a serenade by its content, a dirge by its occasion. But how are
we to define an epic? Consider these statements by Aristotle, Tasso,
and C. M. Bowra:

> As for the art of representation which is narrative and in
> metre... there must be the same varieties of epic as of tragedy
> ... and the constituent parts (with the exception of song and
> spectacle) must be the same.... Epic differs from tragedy in the
> length of the composition and in metre.
>
> A heroic poem (that is, an epic) is an imitation of noble action,
> great and perfect, narrated in the loftiest verse, with the aim of
> giving profit through delight.
>
> An epic poem is by common consent a narrative of some length
> and deals with events which have a certain grandeur and impor-
> tance and come from a life of action, especially violent action
> such as war. It gives a special pleasure because its events and
> persons enhance our belief in the worth of human achievement
> and in the dignity and nobility of man.[1]

Aristotle fixed on the form of epic—narrative not dramatic form—

1

because he wanted to distinguish it from what he thought was a near relation, tragedy; Tasso on the moral purpose because he feared confusion with romance; Bowra on the content and spirit lest we should admire the many kinds of primitive song—stories of shamans, culture heroes, magicians, and gods—and call them all epics. Aristotle's comparison of epic and tragedy served him also to distinguish epic poetry from history: poetry universalizes, history concerns itself with particulars. A versified chronicle therefore was not an epic poem. These are not negligible distinctions, and we should bear them in mind; it is the affirmative parts of the definitions that cause unease. What is all this about representation and imitation, profit and special pleasure? Are we not being bullied with theoretical abstractions? And the real literary bullies in this field, men like Scaliger, Le Bossu, and Addison himself, are more irksome than the clear-thinking philosopher, sensitive poet, and broad-minded scholar. Le Bossu forbade the action of an epic poem to take place in winter, because he could find no precedent for that season. The trouble is that generalizations are made from particular poems. Aristotle defined epic in terms of the *Iliad*, Tasso in terms of the *Aeneid*, and Bowra in terms of the poems examined in his *Heroic Poetry* (London, 1952), especially the Homeric epics, the Anglo-Saxon *Beowulf*, the Old French *Chanson de Roland*, the Kirghiz *Manas*, and the Serbian epics of Kosovo. But can one poem, or group of poems, define the genre?

Epic poetry has many aspects, and an excess in one quality must be allowed to compensate for a deficiency in others. To go into detail, to insist on this and that, is to make one sort of epic poetry the touchstone for all the rest. Against such a course there is an awful warning. In his *Essay on Epic Poetry* (1726; French version, 1733) Voltaire satirically alleged that the savants of his day defined an epic poem as "a long story invented to teach a moral truth; in it the hero performs some lofty deed, with the aid of the gods, in the space of a year." By the savants Voltaire meant Le Bossu, whose long and exhaustive *Traité du poème épique* had been published in 1675 and had enslaved the imagination of two generations. "But the English," Voltaire went on, for he loved to be Anglophile as well as provocative, "The English have an epic poem whose hero, far from succeeding in some notable enterprise in a year, even by divine assistance, is deceived by both the Devil and his own wife in one day and is thereupon expelled from the terrestrial paradise. This poem nevertheless is ranked by the English as the equal of the *Iliad;* in fact many people prefer it to Homer, with some apparent justification." There were indeed those who did say that *Paradise Lost* was not an epic, but the point holds. Accidents must not be taken for essentials. The savants' stress on moral truth, lofty deed, aid of gods, and a particular span of time reflected the concerns of European literary men between the Renaissance and the Romantic movement; even more so did their inferences about unity and completeness of plot, variety and novelty of character, and propriety of sentiment and language.[2] All this critical attention would have amazed the anonymous epic poets who stand at the head of most of the literatures of the world.

But what are the essentials of epic? We are looking at the longest-lived and most widely diffused of all literary forms. Epics have sprung up with every appearance of spontaneity whenever societies throughout the world achieved a certain stage of development or a certain kind of culture. The Sumerians sang of Lugalbanda and Enmerkar in the third millennium B.C., and if the epic itself in Western literary tradition seems not to have survived the nineteenth century, its offspring are still with us. There are very early poems, like the Babylonian *Gilgamesh,* the Greek *Iliad,* and the Indian *Mahābhārata,* with complex literary histories. There are the monuments of Graeco-Roman literature that modeled themselves formally on the *Iliad* and *Odyssey* of Homer. There is the heroic epic of medieval Europe—*Beowulf, Chanson de Roland, Canto del mio Cid, Tale of Igor's Raid, Digenis Akritas, Nibelungenlied,* and the like.[3] There are the masterpieces of Renaissance literature that combined the example of Virgil's *Aeneid* with, it was hoped, the precepts of Horace and Aristotle. And there is the vast literature of contemporary, preindustrial Africa, southeastern Europe, and many parts of Asia, which modern scholarship has partially preserved. What unites this enormous production of the human imagination? Is there a Platonic form (in Greek, *eidos*), so to speak, in which "epics" participate more or less imperfectly?

At times, favorite exemplars have been elevated to such a status. The Greeks idolized the *Iliad,* Europeans of the Renaissance the *Aeneid.* But whether we draw our criteria from an exemplar or invent our own, the procedure has two disadvantages. In the first place, it is exclusive and inward-looking. It operates so as to disqualify candidates for epic status and offers no encouragement to those who wonder how *epic* became a term of praise (sometimes faint praise) in the jargon of literary reviewers or in what sense a critic tentatively describes, for example, Pound's *Cantos* as an epic poem. Secondly, the concept of an ideal form results in interpreting distance from the exemplar as a failure in aim. Serious misjudgments can follow. Longinus (as we may call him), best of the ancient critics, deprecated the *Odyssey* because it fell short of the standards of the *Iliad* and so seemed the product of a great genius in decline (*On the Sublime* 9.12–14). That evaluation, though unlikely, could just possibly be true. The critics of the Renaissance, however, with Cardinal Vida at their head, condemned Homer by the standard of Virgil: a persistent view but patently wrong. Virgil displayed decorum, or sense of propriety and order, and also a moral purpose, all of which the age desired and lacked and did not find in Homer, a barbarian author whose style seemed prolix, inconsistent, and repetitive and whose heroes were too earthy for cultivated readers. Stated in neutral terms, these qualities describe real differences between the Homeric poems and the *Aeneid*. But the *Iliad,* the *Odyssey,* and the *Aeneid* are not attempts with varying success at the same form but different forms of the epic.

Must we then retreat into some wide generalization and hope that is will cover all the poems that have reasonably been called epics—the narrative mode, the verse form, a certain scale, a conception of character that compels respect, a public voice, and therefore an end outside itself? But what conception of character? What scale? To what end does the epic address itself? We can answer these questions for one epic or another but not at the same time for every work with a just claim to the title unless we make the form very loose indeed. Then, of course,we begin to include too much: we may wish to say that Lucretius' didactic poem *De Rerum Natura* shows the influence of the epic tradition, but it would be misleading to call it an epic. Nor do any of our criteria seem to be indispensable. Narrative may be reduced to a succession of tableaux. The verse form may yield to heightened prose—or nowadays to the visual images of film. Scale is always relative. Fantasy, to which the proper response is astonishment, may cloud respect for heroic audacity and will. Personal feeling may infect the objective style and the public voice scarcely conceal a private standpoint. Heroes flit between the worlds of history and folktale. The techniques of ancient oral composition linger into the literate age. The use of a literary form, like the usage of a word, creeps this way and that, and limiting cases may turn out to have little in common. For the truth is that literary artists would be held in little regard if they did not give some impetus to the evolution of their genre. A long history, as in the case of the epic, or sheer volume of production, as with the novel, breaks up the form into subgenres. Hence the term "epic" often receives from its critics a determinative epithet: heroic epic, historical epic, romantic epic, primary epic, or literary epic. Few instances are pure examples of their type, for the subgenres intersect, and some examples—Ovid's *Metamorphoses*, Dante's *Divina Commedia*—are sui generis.[4]

Narrative is the formal root of the epic, but not just any narrative. The primitive phases of most cultures provide examples of myths and folktales, stories by which men and women have sought to explain the world or escape from its miseries. There are also sagas to record success and eulogies to commend it. The seed of the epic is sown when these are blended, given metrical form, and cast into the narrative mode of heroic poetry.[5] Eulogy is a decisive element; for eulogy implies the hero whose successful struggles are celebrated, and none of the primary epics lacks a hero. Against whom the hero struggles and by what means depends on the forces ranged against the community for which he fights. Heroes who are little more than sorcerers, like the Finnish Väinämöinen, express the desperation of those who live on the edge of survival. Heroes like the Greek Heracles, who fight against monsters or natural forces, celebrate the victory of civilization. But for the most part heroes fight other heroes. Naturally they are supermen, and they may possess supernatural powers or supernatural weapons; but in what may be called his purest form the hero dispenses with such aid:[6] Beowulf, in a remarkable passage (*Beowulf* 669–74), will not wear even normal battle gear to face Grendel. Without magic to help him, the hero must rely on himself, on his physical and moral strength. Physically powerful heroes are ambiguous figures, better described as awesome rather than admirable. The important heroes for literature are those with moral strength, for however ferocious, egotistical, and violent they may be, they are capable of refinement and development. The greatness of the deed may then be made to lie in its daring, as in the quest of the Argonauts for the Golden Fleece or, on the spiritual plane, in the quest of Gilgamesh for immortality. Or the greatness may be altogether the hero's, the deed itself being unexceptional, as when heroes who know they are doomed face death unflinchingly.

Like most kinds of traditional art, heroic poetry has no author in the literal sense. A lyric poet can compose for his own satisfaction, and a literate artist can hope for posthumous fame, but the oral poet-performer of traditional songs cannot be so self-indulgent. He and his audience, which is effectively the whole community, are one.[7] It creates his repertoire, directly by the songs it demands, indirectly by its reactions to his performance. Traditional art is a public art, and when art has a public character, we should look for its social function. In the most general terms a community sees reflected in heroic poetry an image of itself that it likes to see, and in seeing it the community is encouraged.[8] Courage may be everywhere the same, but it is more natural to admire our ancestors, our friends, and ourselves than to admire some remote and alien paragon of virtue. For this reason heroic poetry has a tendency to show patriotic overtones, usually tribal or national but sometimes religious or cultural. The common factor is that heroic poems celebrate, affirm, and confirm something; they do not, as the epic can and does, explore and question at the same time as they celebrate. The difference is easily understood if we compare the Old High German *Hildebrandtslied* with the medieval *Nibelungenlied*. The *Hildebrandtslied* is a lay, a short narrative poem surviving from the end of the age of migrations, the Germanic Heroic Age; its ethos is strongly heroic, tragic, and rooted in feudal custom: two champions engage in a duel between their armies. The older man recognizes the younger as his son but is forced by honor to fight and slay or be slain. The *Nibelungenlied* is a complex epic of jealousy and vengeance built around the theme of the sin of avarice.

Heroic poems like the *Hildebrandtslied* tend to have simple linear plots, long enough to fill their audience's leisure but short enough not to try its patience. For a narrative on this scale, the shape of the story itself imposes all that is needed in the way of formal structure. A limited scale naturally engenders a succinct, panoramic style:

> As he came forward I struck him with my bronze spear, and down he fell in the dust. Leaping into my chariot I took my stand beside the foremost, but the gallant Epeians fled this way

and that when they saw the leader of their horsemen fall, the
man who was best in battle. Like a black whirlwind I leaped
upon them. Fifty chariots I took, and by each two men bit the
dust, slain by my spear. (Nestor to Patroclus, *Iliad* xi 742–49)

That tells us what was done, and little more. We may exult with the
youthful Nestor, but if we do, all the effort of imagination has been
on our part. For though a story is essential to a heroic poem, it is, in
E. M. Forster's words, "a low atavistic form," a mere list of events.[9]
The involvement of the audience calls for some expression of the
quality of a scene or act, as one singer explained:

Well, for example, [a good singer] adds what the heroes were
wearing. He says that they were carrying knives, and saddle
pistols, and Osmanli saddles. Then he says: "Over the saddle,"
he says, "are fine blankets, over the blankets," he says, "are
scattered thin rupees. And in the middle," he says, "are small
mahmudis," and so forth. He ornaments it. He tells that the hilt
of his sword is of gold, and the blade of deadly steel, and there is
a bit of twelve pounds in the [horse's] teeth, and he adds more
. . . and in that way he sings it longer and better. People say it's
better that way.[10]

—as well they might, for the bare event of panoramic narration has
been replaced by the stimulating color of a detailed picture.

This expansiveness is at the foundation of epic, for primary epic
poetry is heroic poetry writ large, its range extended and its insights
deepened. At the very least the epic puts people, and therefore
feelings, hope, despair, sorrow, and triumph, into the events of the
heroic lay; at its best it spreads itself over the whole mass of traditional knowledge. A deeply serious genre, the epic must be more
than storytelling.[11] Stories allow surprise, suspense, and climax; they
provide memorable moments. But it is significant that they take their
titles (which are, or ought to be, the ultimate summaries of their
contents) from their characters or their events. One would not
naturally refer to *Cinderella* or the *Saga of Eric the Red* in any other
way. But the higher genres of the drama and the novel often take
their titles from their themes—*Pride and Prejudice*, for example, or
Measure for Measure—thus proclaiming they offer an explanation of
the events they depict. The writers of literary epics sometimes make a
sort of compromise, as does Tasso with *Gerusalemme Liberata* or

Milton with *Paradise Lost,* titles that add a certain overtone to the description of the subject. The epics that first emerged from the background of heroic song usually announced themselves similarly as stories—"O Gilgamesh, lord of Kullab, great is thy praise!"; "Sing, Muse, of a man [Odysseus] of many wiles"—and the titles subsequently bestowed on them reflect the centrality of narrative, although such titles are inadequate descriptions. But even then there were exceptions. Homer did not call his major poem the *Iliad,* which means "tale of Troy," a title first attested in the fifth century B.C. The real title is provided by the opening phrase, "the devastating wrath of Achilles." In short, the *Iliad* is aware that it has a theme; it is about heroism, specifically about heroic honor, and its effects and price. It is not a modest poet who dares to compose on such a scale. He must be, like the heroes of whom he sings, "great-souled" and not flinch at the problems posed by grim fate, stern duty, and the inscrutable purposes of the gods. The epic poet extended the tales of heroic vengeance that lay at the heart of the *Iliad* and the *Odyssey* into extended homilies on the meaning of life as their audiences would have understood it. He aimed high, and it was needful that he did, for there is a certain pretentiousness about the mere size of an epic that calls for a corresponding grandeur in conception to sustain it.

The usual fate of a tradition of heroic poetry, even if it achieves epic form, is a slow death. Its patrons widen their cultural horizons and learn that it is crude and primitive. Hack poets fill the gaps, if the master poets seem to have neglected a detail—how Roland and Oliver became friends; how the vanity of goddesses began the Trojan War; how a reluctant Odysseus came to be at Troy. It was a doubtful service. In Greece the patrons of Homer were succeeded by the patrons of the lyric poets. That the Homeric poems survived at all is the consequence of two fortunate accidents, the introduction of alphabetic writing into Greece in the eighth century B.C., which made it possible to preserve them, and the development of an attitude of respect for Homer that made preservation of the poems seem worthwhile. More accidents of history brought it about that Greek literature shaped Roman literature and that the two literatures together molded the literary ideas of the Renaissance. A different history would have produced a different idea of the epic, or perhaps no epic at all. As it was, the Homeric poems bequeathed a form, a style, and a whole armory of narrative devices to European literature, whereas their Germanic, Romance, and Slavic analogs have died without issue.

Literary epic is a "sentimental" revival of the Homeric form of epic.[12] It began in Greece in the late fifth century B.C. and has never quite expired. That the legacy of Homer was taken up, however, remains one of the most extraordinary facts of literary history. It is easy to understand that the Renaissance emulated the literary achievements of a classical age that it profoundly admired but harder to see why the civilized and sophisticated periods of Greece and Rome took up a form created by a barbaric age. The historian Thucydides, writing in the fifth century B.C., could find nothing in the times that produced the Homeric poems but piracy and poverty. Art and material culture, however, are not correlated. Though the *Iliad* and the *Odyssey* tell of violent and brutal deeds, they do so in a form and language that makes them highly sophisticated works of art. They passed the tests of criticism. They also enjoyed an impregnably entrenched position in the life of Greece. Yet the heroic outlook of Homer was not the outlook of the citizens of the classical city. The poets of the revived epic found new subjects or new interpretations; what they revived was the form of the Homeric epic. There was nothing remarkable in their so doing, but the step was crucial. Henceforth the idea of the epic and its Homeric form are interlinked.

Yet there is something self-indulgent about the resuscitation of an obsolete form. Can it be more than an elegant and ingenious diversion for scholarly poets? A vital epic must be something other than a combination of Homeric structure, elevated language, funeral games, and divine machinery. In practice there is more than a suspicion that many of the epic poets who invoked the Muse during the eight centuries between 400 B.C. and A.D. 400 were studiously ventilating a corpse. Yet there were successes. Three Greek and five Latin epics have survived, although survival is not a sure guide to quality. The loss of Valerius Flaccus' *Argonautica*, Silius' *Punic War*, Quintus Smyrnaeus' *Posthomerica*, and Nonnus' *Dionysiaca* would be no great cause for lamentation; not many would miss Statius' *Thebaid*; but literary history must always reckon with Apollonius' *Argonautica* and Lucan's *Bellum Civile*, and Virgil's *Aeneid* has a permanent place in world literature.

What has been said of the greatness of soul of the primary epic applies as strongly to its imitators. But the poet of a literary epic is not the anonymous spokesman for his age, and he cannot help but add a private note to his public voice. Where Homer expresses the accumulated experience of his tradition, Virgil expresses a Virgilian view of Rome. Because they have this personal aspect, literary epics display a broader range of themes than the primary form. Poets continued to respond to the idea of heroic action but blended it with other themes. National and party patriotism are prominent and gave rise to their own subgenre, the historical epic. Religion, a weak force in the main classical periods, enters at the end of antiquity and was productive during the Renaissance. The purely mythological epics of Apollonius and Statius have had a more limited appeal. To many their brilliance has seemed to overlie a hollow shell, elegant but arid. We readily understand the march of history and the idea of liberty crushed by despotism because these things are always with us, but unfamiliar assumptions have to be made to come to grips with the aestheticism of Apollonius or the harsh rhetoric of Statius.

The evolution of the epic genre has been a cumulative process. Its roots are infinitely old, for they are the roots of narrative speech itself. Any kind of narrative, including the ubiquitous modes of myth and folktale, will develop the arts of storytelling. What determines that storytelling leads in the direction of the epic is the emergence of a certain idea, the idea of heroic action. The greater the scale on which circumstances permit him to work, the more easily can the poet expand heroic poetry so as to give expression to the qualities of mind that fit the hero to perform great deeds. If he can then relate the hero and his deeds to the cosmic order and give his poem the sort of general relevance that persuades his patrons not to let it perish, the epic has arrived. The poets of the literary epic, whatever the subgenre in which they write, add a sharper personal viewpoint, what Milton called a "great argument," to these age-old components. They set out to be at once masters of narrative style, like romancers, and masters of characterization, like dramatists, and to combine these with the vision of a philosopher and the urgency of a prophet. Not many have succeeded.

II

Greek Primary Epic

The Heroic Age and Heroic Poetry

Epic singers from the dawn of human
consciousness have been a deeply significant
group and have contributed abundantly to the
spiritual and intellectual growth of man.

Albert B. Lord

The earliest artistic form recognized in the history of criticism is
that which the Homeric poems called simply song. The term covered
many kinds of composition we nowadays are accustomed to separate:
dirges, didactic verses, and narratives in praise of gods and heroes.
The Greeks were always apt to call them all verses without distinction, and they were justified insofar as each employed the same
language, diction, and meter. Naturally the Greeks knew a dirge
when they heard one, and though they blurred the distinction (if it is
a real one) between stories about gods and stories about heroes, they
recognized as one of the chief topics of "song" the "famous deeds of
men," what we call heroic poetry.[1]

The Homeric epic is the child of Greek heroic poetry. Of course,
the parent did not die with the birth of the child, but for the literary
historian the long generations of anonymous singers whose art made

11

Homer's possible had played their part when the great epics came into being. Their successors are an irrelevance. But when was Homer? The Greeks themselves had really no idea. When they addressed themselves to the question in the fifth century B.C., Homer lay beyond living memory, so he (as well as Hesiod and the mythical poets Musaeus and Orpheus) must have preceded the earliest elegiac and lyric poets. The elegy and the lyric flourished from the early seventh century, and Hesiod seems to have lived around 700 B.C. Although the Greeks tended to mention Hesiod before Homer when they listed their poets, modern opinion is usually impressed by the relatively more archaic form of language found in Homer and assigns him priority by a decade or two.

If Homer sang c. 725 B.C., when did the great exploit of his heroes, the siege of Troy, take place? Here the Greeks thought they were on firmer ground. The kings of Sparta (about whom, it was presumed, there could be no reasonable doubt) descended in two lines from the demigod Heracles, whose generation was the last before the siege of Troy. The gallant Leonidas, who defended Thermopylae against the Persians in 480 B.C. in a truly epic manner, was twentieth in line. A dozen different dates were calculated for the fall of Troy from this evidence, with a mean around 1200 B.C.; that of the scholar Eratosthenes (fl. 230 B.C.), 1183 B.C., became canonical. Modern authorities give c. 1240 B.C. for the destruction of Troy VII A, the seventh city built on the site of Troy.[2] The close coincidence of ancient and modern science is impressive, but the ancients stretched and fudged their generations, and the moderns are at the mercy of the classification of ambiguous potsherds. What is certain, however, is that the distance in time between the *Iliad* and the world of the *Iliad* is considerable. Heroic poetry contrived to bridge the gap.

The "famous deeds of men" normally rest on some fragments of genuine history celebrated while they were still remembered and appreciated.[3] But heroic poetry is not history as we have come to understand it. Strictly speaking, it does not even preserve a record of events if that means preserving them in proper sequence and proportion. Writing is a necessary condition for that sort of history, and there is no evidence whatever that anyone in Greece between c. 1100 B.C. and 750 B.C. could so much as sign his name. The oral techniques of heroic poetry select what is appropriate to famous deeds and forget the rest; they confuse times and places; they impose the heroic ethos on shabby deeds of treachery and vengeance.

The world of the *Iliad*, insofar as it is not fiction, is the period known informally as the Mycenaean Age and to archaeology as the Late Helladic III (LH III), the mature phase of the Greek Bronze Age. It is held to have begun about 1580 B.C. and to have ended with the destruction of Mycenae about 1150 B.C. The high point in material and artistic achievement was the second phase of LH III, known as LH III B, c. 1300–1200 B.C. Impressive monuments of the LH III B period exist to this day in most parts of Greece as far north as Thessaly, but especially in the Peloponnese. There was a great fortress at Troy but not much else on the Asiatic side of the Aegean.

It has been known since 1939 that the LH culture was literate and since 1955 that it used its literacy to keep administrative records, though apparently for no other purpose. In Pylos in the southwestern Peloponnese, where hundreds of documents have been found, officials checked the production of wool and cloth, issued raw materials to workers, counted the labor force and doled out its rations, inventoried the contents of palatial residences, listed the command structure and deployment of the armed forces, and arranged for the due observance of religion.[4]

Pylos lay on the edge of the LH world. To the west and south was sea, leading nowhere. It did not even seem necessary to turn the palace into a citadel. Even the army was on the defensive. It all looks very unheroic. Can these be the people for whom it would be fun to go out and steal cattle, or a princess? But the king of Pylos is not mentioned in his documents and seems to have moved in a different sphere. Perhaps his view of life and *gloire* was different from that of his administrators. Other LH kings felt closer to their neighbors, and the nearer one approaches the center of the LH world, the higher and thicker the fortress walls become. At Mycenae and Tiryns the well-preserved bastions, casemates, and sally ports are more than regal ostentation. Late Helladic kings feared each other, and with good reason. During LH III Cnossos, Thebes, and Troy were sacked and burned. For the victors there was something to celebrate. On the walls of the throne room at Pylos a fresco depicted a seated singer holding a lyre before him. The pose is that of the epic singer described in *Odyssey* viii.[5]

A generation later literacy and luxury had vanished as if they had never been, and Greece had entered what English-speaking scholars have long been accustomed to call the Dark Age. The Greeks remembered this collapse as a political overturn: the descendants of Heracles returned to Mycenae at the head of the tribe of Dorian Greeks to claim their just inheritance and dispossess the house of Atreus. We cannot verify this story, for the mute stones do not speak and tell us who threw them down; but whatever the cause, the collapse was real, and so was its aftermath: the migration of many Greeks to the Asiatic shore of the Aegean. Naturally they kept alive the memory of past glories.

All the circumstances that lead to the idea of a past Heroic Age were thus present: disaster certainly, probably conquest, and migration from the former homeland. The idea did not fail to develop, and it became one of the most important legacies inherited by the epic tradition from its progenitors.[6] Almost without thinking, generations of classical epic poets would cast their imaginations back into the Greek world of the second millennium B.C., and their modern descendants have groped to find an appropriate equivalent.

Only in a general way, however, did Greek heroic poetry reflect the world of the archaeologist's LH III. There was uncertainty about the location of Pylos (a site that ceased to be inhabited), but most place names survived into classical times even if the cities they designated had, like Mycenae, sunk into villages or ruins. Legends clustered round the major LH sites in proportion, more or less, to their LH importance, as that importance might have been viewed from Mycenae itself. So Mycenae, Tiryns, and Argos figured prominently, and so did their rival Thebes to the north. Remoter places, such as Iolchus and Calydon in northern Greece, or Elis and Pylos in the western Peloponnese, were mentioned in one or two tales but have connections with the central area. Athens stood to one side, the Belgrade of the Mycenaean world, aloof from the rivalries of the great powers. Corinth, to its later vexation, did not appear at all.[7]

It was known that the age of the heroes was an age of bronze, not iron, an age when cities were ruled by kings, not magistrates; when palaces, not temples, crowned the citadels; and when, of course, gold burst the treasuries, and there was never lack of meat and wine for the daily banquets of god-descended nobles. No memory, however, survived of Mycenaean literacy, bureaucracy, and social organization; such things did not interest those who created the tales of

Heracles and the Argonauts, of Thebes and Troy. The chronology of these stories is sharply defined, so sharply that when the didactic poet Hesiod surveyed the history of the human race he could speak of an age of heroes, the men who died before Thebes and Troy (*Works and Days* 156–73). One generation assaulted Thebes and sailed in the Argo; their sons sacked Troy. Sometimes we know the names but not much of the deeds of their ancestors and progeny. In archaeological terms the so-called Heroic Age is the latter half of LH III B, and the dominance of the two generations in legend rests to a great extent on the genuine brilliance of that period.[8]

Into the Heroic Age went the whole legacy of the past in enhanced heroic color. "There were brave men before Agamemnon," said the Roman Horace (*Odes* iv 9, 25), rehearsing the cliché that there was no renown without poetry; but it is most unlikely that those pre-Trojan heroes lacked a singer.[9] They were simply outshone by the dazzling brightness of those who fought at Thebes and Troy. Some, however, were too good to lose. According to his official genealogy, the great Ajax, the son of Telamon, was cousin to Achilles—but appearance is sometimes a better clue to paternity. Achilles was the most handsome of the Greeks, but Ajax is described as "monstrous," a perfect bear of a man, who sheltered his bulk in battle behind a shield "like a tower." For three thousand years, till the late nineteenth century, it is doubtful if anyone had any notion what this object was, for it is the huge shield depicted on the inlaid blades of daggers found by Schliemann in the Shaft Graves at Mycenae and dated to the beginning of LH I (c. 1550 B.C.).[10] Soon afterward it was discarded in favor of more manageable gear. Along with his outmoded shield Ajax preserved some obsolete language: in several places in the *Iliad* the dual number *Aiante*, which we should expect to mean "the two heroes called Ajax," has the curious sense "Ajax and one other [viz. his brother Teucer]." Foreign to classical Greek, this usage is paralleled in Vedic Sanskrit; it might even be Indo-European, a hint perhaps of the extreme antiquity of this tradition of heroic poetry.[11]

Though the Heroic Age was happy to accommodate a few dinosaurs, it was totally inhospitable to anyone who lived afterward. Careless of anachronisms in the material world, the poetic tradition was vigilant about its personnel. Whole tribes of Greeks had no role whatever. There was a literary consequence to this omission: Greek heroic poetry, and therefore Homeric poetry, faced firmly toward a distant past. Without consciously meaning to, they archaized. Later epic poets had to archaize deliberately and risk breaking the dramatic allusion with anachronism; some ingeniously contrived to interweave the Heroic Age and the contemporary world.

Heroic poetry comes cheap, and the Dark Age was not so impoverished that those who claimed to be descended from the heroes could not pay for the celebration of their ancestors. But the external circumstances of Greek heroic poetry made a dismal contrast with its potential. In an aristocratic world the singer, though he might be inspired by a god, had a low opinion of his place. He was a member of the demiurgic class, plying a trade like a soothsayer, a doctor, or a carpenter (cf. *Od.* xvii 384–85). His job, as he saw it, was to entertain. This is how heroic poetry always appears in Homer: Phemius sang to amuse the suitors of Penelope (*Od.* i 325), Demodocus to divert Odysseus and the Phaeacians (*Od.* viii 62), and Achilles to amuse himself (*Il.* ix 186). These were ordinary secular occasions, not public ceremonies. Phemius seems to reside in the palace, but then the suitors demanded continuous festivity. Demodocus, who is said to be "honored by the people," had to be fetched, presumably from the marketplace or wherever his vulgar audience might assemble. At an appropriate moment he took his lyre, seated himself at a strategic point, and struck up a prelude. Since all this had happened many times before, he did not need to explain his song: it would be taken from the great sagas of the Heroic Age. Naturally he selected a portion that would be well received by his audience. That was why the suitors, who had not been to Troy, were regaled by Phemius with the disasters of those who had. But suppose the singer misjudged the feelings of his hearers? In that case they felt no obligation to hear him out. Penelope made a rare sortie from her chamber, made derogatory remarks about Phemius' song, and silenced him (*Od.* i 337). Among the Phaeacians Alcinous was even more high-handed: he put the same value on song as he did on wrestling (*Od.* viii 97) and made the bard provide the music for a public dance (*Od.* viii 254). Sometimes the audience would suggest its own subject, as Odysseus did at *Od.* viii 492, knowing or presuming that the singer could cope.

Where the singer was at the mercy of an audience well aware of its status and superiority, what sort of art was possible? Professionally the singer was an entertainer, whatever his pretensions to a special relationship with the Muses. To live he had to please. Patrons were mean (they always are) and scarce; there were rivals at the door; to the next town the way was long and the welcome uncertain. All in all, it was best to stick to the old songs, to keep to the familiar plots, to avoid what would trouble or disturb, to aim to please. In telling the tale, there was nothing for it but to add scene to scene in the manner scholars call parataxis. No one could say at the beginning where the end would be. The singer proceeded step by step, his attention on each episode in turn, lingering or hastening as he observed the signs of interest or boredom. He might digress or change course. Obviously, this could not be conducive to any refined concepts of literary form beyond the structure provided by the story itself. There could be no notion, such as later endeared itself to Aristotle, of the well-rounded plot with each of its well-articulated parts subordinated to the whole.

The picture, however, is not without its brighter spots. The heroic tales were a kind of encyclopedia of morality, reflecting an image of men as they should be: honorable, brave, courteous, and pious, surrounded by deferential youths and chaste wives. Subconsciously perhaps people perceived that heroic poetry reinforced these values and was therefore something to be esteemed as well as enjoyed. From the time of Hesiod the art of song is attested on ceremonial occasions. This development was not early, for the arts did not enter into the funeral games of Patroclus in the *Iliad* (xxiii 257–893), but it was most important for the future. Until there was a reading public, a thing unknown before the fifth century B.C., such official occasions were a principal means whereby singer and epic poet reached a wider audience. Games and festivals were also organized events and lent their authority to the singer. He could plan and prepare his song with some expectation of being able to finish it. Until that happened, unless some poet insisted on it by sheer force of personality, the singer could not be master of his craft, so as to make it do as *he* wished and not as traditional sagas and fickle patrons led him.

To recount the tales of the Heroic Age was no task for amateurs. The events and personnel of that distant epoch constituted a corpus of "knowledge" that was not to be learned without much application. But that knowledge, though necessary, was not sufficient to tell the stories. The singer had to tell the tale in verse, and at short notice or none at all. He had, of course, no song book, for this was an illiterate age. Good analogical arguments show almost conclusively that he did not memorize as we understand it. He was well rehearsed, since his material was all traditional and had been sung by him many times before, but what he actually did was re-create the song in the act of performance.[12] "Improvise" is too strong a word, although some have used it, but it hints at the uncanny skill of the singer, to which a Homeric simile pays tribute: "As one gazes in wonder at a singer who is taught by god and sings words of delight to men, and ever eagerly for as long as he sings do they desire to hear him" (*Od.* xvii 518–20). For the gods and muses of Homer, scholars of today have substituted a "poetical grammar," a variety of linguistic skills superimposed on the skills implied by ordinary speech. Practical in origin, these gave the traditional narrative style its peculiar quality. In his excellent tract *On Translating Homer* (London, 1865) Matthew Arnold wrote, "The translator of Homer should above all be penetrated by a sense of four qualities of his author;—that he is eminently rapid; that he is eminently plain and direct, both in the evolution of his thought and in the expression of it, that is both in his syntax and his words; that he is eminently plain and direct in the substance of his thought, that is, in his matter and ideas; and finally that he is eminently noble." Much of that indeed describes Homer, for in the same medium Hesiod did not achieve any of these qualities in the same degree. But some credit is due to the medium, one that Homer had inherited from the singers of heroic poetry.

The verse the singer chanted is one of the most famous in literary history. It is called in technical language the dactylic hexameter, a sequence of long and short syllables arranged according to the following pattern, with two short syllables (˘ ˘) taken as equivalent to one long (–):

– ˘ ˘ /– ˘ ˘ /– ˘ ˘ /– ˘ ˘ /– ˘ ˘ /– ˘

Those whose native language is English will probably read this pattern as a succession of stressed and unstressed syllables. That is barbarous, but the melody of a language whose accent is one of pitch and whose metrics rest on a feeling for quantity is not accessible, without effort and training, to those accustomed to the dominance of stress. Read it as we may, the hexameter verse is a remarkable instance of Greek serendipity. It had to be repeated, according to the almost universal practice of heroic poetry, hundreds of times in a song. It was therefore a matter of the greatest consequence that the hexameter came in thirty-two rhythmical varieties. The monotony of which observers of modern heroic poetry complain was thereby avoided, and there was ample opportunity to match the pattern of the verse to the mood and tempo of the thought.

The hexameter is also a long verse in comparison, say, with the eight syllables of the Finnish *Kalevala* (the meter of Longfellow's *Song of Hiawatha*) or the ten syllables of the South Slavic tradition. The effect of a long verse is not only a certain dignity but also a certain variety, since strong syntactical pauses are likely to occur within the verse as well as at its end. About a third of Homeric verses finish a clause in mid-line. Consequently the best hexameter writing displays a satisfying harmony of meter, language, and sense. After Homer Virgil was the conscious master of this art, yet what he exploited was a potential inherent in the hexameter.

Into the verse according to Arnold went a swift-flowing simple sentence: "[Idomeneus] struck him in the right shoulder as he was about to mount his chariot. Down he fell from his car, and dread darkness seized upon him" (*Il.* v 46–47). These two modest verses exemplify much that is characteristic of the heroic narrative style. In the original they are indeed rapid and clear, because the style is additive. The phrases are distinct, not interlaced as they are in the involved and stately styles of Virgil or Milton. Each half-verse is a complete phrase stacked against the one that precedes, enlarging the syntax without obscuring it and drawing the reader's mind along.

The four phrases that make up *Il.* v 46–47 are, as it happens, formulas. Heroic poetry everywhere is full of such repeated expressions, and in Homer there are hundreds of them. But the long hexameter called forth a special and conspicuous kind, noun + epithet formulas, where the epithet, if we consider only the essential meaning of the phrase, is redundant or at least has no direct relation to its context. At *Il.* v 47 "dread" adds little to our concept of the darkness of death. In the verse preceding those cited the poet had to express the thought "Him Idomeneus with his spear struck." What he sang was "Him Idomeneus *famed for his lance* with his *long* spear struck." The two epithets are apposite, but only in a general way. Spears are naturally long, and Idomeneus was indeed a warrior of high repute. But any suspicion that the epithets are specially appropriate at this point in the *Iliad* must be dispelled by the observation that when a hero in Homer has an epithet in this position in the verse, he is regularly "famed for his lance", and that the spear is always "long" when it occupies the last feet of the verse. This economy of the diction—enough expressions, but only enough, to meet the metrical requirements—shows that in the first instance the formulas are an aspect of the singers' technique, not the product of some exotic aesthetic predilection.[13] Indeed the formulaic diction was a problem for Homer's critics and imitators. It was often highly colorful: "dark-clouded blood," "deep-eddying river," "wine-dark sea," "cloud-gathering Zeus." Long epithets in Greek mean compound epithets, and compounding opens up infinite possibilities for the artist in words. But in the systems of formulas the colorful effect is a bonus: the singers were often obliged to meet their needs with something tautologous and gray: "sharp swords," "swift arrows," "fast horses," "sweet wine," "noble heroes," and so on.

Besides his special diction the Greek singer had also to arm himself with a special language. Poetical speech is always artificial to some extent, but that of the Greek art of song was exceptionally exotic. The singer preferred the forms and grammar of the dialect of Ionia, the middle zone of Greek settlement on the eastern shore of the Aegean, where the mainstream of heroic tradition was preserved; but he admitted a liberal admixture of archaisms, neologisms, dialect forms, and even certain abuses of syntax. There was method in this confusion. Intuitively the singers sought out and kept as many word forms of the same sense but different metrics as they could find. They did not choose outlandish words for their own sake, as if deliberately seeking a language redolent of the Heroic Age, for the Ionic prevails wherever it is metrically accommodated to the hexameter.[14] Of course, by being associated with heroic poetry, the special language could not help sounding like the language of the heroes. No Greek epic poet failed to take advantage of it.

But what about the story itself? How was the singer to describe the heroes doing battle over the flocks of Oedipus or the injured honor of the house of Atreus? Heroic poetry puts the emphasis on the art of storytelling. An audience, according to the comment in the *Odyssey* (xvii 520) cited above, feels an "insatiable desire to hear," and frequent allusion is made to the hold a storyteller exercises over his hearers: Alcinous was ready to listen all night (*Od.* xi 375), Eumaeus for three days (*Od.* xvii 515), Aeolus for a month (*Od.* x 14), and Telemachus, with youthful enthusiasm, for a year (*Od.* iv 595). It used to be the fashion for critics to praise what they called the invention of Homer. In fact, like his forebears, Homer probably invented very little in the way of incident. The epic poet's contribution, what helped turn heroic poetry into epic poetry, lay rather in the critical attitude he took toward traditional stories. Obvious pitfalls lay in the way of the oral singer who sought, without the rehearsal of repeated performance, to create a new kind of battle: better to stick to the traditional "themes."[15] The sequence of motifs and topics seems to be the form in which a song exists in the minds of many oral singers at the present day. It was also the means by which the poet of the *Odyssey* was able to summarize the episode of the wooden horse so succinctly (viii 500–520). He defined the starting point—the abandonment by the Greeks of their camp—and proceeded to list the constituent themes of the story:

1. "Odysseus and his friends were sitting in the wooden horse." (A catalog of the great and the good who entered the horse is an appropriate item at this point. In the *Iliad* a catalog is common form at the beginning of major episodes, e.g. ii 484–759, xii 89–104, xvi 168–97.)

2. "Around it the Trojans debated" (an assembly, disputatious and prolonged, as at *Il.* i 53–303, *Od.* ii 1–256).

3. "Troy was fated to fall" (a comment on the higher powers and their purposes, often expressed through the personal interests of the Olympian gods, as at *Il.* i 493–527, xvi 431–61, xxii 166–86, *Od.* i 26–95).

4. The fighting, consisting of a general description leading to a list of the exploits and victims of the major heroes. (This is standard practice in the *Iliad*, e.g. v 37–83, xvi 306–50.)

5. The *aristeia* of Odysseus and Menelaus, culminating in the duel with Deiphobus, with a hint of divine intervention. (The *aristeia*—a series of exploits performed in quick succession by a single hero or a pair of heroes fighting together—is one of the commonest Iliadic themes; so, of course, is the duel; for the sequence cf. *Il.* xvi 394–486.)

These are quite general topics, and within each are others of narrower scope, such as the arguments pro and contra in theme 2 and various sorts of fight and duel in themes 4 and 5.

The tale of the wooden horse is a precious example of the sort of heroic song that formed the immediate background to the *Iliad*. In fact, it is too close in all respects to the *Iliad* to be informative. There were many paradigms of valiant action in the stories of the Heroic Age—sieges (Troy, Thebes, Calydon); cattle raids (Nestor, Idas, Achilles); marriage quests, called rapes in Greek legend (Helen, Iole); ordeals (Argonauts, Heracles); and fights with monsters (Perseus and the Gorgon, Bellerophon and the Chimaera, Heracles and the Hydra). Two of these tales are told in summary form in the *Iliad* itself: the stories of Bellerophon (vi 157-211) and Nestor (xi 670–761).[16] By a happy chance these two stories seem to define the limits of Greek heroic poetry.

Nestor's tale is pure heroic narrative. Realistic and historically plausible, it is set in a genuine landscape. The men of Pylos, it begins, made a cattle raid on Elis in the course of which the youthful Nestor slew the mighty Itymoneus. A vast booty was driven back to Pylos, the more welcome because Augeas, the lord of Elis, had earlier taken advantage of the defeat of Pylos by Heracles to renege on his debts. The men of Elis did not submit tamely to Nestor's depredations but, led by the formidable Siamese twins, the Molione, laid siege to Thryoessa. Inspired by the goddess Athene and fortified by sacrifices to her, to Zeus, and to Poseidon, the Pylians rushed to the rescue. Nestor frustrated his father's efforts to detain him, joined the fight, laid Moulios low, and would have the slain the Molione too had not their father, the god Poseidon, rescued them. Victorious, the Pylians returned home giving equal honor to Nestor and Zeus.

The sequence of events in this tale is well ordered, but it is highly predictable within the framework of Greek heroic poetry.[17] Consequently, cognitive interest (or interest in the story qua story) would depend to a great extent on qualities of performance, that is, on the singer's mastery of the traditional apparatus of themes and formulas. The climax is weak, since the Molione—the only really salient feature of the story—are tamely allowed to escape. The preliminaries are drawn out and constitute a separate story on their own. Emotional interest, however, would be high. The story concerns a famous figure of legend; it sets him in a situation of pathos (he is the youngest and sole surviving son of his family); and it pits him against a monstrous opponent. Evidently, the point of this story is the spirit and love of honor of the young Nestor. (In its context in the *Iliad* the tale is told in order to shame Achilles into fighting.) When we read this tale, it is easy to see how the concept of heroism it embodies could grow into the spirit of the *Iliad*.

Bellerophon's story, which is told as the foundation legend of the royal dynasty of Lycia, is a combination of two folktales, the story of Potiphar's wife (cf. *Genesis* 39: 7–20) and that of the prince's ordeals. Anteia, wife of Proitos, king of Tiryns, fell in love with the hand-some Bellerophon. The virtuous youth rebuffed her immoral advances and was rewarded with a false accusation. Proitos was resolved to defend his honor, but to avoid the guilt of straightforward homicide, he sent Bellerophon to Lycia with a message designed to bring about his death. So the king of Lycia set him ordeals to perform: first, to dispatch a monstrous beast, the Chimaera; second, to subdue the savage tribe of the Solymi; third, to slay the Amazons. Bellerophon performed every task and for good measure beat off a Lycian ambush on his return. Such single-handed prowess, itself proof of innocence and divine blood, had only one obvious reward: Bellerophon was invested with half the kingdom and the hand of a princess.

Heroization is here no more than skin-deep. The characters of the tale and its geography are real, at least until Bellerophon marches up-country from Lycia. He fights "trusting in the omens of the gods" and does not use magic or trickery. But that is all: these single combats do not fall within the same frame of reference as the exploits of the juvenile Nestor. Nevertheless they do fall within the limits of heroic action as Greek legend conceived it. Heracles was the arche-type of those who did battle with monstrous beasts, Jason and the Argonauts of those who traveled to distant places where untold horrors awaited discovery. As a story, therefore, Bellerophon's tale has much in its favor: striking events, a coherent but unpredictable plot, and a morally satisfying conclusion. There is much here that would have interested the poet of the *Odyssey*.

But the story of Bellerophon *is* a folktale, with a fragment of the Heroic Age imposed on it, and folktales fascinate their audiences by their qualities as stories. Since they are pure fiction, there is nothing to interfere with the coherence of the narrative or downgrade the salience of incidents. Folktales are ideal material for the theoretical study of the narrative mode. But those who sang songs of a more purely heroic character were creating something closer to reality. They were relating events, and that was their problem. The natural course of events seldom has a pleasing aesthetic structure. There is too much chance and coincidence to satisfy the artist's craving for coherence, too much banality and disappointment to furnish the narrator with a good plan and an attractive goal. It would have been easy, when the epic used the arts of heroic poetry to build a great poem, to pile story on story. Easy, but not satisfying. How then to combine heroic spirit with dramatic movement? The answer was to select the smallest part of "reality" (the heroic tale) that the poet dared and expand it with fiction.

Besides material and means the creation of an epic required also an opportunity and a motive. Motive (it may be conjectured) resided in the contribution that the Homeric poems made to the idea of the epic, a willingness not only to celebrate but also to explore and even question the implications of their themes. Opportunity would be found in new audiences and new circumstances as society evolved. The audiences of heroic songs described in the *Odyssey* are, literally, those present and listening. Yet an audience, if circumstances are right, can include the singer's potential listeners in addition to those before him. In their ideology the Homeric epics are Hellenic, not Ionian, poems and imply a Hellenic audience.[18] This wider appeal was a decisive addition to the simple ethos of Nestor's and Bellerophon's heroic lays. The epics of Homer gave form to a myth: the idea of Greekness.

Homeric Epic

> A man may be either the master or the slave of
> the rules by which he lives; the conventions of
> an art have never yet confined genius and
> mediocrity in equal chains.
>
> D. L. Page

Of all the heroic tales bequeathed them from the former age, the tale of Troy must have seemed to the Greeks of Asia the most relevant to their own situation, especially to the aristocracies who continued, it was supposed, the lineage of the heroes who had fought at Troy. Thus a simple story of siege and plunder became the focus of a cycle of heroic tales.[1] Growth meant fiction but not invention: fiction because the elements of accretion had nothing to do with the real Troy, derivative because they recast some archetype.

A rape-and-rescue myth provided a cause for the war—and put the Trojans in the wrong. The leaders quarreled and jeopardized success. A divine mother was given to the chief warrior, and his life was darkened by frustration and tragedy. The city was mystically preserved and could not fall but by extraordinary means, a special weapon (the bow of Philoctetes) or hero (the son of Achilles), the theft of a talisman (the Palladium), and the making of a diabolical device (the wooden horse). Nor could so great a war be without its aftermath—disaster, for the natural excesses attendant on a sack ensured that offended gods were nursing their resentment. Thus expanded, the story easily absorbed other tales and heroes: it needed to in order to find enough action to fill the ten years of war. In the end all Greece and all the known parts of Asia were involved. And there were questions to be answered, whether trivial, such as how the indestructible Odysseus met his end, or profound, such as how the long struggles of the heroes related to the obscure purposes of the gods. Even if it were succinctly told—and the singers of heroic songs are not naturally inclined to brevity—it added up to an enormous quantity of verse, far more than the most patient audiences could hope to hear before sleep or hunger overcame them.

The tale of Troy thus posed a formal problem. The singers found an answer and thereby affected the form of epic from its inception. They assumed that the saga, or at least its outlines and its characters, was known to their audience: no one needed to be introduced; nothing needed to be explained.[2] The singer simply announced what segment of the tale he intended to sing or at what point he proposed to begin if he had no end in view. This was the kind of exordium attributed to Demodocus in *Od.* viii and implied in Phemius' case in *Od.* i. Having found the way to begin, Demodocus faced no other serious problems. His song would fit into the compass of two Homeric "books"—say, two hours' recitation. The story of the sack of Troy moves from the general to the particular and ends with the big fight: an effective movement, but above all a natural one. The steps from one episode to the next are easily understood, even if they lack the compelling logic of some fifth-century tragedies, and lead by the most fundamental of narrative principles to a climax.[3]

Demodocus chose his episode well, for the tale of Troy as a whole has the low literary qualities of a chronicle; it purports to recount a historical event as it happened. "Recount"—the Greek word is cognate with "catalog"—is the Homeric term (cf. *Od.* viii 489), and the demands of recounting as it happened are met by an additive, formless narrative. Now let the impulse arise to turn such heroic poetry into monumental epic, to multiply the short lay by a factor of three or six or twelve. There were those who saw no resulting problem: in the *Little Iliad*, an early post-Homeric epic now lost, eight unrelated tales were strung together—such is the allegation of Aristotle (*Poetics* 23.1459b), admittedly a hostile witness. But mere addition will go only so far. If the poem does not fall apart, we lose direction: interest wanes, and tedium threatens.

The epic therefore demands form. The singer who transformed a chronicle transformed it into what was essentially fiction, and fiction cannot be justified, or excused, by an appeal to what happened. Fiction must hold its audience by its intrinsic interest and the way it is presented. It helps if the material has some form of external articulation: hence the popularity of the biographical principle, especially if it is more sharply defined as the adventures of the Argonauts or the labors of Heracles.[4] Such articulation, however, is quite arbitrary unless it is supplemented by some such principle as that of balance: the two great fights of the young Beowulf, for example, followed by his last struggle. In its purest form the working of this principle seems to have been seen in another early Greek poem, now lost, the *Aethiopis*. In its first major episode a Trojan ally (the Amazon Penthesileia) arrives, drives the Greeks before her, is slain by Achilles, and is buried with due pomp; in the second episode another Trojan ally (the Ethiopian Memnon) repeats the exploits and suffers the same fate as Penthesileia; in the third episode Achilles attacks, drives the Trojans before him, is slain by Paris, and is buried with full ceremony. Arctinus, the supposed author of the *Aethiopis*, had a sense of climax but not much sense of connection: Memnon could as effectively precede Penthesileia as follow her. Beowulf's first two fights have at least a natural sequence when the triumph of his first victory is cut short by the revelation that the repulsive Grendel had—a mother! But no form imposed from without can create an inner unity, and this matters to some critics.[5] Aristotle detested the merely conglomerate, and so therefore did the Renaissance writers on the poetical art. It obviously bothered Homer (as the Greeks called the author, or authors, of the *Iliad* and the *Odyssey*), for he devoted particular care to the construction of both epics.[6] In doing so, he employed, surely in some cases for the first time, a number of devices that have formed part of the armory of narrators in verse, prose, and image ever since.

First, Homer took advantage of the singer's prerogative of beginning in medias res, without more preliminaries than a formal invocation of the Muse. Action follows at once. However, beginning in the middle means the middle of the siege of Troy or the return of Odysseus, which consist of many smaller stories. Like Demodocus, Homer respected the integrity and chronology of the episode he selected. Second, the time span of the epic is enormously compressed. The siege of Troy may have lasted ten years; the *Iliad* spans fifty-two days altogether, and squeezes its action into no more than ten days and a night. The *Odyssey* is still more succinct. The careful attention paid to intervals of times, especially in the *Iliad*, suggests that the compression is deliberate and not just the result of the sort of story chosen for telling.[7] A poet who sets out to relate the events of a span of years is doomed to paratactic incoherence.[8] Third, the coherence of the story is made tighter than the natural sequence of events. In the *Odyssey* this is manifested in the engineering of suspense, in the *Iliad* by a plot analogous to that of a tragic drama, each step reasonable and logical, at least to one of Achilles' mentality, but leading inexorably to an Achilles famed but doomed and friendless. Fourth, having conceived an action of comprehensible scope, and therefore quite short, Homer expanded it to the monumental dimensions he desired by incorporating at a logically subordinate level much of the saga of Troy or the tale of Odysseus that fell outside his chosen fragment. Aristotle, who admired logic, was ecstatic: "In this respect also, compared with all other poets Homer may seem, as we have said, divinely inspired. . . . He takes one part of the story only and uses many episodes [parts of a composition not forming part of its central action], such as the Catalog of Ships and such like, with which he intersperses his composition" (*Poetics* 23.1459a). In the *Iliad* this end is achieved by a simple plot setting up situations, mostly battles, that can then be indefinitely extended; in the *Odyssey* characters are made to narrate what had happened before the poet took up the story and prophesy what would happen after he concluded.

These points define the characteristic form of the Homeric epic. It can hardly be doubted that they represent the deliberate contribution of a poetical genius who was moved to transform heroic lays into monumental epic. But the transformation could not have succeeded if the genius had not also been a master of the craft. Homeric narrative style always reads fast: simple syntax and cumulative manner see to that.[9] But the pace varies in the sense that the ground covered in a paragraph may be much or little. The average passage, however, packs in considerable detail. Here is Odysseus in the last stages of shipwreck:

> The while he pondered this, a great wave was bearing him towards the rock. He would have had his skin torn off and his bones broken, if Athene had not prompted him. With both hands he quickly seized the rock and held on groaning till the wave passed. So he escaped one danger, but as the wave surged back it struck him and flung him off into the sea. The skin was torn from his hands and left on the rocks, like pebbles clinging to the suckers of an octopus dragged from its lair. . . . He swam on and reached the mouth of a river. The place looked good, smooth without rocks, and there was shelter from the wind. He felt the current and uttered a silent prayer, "Hear me, Lord, whoever you are . . ." (*Od.* v 424–45, omitting decorative epithets and other formulaic pleonasms)

This passage moves, but it also pauses. Similes and direct speech are variously serviceable. They are much the best way in which Homer can talk about character and feeling or highlight a particular scene; but for the narrator their prime value is that they are not narrative. The human mind best comprehends a string of events or arguments if it can stop after every few steps to recover its bearings and regroup its ideas for the next thrust forward. Similes and speeches, together with anecdotes and descriptions, are an old part of the singer's craft; the formulas that embed them in the narrative show as much. Short similes are universal. "He himself [Hezekiah] I shut up like a bird in a cage in Jerusalem, his royal city," boasted Sennacherib in 691 B.C. in what was already an ancient style; "I shut him up like a pig in a sty" had been the boast of Hittite emperors in similar circumstances seven centuries before. But Homer is rarely content with the short comparison, however graphic; the simile becomes a little picture in words. The retreating Ajax is not merely "stubborn as a mule" nor even "stubborn as a mule in a cornfield"; we must imagine the mule shouldering aside the children who are leading it, breaking into the field and chomping down the crop while ignoring the blows from its helpless keepers who can only get it out, when it has stuffed itself full, with desperate effort (*Il.* xi 558–62). This extended simile is the special contribution to literature of the Greek epic tradition. It is rare in the epics of other nations and uncommon in Greek outside the epic genre. But within the epic it is frequent enough to be one of the characteristics of its style. There are about two hundred long similes in the *Iliad*, with a concentration in the episodes of battle, and about forty-five in the *Odyssey*. Since their content is not at all confined to echoes of the heroic world, the similes make an important contribution to the epic breadth of view. And they are useful for another reason. Much of what Homer described was outside his audiences' direct experience. It could be stirring stuff for all that, but how much more effective if it could be brought within the imaginative experience of an audience.[10] The simile invites, almost compels, its hearer to visualize the two scenes, the action and its likeness.[11]

Descriptions that paint the scene, which are more common in the *Odyssey*, fulfill the same function; but the scenery of the *Iliad*, a level stretch of dusty battleground, gives the poet little scope for this aspect of his art. Devices like similes, descriptions, speeches, and conversations help create the narrative illusion. For a moment the audience lives in the heroic world, as the heroes themselves relived their adventures as they heard them recounted by the singer (see *Od.* viii 487–91). Did the audience applaud? No. "All were silent. Throughout the dark hall they were in the grip of *kēlēthmós*" (*Od.* xi 333–35). The word has magical overtones. The audience was bewitched, enraptured, and transported into a distant world of bronze weapons and mighty deeds. The illusion is well maintained for thousands of lines on end.[12] We are accustomed to this situation in the theater or cinema, where the intrusion of the author or the director and his camera is contrived only with some difficulty and for special effect. So we do not notice how self-effacing Homer is and are mildly disconcerted when the poet steps forward to appeal to the Muses or confess his inadequacy to describe a scene.

For an oral narrator nothing is so easy as to intrude himself, to appeal to his audience directly and dictate their response. In some traditions of heroic poetry the narrator uses the first person and surveys what he (or, often, she) describes as it were in a trance. But

the tradition of heroic poetry that Homer inherited prescribed that
the singer should use the third person and the past tense. In fact, he
was pushed as a narrator so far outside the actions he related that he
could see them in their totality. In relation to them he was omni-
scient. He knew the will of Zeus and could see the gods at work.
When in his rage at Agamemnon Achilles made to draw his sword,
the watching Greeks saw only the hand on the hilt, the heroic brows
knitted in thought, the blade returned to its sheath. But thanks to
the Muse Homer knew and told how the goddess Athene had
intervened in person to restrain Achilles "appearing to him alone"
(*Il.* i 198).

No narrator, however, can be so far outside his narrative that he is
totally objective. It does not matter greatly that Homer comments
from time to time on the action—he is only pointing out the details
of the picture like any good observer. But it does matter what he
selects, what he emphasizes or plays down, for these betray attitudes
to the events described. But whose attitudes? Who is the "me" of the
first line of the *Odyssey*? The real Homer or, as is more likely, the
character he assumed for the purposes of his epic? In the latter case
his narrative will express, in the first place, the attitudes that had
been built into the content of heroic poetry by its tradition; in the
second place, those of its audiences who were the singers' masters;
and last, those of the poet who was sufficiently master of his situation
to create the great epics.

In the *Iliad* the focus of the world the poet describes is the deeds
and feelings of the great heroes, but the very fact that the poem is
concerned with the effects of heroic postures broadens its viewpoint.
Old men, queens, and princesses comment on the war, and comment unfavorably. The *Odyssey* goes further and sees the heroic
world from the standpoint of a dispossessed heir and a supposed
beggar. In both epics similes insinuate the contemporary world and
the world at peace; from time to time we join the gods on Olympus
to view the strife of men from a distance, like amused spectators in a
sports arena. What is it that we see when we view the sport of war?
The triumph of victory, naturally, but also for those with eyes to see,
the pathos of defeat.[13] Pathos appears repeatedly in the anecdotes
that embellish the fates of minor figures; the high hopes with which
they came, the fears of parents, the horrors of widowhood and
bereavement. The truest reaction, truest to the intention of the poet

if it is possible to divine it, is a kind of horrified fascination,[14] exemplified by the tears of Menelaus and Odysseus when they hear again the tale of Troy (*Od.* iv 183, viii 83, 521) and the philosophy of Eumaeus ("Let us enjoy the recollection of each other's painful sorrows; afterwards even misery gives a man pleasure" [*Od.* xv 399]). There were doubtless those in Homer's audiences who enjoyed a good killing, especially when men died quickly and the narrative did not linger. Few tears are shed when the Indians are shot off their ponies at the climax of a traditional western; so too in the *Iliad* what matters in a battle scene is the visually striking motif: heads rolling like logs, spectacular falls from chariots, berserk heroes foaming at the lips. But there is an ambiguity even in the traditional attitude to war. There are formulas that tell of "battle that brings glory to men" but also of "war that brings many tears." Achilles has much to say about his short life, but his death at Troy (an early death) was part of his story, not Homer's invention.

Can what Achilles said be evidence for what Homer thought? Both epics are thoughtful poems, but most of the expression of their thought comes in what the characters are made to say. It is striking when Homer is contrasted with his followers (and it clouded classical attempts to devise a criticism of the epic) how much Homeric characters are allowed to speak and to become actors in their own drama. Reciters of Homer found great scope for their histrionic talents, for over long stretches the epic can be almost dramatic in form, speech answering speech with laconic stage directions. Thus the quarrel of Achilles and Agamemnon (*Il.* i 53–303) is not so much told as presented.

This mode of telling the story distances the author still further from his public, for what his audience hears in the first instance is Achilles putting *his* case. Authors of course habitually use the dramatic mode to make an argument indirectly. They betray themselves if they allow the argument to develop beyond the needs of the dramatic moment. Yet even where the philosophy of the *Iliad* is closest to the surface, in the long discourses of Odysseus, Achilles, and Phoenix in *Il.* ix, there is no loss of contextual relevance. They say what heroes have to say, just as they do what heroes have to do, and the mind of Homer eludes us. Later poets of the epic were much more inclined to raise their personal voice and lay bare in their own words, not the hero's, the turmoil of the heroic soul. The tendency is naturally greatest in those epics that are openly argumentative or didactic, such as those of Lucan or Milton.[15] Sometimes a character may become the poet's mouthpiece; in the speeches of Raphael in *Paradise Lost* v–vii it is not always clear whether we hear Raphael speaking to Adam or Milton speaking to us, not is it of great consequence.

To classical and later times, when rhetoricians had learned to distinguish such qualities, the Homeric syntax exemplified what was termed the plain style. Its virtues were that it was clear and to the point and therefore particularly suitable for the presentation of facts.[16] But simplicity is an art, and those who affected the plain style risked seeming flat and unimaginative—prosaic, in fact. In the old poetical language, however, when it is used to express the thoughts for which it was designed, it is almost impossible to be prosaic even in the most routine episodes. Add to this the fullness and detail of the Homeric style, and a singularly graphic effect is achieved, "as if the poet had been present himself or heard it from another" (cf. *Od.* viii 491). Homeric narrative according to various critics is direct, explicit, externalized, a succession of events taking place in the foreground of our vision. They mean that the events described are easily visualized, undistorted by rhetoric or hyperbole.[17] It is the style of an observer painting what he sees. If we are not devoid of imagination, we can join in the fight before Troy, but the Homeric style is not empathetic like that of Virgil. That is not to say the style lacks depth. Just as men and women, before civilization restrained them, used simple acts (tearing clothes, cutting the hair, sitting in dirt, throwing down gauntlets) to express emotion, so the Homeric narrative habitually hits on the emotionally significant object or action: Odysseus seizing the rock for dear life (*Od.* v 426); Achilles flinging down the scepter (*Il.* i 245); Andromache casting off her veil (*Il.* xxii 468); the Trojans, who so frivolously disregarded the laws of god and humanity, going to war in fancy dress (*Il.* ii 872, iii 17, xvii 51); or King Priam kissing the hands of Achilles (*Il.* xxiv 478).[18]

A corollary to this emphasis on doing is that if the hero is condemned to inaction, with its concomitant boredom and frustration, Homer has nothing to say: Achilles is abandoned in his hut for thousands of lines while his rivals enjoy our sole attention. If there are no others to come forward, Homer simply notes the passage of time. The plague ravaged the Greek army for nine days before the soothsayer was consulted; for nine days too Hector lay unburied while the gods argued about his fate. In an extreme case Odysseus spent eight uneventful years between his landing on Calypso's island and his first opportunity to leave.

The two Homeric poems have so much in common; yet in temper they are very different. The *Iliad* is austere, gloomy, and realistic. The only fantasy, as a pious age understood fantasy, is the talking horse Xanthus at *Il.* xix 408, and Xanthus talks of death and fate in the highest heroic tones. Friendly or hostile gods may intervene at moments of crisis but rarely in a way that does more than personify the hero's own efforts. A comparison with what we know of the rest of archaic Greek epic underlines the *Iliad*'s self-denial in this respect, a self-denial that is no more starkly evident than in the poem's refusal to contemplate any balancing of good and evil in the hereafter or any just governance in the present. The hero, and therefore the idea of heroism, stands alone. Beside this disquieting vision the *Odyssey* seems at first altogether slighter. Its moral tells us what, in this confusing world, we want to hear, that god is on the side of virtue and justice and that wickedness will be punished. But then the *Odyssey*, so strong is its narrative line, might easily have been a story pure and simple and have had no theme in this sense at all. As its first line announces, it is the story of a man. It is not necessary to say that he is brave and tough. The attraction of his character is that he is loyal, tenacious, and also crafty, an ambiguous virtue that did his later reputation no good but is needful in his epic, where the interest lies not only in the man himself but in his adventure too.

The *Odyssey*, in the common and reasonable view, was created later than the *Iliad* and was perhaps inspired by it, but in the evolution of the concept of the epic poem it is the more primitive. It draws its strength from ideas more fundamental and permanent than the transitory ideals of a militant warrior class and places a greater reliance on narrative effects. This is easily apprehended if the plots of the two epics are reduced to their barest outline. The *Iliad* is a brief episode in the life of Achilles, and for most of the time the hero does nothing but brood and wait; action is the preserve of secondary characters. A hero, the poet sings, is slighted by his sovereign and withdraws from the fight. Without him his compatriots are beaten. He rejects the appeals of his friends. His compatriots are again beaten. The hero's closest companion then saves them but is slain.

The hero then permits himself to be reconciled, and though warned of the fatal consequences returns to the battle and avenges his friend. In the *Aethiopis* Achilles fought an Amazon queen and the son of a goddess from the ends of the earth, both tales promising rare thrills and excitements; but in the *Iliad* Achilles is never in danger, and once he has caught up with Hector, he slays him in almost perfunctory fashion. Any romance or folktale has more narrative appeal, more suspense, and more riveting action than this story of Achilles. It follows that the attention of the *Iliad* is not focused on what Achilles does but on the spirit in which he does it. It is the story of his soul.

By contrast, the immediate affinities of the *Odyssey* are with the tale of Bellerophon. At its heart it is a folktale, the Return of the Lost Husband.[19] Within this tale are many others, for the scope provided by an absent and wandering hero has no obvious limit: he visits the ends of the earth—or beyond, the world of the dead; he meets the horrors of nightmare, ogres, cannibals, witches, and (since romance and folktale overlap) divine mistresses and alluring princesses; he sails waters where the sea is turned into whirlpools and reefs have the power of movement, and where the fortunate few dwell in a remote utopia that the wretched mortals before Troy could only dream about; he is the victim of one god's anger and the favorite of another; he is a hero unsurpassed in strength and guile but is dressed and treated like a beggar.[20] Apart from the hero himself none of this has the slightest connection with the Trojan War; some of it indeed appears to have been purloined from another popular saga of distant travels, that of the Argonauts.

Put in linear form, the essential content of the story begins with the departure of Odysseus from Troy. He is laden with loot and glory. His goal, of course, is to return home to Ithaca, but fate and god put obstacles in his way, as narrated in what are now books ix–xii. The loot and the glory are now gone, and the hero has become a lonely castaway on the shore of an unknown island. The inhabitants prove to be friendly, load him again with treasure, and send him on his way to Ithaca. Here he meets his sharpest setback. His wife is beset by a hundred suitors and, presuming him dead, is on the point of remarriage. She sets an ordeal for her wooers, to decide the fittest. Who should pass the test, however, but Odysseus himself! The goal is thus attained and the suitors disposed of, but by unexpected means and a circuitous path.[21]

Like most folktales, this story is rich in mystery and suspense, and by exploiting these qualities it has grown into a romance. Many incidents are irredeemably unheroic. When, for example, Odysseus sets out to meet the witch Circe (whose habit it is to turn her visitors into animals), he encounters on the way a "helper," as the heroes of folktales so often do. It is the god Hermes. He provides Odysseus with a talisman, the mythical herb moly, which will give him immunity against the witch's spells. Circe's wand accordingly proves useless, and she falls back on more universal charms—she is not one of the haggish witches of Germanic folklore—and proposes they retire to bed. The heroes of epic are not given that sort of assistance, nor do they receive that sort of reward. The problem, then, was how to make heroes out of this material and moralize it. The fundamental step was to perceive the killing of the suitors as a punishment. In the folktale we were not interested in their discomfiture; they could dissolve into smoke, like the evil magician, in fits of frustrated rage or meekly promise amendment without much effect on the tale. But in the *Odyssey* they are killed, and this is a punishment. As to their offense the poet is vague; after all, overtures to a supposed widow are scarcely criminal, and death is a harsh penalty for overstaying one's welcome. But in general terms the suitors exemplify excess and arrogance—hubris—nor did they count the consequences. All this the *Odyssey* calls reckless folly, a breach of the limits that god, society, and good sense have placed on human behavior.[22] Obviously, the point cannot wait until we meet the suitors near the end of the story, as was the case in the folktale; it must be made at or near the beginning of the epic.

In the folktale the hero worked a clever trick: the arms that decorated the walls of his great hall were removed (for cleaning, as he said). That left the suitors without defense. The ordeal, the stringing of the bow, put a weapon into the hero's hands, and he proceeded to shoot them down without compunction. But compunction in such matters is precisely what the hero is expected to show. There is no glory in the unfair fight. The solution to this problem is not difficult: provide the suitors somehow with arms—the spears with which heroes fight; prolong the battle; and put the hero and his little band of helpers into peril before they are victorious. The odds are twenty-five to one, but he does not flinch.

A more intractable problem was that of the wanderings in fairyland. For most people these are the essence of the *Odyssey*. The

Cyclops, Circe, the underworld—these were episodes too good to be discarded, even if the hero escaped their perils more by luck than by valor. But it would not do to have them in the foreground of the poem. They must be there, but they must be distanced and subordinated.

No one can say whether the need to moralize the folktale or the need to heroize it weighed more heavily with the poet. Both pushed him in the same direction: to begin with the return itself and have Odysseus narrate the wanderings in his own person to a suitable audience. This arrangement isolated the supernatural elements, compressed their scale, and achieved (though the subterfuge is transparent) a time span similar to that of the *Iliad*. The poet's narrative, by contrast, could be located for the most part in the heroic world. But Odysseus' home in Ithaca lay on the very edge of heroic Greece, and its links with the center were few and tenuous. How could it be made to seem a genuine part of the Trojan saga? The poet had recourse to a subplot. He begins with the story of the hero's son, Telemachus. A few scenes delineate his moral worth and the worthlessness of his oppressors, the suitors of Penelope. A voyage to southern Greece—pointless, for we know that Odysseus waits forlorn in quite the opposite direction—takes him to the Iliadic heroes, Nestor and Menelaus. Their stories tell of the aftermath of Troy. What these digressions contribute to the idea of the *Odyssey* is a point of anchorage. We start off in the Heroic Age and for four books remain in it. From such exposure the imagination does not easily recover; Odysseus remains the hero of Troy and, whatever his strange adventures, is safe from becoming an anonymous folktale figure. But in literature, as elsewhere, the cure to one problem is apt to create another. The beginning of our *Odyssey* calls for a Telemachus who is at least a mature adolescent. The return of Odysseus to Ithaca must therefore be proportionately delayed. (There was a legend that Telemachus was an infant at the outbreak of the war.) Yet even the poet's pillage of unrelated tales of wanderings could hardly provide enough material to fill ten years of sailing back and forth beyond the limits of the human world, nor is the appetite for such things insatiable. The answer was to cast Odysseus away on the island of the nymph Calypso. There he could be confronted with a different sort of obstacle to his return—temptation. The nymph offers him immortality and love and enforces her demands by virtually imprisoning him for eight years. When he leaves her, he must be shipwrecked again, to resume the thread of the story, on his penultimate stopping place, the utopian land of the Phaeacians. To them, and through them to us, he tells his tale.[23]

The ingenuity of this arrangement has always had an attraction for narrators who wished to impose structure on a picaresque plot or subordinate part of their story to a dominant theme.[24] But it is an arrangement that is well calculated to punish with perplexity an inattentive audience, even if we grant prior knowledge of the story. Its defects are easy to see: the fruitless voyage of Telemachus; the long period of dead time while he waits in Menelaus' palace (so that the main plot can catch up with the subplot); the featureless detention of Odysseus on Calypso's island; his implausibly prolonged anonymity among the Phaeacians; and the ill-defined attitude of Penelope to the suitors. In the form of our *Odyssey* the story can hardly be traditional. It represents the price that a poet was willing to pay to turn a folktale into an epic.

Some ancient scholars thought they had reason to suppose that the *Odyssey* ended with the scene in Book xxiii where Odysseus and Penelope are reunited. Their judgment is worth considering. In many versions of the folktale of the returning husband he first reveals himself to his wife and conspires with her to destroy her tormentors. On that model the slaughter of the suitors (*Od.* xxii) should be the climax, and Odysseus would be left a simple and unappealing character, the avenger, like some minor hero in the *Iliad*. Instead, the *Odyssey* places the reunion with Penelope after the vengeance. The note, though undeniably romantic, is also more truly heroic than the mere perpetration of a massacre. This, his home, was the goal of Odysseus' twenty years of toil, the goal for which he had foregone the love of goddesses and the gift of immortality and ease. Moral courage and a certain humility of the human spirit are the heroism of the *Odyssey*.

There is nothing humble at his first appearance about the hero of the *Iliad*, Achilles. By his own testimony he is "best of the Achaeans" (*Il.* i 244). The poet adds that he was also the most handsome. (That has no bearing on the story but is a necessary attribute of the perfect man.) He is pure hero, totally committed to the pursuit of glory. No ties to wife, home, or offspring complicate his life, save only the heroic bond between leader and comrade. At his birth, it was said, two lives were open to him—short but glorious, or obscure and long. In the heroic world that hardly amounted to a choice. When the *Iliad* opens Achilles has known nothing but success and cares little about the bargain with Fate. The poet proceeds at once to the quarrel with Agamemnon. Achilles is overborne, and now he must come to terms with rebuff and humiliation. We leave him brooding in his hut, a less than edifying spectacle, while through his divine mother he tries to manipulate heaven in his favor and engineer the humbling of Agamemnon. A prospect is thus set up: Agamemnon will be brought to his senses. Much, however, can happen before then. Indeed, it is dramatically necessary that much should happen, for an instant collapse on Agamemnon's part would be bathetic. Four days of battle—seven books of warfare—follow, with much material borrowed from other parts of the saga. At the end Agamemnon has indubitably failed. Error, if not guilt, is acknowledged and a huge bribe offered to Achilles to undo his humiliation and persuade him back to the fight. Dramatically, of course, Achilles must decline. Alone in his hut he had concluded that not only had he himself suffered an injustice but also that there was no justice in the world: he suffered all the pain, and Agamemnon took all the profit. Accordingly he treats his suppliants to a homily on the vanity of heroic glory, only to receive in his turn from his old friend Phoenix a sermon on the perils of obstinacy. Achilles had overstepped the limits of reasonable heroic behavior. That was hubris, and hubris was something for which a man would surely have to pay.

Six books later—for the Greeks must try and fail again—he relents so far as to send his best and dearest friend, Patroclus, to repel the Trojans. Patroclus' story is a minor tragedy in itself. Inspired by a generous impulse, he fights and wins glory, but he is lured by success to overstep the mark set for him and is slain by Hector. For Achilles Patroclus' death transforms the situation. He blames himself. He has failed his friend, and no dishonor could be greater. To wipe it out, no price is too high, no risk can be refused. The conscious acceptance of risk without too careful a calculation of the odds is the minimal requirement of true heroism. That is why the heroic tale of Nestor is so explicit about it. When Nestor brought down on Pylos the retaliation of the Eleans, it was unthinkable that he should shirk his duty. Like Hector (*Il.* xxii 37–130), he brushed aside the pleas of parents who urged the path of safety and disgrace; even the prospect of the

Molione could not daunt him. The presence of those monstrous twins in the tale is a primitive feature, a simple means of enlisting sympathy and displaying Nestor's heroic resolution.[25] Achilles' courage is morally greater. How high a price he will have to pay appears from the important passage *Il.* xviii 88–126: Achilles will slay Hector in vengeance even though that deed will be the trigger of his own fate. We are left with the impression (which is not strictly correct) that Achilles will die as soon as he has enjoyed his revenge. That is a terrible price, for in the *Iliad* death is absolute, unmitigated by any meaningful hope of survival. The Homeric ghost is a wraith, a gibbering, futile, impotent thing, horrible to think upon. Yet Achilles does not hesitate; he attacks as if he were the scourge of Troy, dealing indiscriminate slaughter. Hector for a moment has courage to resist him, for he too has his honor; a few lines later his corpse is dragged away behind Achilles' chariot.

An inner compulsion drives the heroes on to perpetuate their fame. They strive because that is the nature of their world, and no one of them can be exempt from the struggle and its concomitant grief and pain. "We all suffer; why should you not?" is the answer to those who complain—delivered by Achilles with stark brutality to Priam's son Lycaon (*Il.* xxi 99–113) and, considering his nature, with sympathy and understanding to King Priam himself (*Il.* xxiv 518–51) when he finally surrenders Hector's body to him.[26]

The Homeric epics are not hugely expanded heroic lays. Their vision of the heroic world is a particular one, and though presented in the objective, self-effacing style of heroic poetry, it reads like an individual thing. They are exploratory besides being celebratory; that is, they are concerned with something beyond themselves, with examining heroism as well as exemplifying it. That concern makes their epic poetry, in Aristotelian language, more philosophical than mere annals of events, because it universalizes and shows "what kind of thing such and such a person will naturally say and do" (*Poetics* 9.1451a). In beginning to philosophize about heroism, the *Iliad* sounds a note analogous to those sounded in the *Aeneid* and in the best epics of medieval and modern times, a note that came to separate the epic from the romance and give the secondary epic much of its raison d'être. To achieve it, of course, Homer simplified the moral issues. Achilles is made to acknowledge only two categorical imperatives: the duties of public honor and private friendship. Prudent men in the same world, like Diomedes, would submit to unjust reproach (*Il.* iv 411–18) and would not oppose a god (*Il.* v 818–24); brave men might show their courage in ambush; wise men might win honor in council; spies and snipers could expect rich rewards (*Il.* iv 95, x 321). But Achilles will have none of the oblique approach to glory—nothing but fair fight, hand to hand, on the open plain, with identical weapons. It is easy to understand such a posture as an aristocratic ideal. It was: the lords of Euboea whom Archilochus congratulated in the seventh century B.C. fought with sword and spear, like Achilles, and disdained the sling and bow. But social, political, or tribal overtones must not be forced on the Homeric epics. Their themes are moral, to present and scrutinize heroism in its purest forms.

Naturally, when it is in the nature of the epic to take a comprehensive view of the world, such an intention was not clear to every audience. Many admired the *Iliad* for the qualities it shared with heroic poetry in general: vivid narrative and striking incident. We have interesting testimony to the emotional impact of Homer on Greek audiences in the fifth century B.C.:

> *Socrates:* Well, tell me this, Ion. When you are speaking well, and making the deepest impression on your audience, whether you are relating how Odysseus leaped upon the threshold and poured out the arrows at his feet, or how Achilles attacked Hector, or of the sorrows of Andromache, Hecuba, or Priam . . . does not your spirit seem to take part in the events you relate, whether they are in Ithaca or Troy or some other place?
> *Ion:* How vividly you put it, Socrates! When I speak of something piteous, my eyes fill with tears. When I mention something fearful, my hair stands on end with fright and my heart throbs.
> *Socrates:* And do you not know that you produce the same effects on many of the spectators?
> *Ion:* How well I know it! For when I look down from the rostrum I see them weeping and showing signs of terror and astonishment at what I say. (Plato, *Ion* 535)

Ion was a rhapsode, a professional reciter of Homer's epics. He asked his hearers to feel, not think, and used the language of pity and fear, which soon became the framework for the discussion of tragedy. The *Iliad*, in fact, was adapted for the stage at this time.[27] Epic and tragedy did seem to have something in common. Aristotle suggested that the epic could be subsumed under the tragic, and Goethe and Schiller spent a month airing thoughts on the nature of the difference.

The *Iliad* is heroic because Achilles is made to foresee and confront his fate without dismay; it is tragic because we know that the price will be paid. But when the final moment comes, as it did at the end of the lost poem *Aethiopis*, Achilles dies in his moment of triumph by the agency of a god, as Patroclus died in *Il.* xvi, not by the hand of Paris alone. Why the god, we ask, for the unheralded intervention of an irresistible divinity seems to introduce an additional, unwanted cause of Achilles' end. The answer seems to lie in the role of success in the moral system attributed to the Greek Heroic Age. Failure was shameful—not just a miserable homecoming like that of Agamemnon, murdered by his adulterous wife, or a crushing defeat, the result of bad tactics like those of the Trojans in *Il.* xx–xxi, but any failure.[28]

To be killed, since it cannot be a success, was a failure and therefore shameful unless it could be represented as the work of inscrutable and omnipotent gods to whose arbitrary will all must submit. Apollo saved the honor of Achilles and Patroclus. Odysseus won his fight and saved his own honor. As a result of this viewpoint the classical epic tradition failed to develop one of the most potent of heroic ideas: the hero's gallant end. "Men say he could have escaped. But he turned his horse and drew his sword to make a fight."[29] To be trapped by one's heroic pride and then fight it out to the end is a concept of heroism that developed best in the Germanic tradition of heroic poetry. That is how the Nibelungs met their end, as did Roland (for the Franks were a Germanic people) and the heroes of *Maldon* among the Anglo-Saxons. The halls of the Mycenaean palaces with their single great door would have made a fine setting for such a fight, as the *Odyssey* shows well enough. Yet the idea was not a Greek one, not until it was forced on their attention, long after the great age of the epic, by the self-sacrifice of Leonidas and his Spartans at Thermopylae during the Persian Wars. Of such an end human instinct is to say that it was not in vain. Tragedy may sometimes present a picture of complete waste: in the epic there must be achievement and therefore hope.[30]

The epic, Goethe suggested in 1797, made greater demands on

the understanding than any other form of poetry. It took a broad, slow view of its subject. In tragedy destiny should sway events "or what is the same thing, the decisive nature in man which blindly leads him hither and thither," not reason. "In an epos it is precisely the reverse; reason only, as in the *Odyssey*, or some compliant passion, as in the *Iliad*, are epic agents." Schiller stressed the economy, concentration, and clarity of tragedy as against the breadth of epic and the variety of viewpoints possible within it. Goethe agreed: retardation and movement backward and forward were characteristic of, perhaps essential to, the epic.[31] It is easy to see from these ruminations that without its episodes the *Iliad* is too close in spirit to tragedy for the comfort of those who love definition. Likewise the *Odyssey* is too close to romance.

The term *epic* suggests that we are in the presence of something that is "big" in conception, but this bigness is ambiguous between depth and breadth. The *Iliad* is like a lens that focuses light with intense brightness on one spot—men at war, men confronting death and winning glory; the poem is big in the sense that it grapples with a serious moral question. The *Odyssey* spreads itself. Virtue and pleasure, vice, suffering, slaves, foreigners, women, nobles, animals even, all find a place; and to complete its picture of the world, over and above everything there is a just god.[32]

The fact that there were two Homeric poems, and the difference in ethos between them, was vital for the future of the genre. Either by itself would have defined the genre for Greek literature, and there would have been no obvious direction in which to go. As it was, the idea of the epic was elusive, lurking somewhere behind the forms of the two. Clearly other kinds of epic were possible, and who could tell, it might be possible to combine in one the qualities of both exemplars.

After Homer

I loathe the cyclic poem, the vulgar masses,
The thoroughfare where all that's common passes.
                                        Callimachus

The *Iliad* and the *Odyssey* came into existence at a fortunate moment. Singers, who composed (or at least re-created) their songs as they proceeded, were supplanted by rhapsodes, reciters who

neither sang nor composed. Like actors in the theater, they memo-
rized their text. Perhaps since an epic poem like the *Iliad* was a
valuable property, they formed themselves into societies to protect it
from vulgarization or even wrote it down. At least we hear of people
who called themselves Homeridae (sons of Homer) and Kreophyleioi
(sons of Creophylus), who were supposed to have knowledge about
their masters the general public did not.

This sort of preservation means a stable text, the importance of
which is beyond calculation; the fleeting spoken word was transformed into something permanent. The themes and formulas of the
old art of song made it easy to re-create a story but almost impossible
to perpetuate an individualized conception. It was by necessity, not
choice, that Homer was the most self-effacing of artists. Not so his
successors: the didactic poet Hesiod and the satirist Archilochus are
personalities. It took longer to appreciate that the whole nature of
literary art was capable of transformation too and that it could be
removed from the domain of traditional craftsmen and given the
clear stamp of an individual mind.

The poets (as we must now call them) of the seventh century B.C.
kept much of the language and diction of the Homeric epic. One
does not lightly jettison so perfect an instrument of expression. But
they lost no time in shedding the forms of heroic song. This was the
age of Alcman and Stesichorus, who established the form of narrative choral lyric poetry. Such poets used the same stories as the
singers of heroic songs, but their narrative leaps from point to point
and is balanced by prayers and reflections and a confident use of the
first-person pronoun. Their works were performed at public expense
on solemn civic occasions, and they themselves enjoyed personal
renown. Since the poets of genius were exploiting this new form, it is
easy to see that the continuators of the epic tradition were unlikely
to be men of talent, and indeed their aim as poets was low.

The six minor epics that once completed the Trojan cycle hardly
exist in their own right; they are appendages of the *Iliad* and the
Odyssey. Three other poems covered the whole horrible story of
Thebes and the house of Oedipus. There were *Heracleads* and *The-
seids* too, in honor of the labors of Heracles and Theseus.[1] Some
Greeks attributed the whole corpus to Homer—a grave injustice. But
who the authors of these epics were was of no consequence, for it was
fashionable throughout antiquity to despise these poems.[2] Aristotle

could scarcely bring himself to regard them as poems at all since they seemed to him to lack the very essence of any art concerned with the representation of action, that is, a plot. Indeed, such was the lack of coherent form that it was not always certain where one poem ended and the next began. But there is a more serious charge. The poets did not lack promising material; the content of the second book of Virgil's *Aeneid*—the wooden horse, the death of Laocoön, the horrors of the sack—was told in the cyclic poems *Little Iliad* and *Iliupersis*, and elsewhere there were the sacrifices of Iphigenia and Polyxena, the suicide of Ajax, and the murder of Agamemnon. The charge is that they blunted with fantasy and romance the keen edge of the heroic ideal. It is not so much that the poet of the *Aethiopis* made Achilles grieve for his victim Penthesileia (a fine touch but un-Homeric) as that he translated him after his death to a sort of Elysium, the White Island, and so nullified Achilles' heroic resolve to do his duty whatever the cost. Homer's consistently heroic view gave way, or reverted, to miracle and metamorphosis.[3]

As for workmanship, it was agreed by all ancient commentators that the style of the cyclic poems was dull. The fragments, brief as they are, seem to confirm their judgment; there is no eye for graphic detail, no feeling for the emotional power of an episode. By contrast, the cycle is congested with distracting minutiae. Aeneas' descendants were persons of consequence: what was the name of their mother? Eurydice, according to the *Cypria*, or Creusa, if we prefer the *Little Iliad*. How did Achilles come to have a son on Scyros? The *Cypria* explained about Deidameia. Such attention to the codification of knowledge had an obvious and contemporary parallel, the genealogical catalogs of Hesiod and his school. Nowadays we should call these compilations didactic verse and draw a clear distinction between their intention and that of the epic. Ancient critics, however, made no such division, since all these poems were cast in the same meter and dialect. So far as the cycle went, there was little in the content of the poems to disabuse them. The cycle performed the same service for the heroic world as Hesiod's *Theogony* did for the divine world: codified it, preserved it, transmitted it. The appeal of Hesiod was to puzzled minds who yearned to understand the nature of the world and the place of gods and humans:[4] the cycle and the catalogs confirmed the descent of noble houses (the guarantee of social order), nourished the self-esteem of cities, and justified ritual and custom. Poets, thanks to their special relationship with the divine world, had authority to pronounce on such matters. (A sixth-century Greek term for poetry is *sophía,* "understanding.") If required, they could put their understanding to practical use. Did it irk the Corinthians that they had inherited no heroic glory? By a happy inspiration their poet Eumelus identified their city with heroic Ephyre, an unknown site but home of Bellerophon, no less. In the religious sphere a tale could rationalize obscure anxieties, engendered perhaps by plague or famine; so the Locrians for centuries expiated, as they thought, the rape of Cassandra.[5]

The cyclic poems hardly deserved a more discerning judgment. They represent the spasms of a dying tradition. Yet it is possible to be too harsh with these poems; they, and the parallel tradition of didactic poetry, kept the art of hexameter poetry alive for three centuries. Some powerful didactic works were produced by the philosophers of the early fifth century B.C. At the same time the epic genre regained some of its vitality, but as a revival of the genre, not as a continuation of the old tradition. Its new exponents recognized that the direct line of descent of heroic epic was indeed moribund and self-consciously put the form to new purposes.

III

Hellenistic Epic

The Theory

Hence, meddling tribe of critics, gall and cant,
Who prick and gnaw, uproot what others plant,
Callimachus' curs, whom schoolboys hate,
Who praise Erinna and backbite the great.

Antiphanes

Literary criticism, in any form that we could recognize as such, did not begin in classical Greece until the late fourth century B.C. Even then, with honorable exceptions like Longinus, criticism seemed to avoid the very questions for which we nowadays would read a critical review: What has this author got to say? What is it that makes him worth reading? The classical critics, by contrast, addressed themselves either to imponderables (What is literature for?) or to minutiae. Even Aristotle devoted a chapter (*Poetics* 25) to the rebuttal of obtusely literal-minded objections to passages in Homer. There is an unmistakable whiff of the lecture room about much that passed for literary criticism among the ancients. "Grammarian" (*grammatikós*) means both critic and scholar, anyone in fact concerned with letters. Such men naturally saw their function as prescriptive, to say *how* one ought to write. Their value judgments in consequence tended to be directed toward style, that is, the manner of expression rather than the thought expressed. This approach coincided with the view that literature was a matter of art, a view that from the beginning of the fourth century B.C. displaced the old idea that poetry was inspired. Often it was the commentators or "scholiasts" on Homer and other works who had better things to say than the critics.[1]

Nevertheless, the limitations of professional criticism did not prevent views being held and judgments passed, however inchoate, about poets and poetry. Much, of course, was hardly more profound than "I know what I like." There is no doubt that the Homeric epics were well known and held in high regard. Since the time when the tyrant Pisistratus had reorganized the program in the late sixth century B.C., the entire *Iliad* and *Odyssey* were recited regularly at the Athenian Panathenaic festival. It would be incredible if such an attraction had been unique in the Greek world. Moreover, epic poetry was extensively used as an instrument of primary education. The schoolmaster read it to his pupils, as charmingly depicted on an Attic red figure cup by Douris of the early fifth century B.C.[2] Indeed, he probably taught it to them, for many well-educated men knew the Homeric poems by heart. But the schoolmasters of classical Greece did not teach Homer as ours teach Shakespeare or Milton. They were not interested in his characterization or his narrative technique, nor in his vision and understanding. Education in Greece, before it was complicated by the thinkers of the late fifth century B.C., had little to do with the training of the mind. Its aims and methods have been conveniently set out by Plato. He writes that when their pupils have learned their letters and can understand what is written, schoolmasters give them the works of poets to read and make them learn the poems thoroughly; and there they find much good advice and many stories in praise of the virtuous men of old, so that the pupil may aspire to become like them. The music teacher likewise is concerned with *sōphrosýnē* (self-control) and with restraining young men from reprehensible conduct. "Lastly, parents send their sons to the wrestling school so that they may have better bodies to serve sound minds and not be forced by feebleness to play the coward" (*Protagoras* 325–326, the sophist Protagoras speaking). This might well have been an account of the education of Achilles at the hands of the centaur Chiron. Nor was this coincidence accidental. The epic incorporated a serious description of an admired world.

For those who read Homer in that light, the godlike men of the Heroic Age were the example toward which all right-minded Greeks should aspire, and the best interpreter of that moral example was Homer.[3]

Such a use of the national literary heritage almost precluded any real understanding of poetry. In its crudest form everything was reduced to the didactic mode. "Orpheus taught us sacred rites and that we should abstain from bloodshed, Musaeus oracles and cures for disease, Hesiod how to work the ground and times to reap and plough. And as for the divine Homer, to what does he owe his fame and honor if not to the fact that he taught good practice, how to arm, form ranks and be a man?" (Aristophanes, *Frogs* 1032–36). That one might learn generalship from Homer (cf. Plato, *Ion* 541) was probably an extreme view, but it was thought perfectly rational to take Homer, and of course the didactic poet Hesiod, as authorities on religion. In Herodotus' pronouncement (*History* ii 53) the two poets had defined for Greece the names, titles, attributes and provinces of the gods. Did they deserve the compliment? From the beginning of the fifth century B.C. the philosophers had had doubts. It was not disputed that Homer and the rest were teachers, but did it make sense to attribute such a breadth and depth of knowledge to them? Was Homer master of all the arts of war and peace? Did he know what virtue was? Did he actually know anything?[4]

Plato, like any skilled controversialist, saw the weak point at once. It was the poets' presentation of the gods—those stories of Cronus devouring his children, of the intestine wars of heaven, of adultery, deceit, and treachery, "dangerous stories which should not be permitted in our city, for a young man must not be allowed to think that he does nothing strange when he commits the most shocking offenses" (*Republic* 378). Nor from this viewpoint was Homer's dismal afterlife much better, nor his penchant for lamentation, unseemly laughter, and similar instances of an unedifying lack of self-control.

All this was dangerous because poetry was seductive; its charms beguiled like the blandishments of Paris on Helen, and with equally disastrous effect. In the souls of its victims reason was deposed and emotion reigned.[5] A *fortiori* what applied to his readers applied to the poet himself. He was the mouthpiece of the Muses; he had surrendered his reason to their inspiration; he was "a light, winged, holy creature, that could not compose until he was possessed and out of his mind" (*Ion* 534b). But he was not so far out of his mind that he was above pandering to the prejudices of the vulgar and the igno- rant, like a politician in the popular assembly. How could such a creature, in such a state of mind, have had knowledge of moral virtue? Poetry was tainted fare and corrupted all who touched it—poet, reciter, and actor as well as the participating audience. It did so because it involved what Plato called mimesis, a scarcely translatable term since it is a technical expression in a theoretical structure unfamiliar to us. We may say "impersonation" when the object is people, "representation" when it is action. Mimesis is an idea that naturally occurs to anyone considering the art of the theater, and it dominated critical thinking in the fourth century B.C. because in the course of the fifth century the drama had become the dominant literary form. Indeed, at first Plato distinguished the mimetic component of the epic, that is, the direct speech, from the narrative, but as his argument progresses, the sense seems to widen until it comprehends the whole poetical medium.[6]

Pleasure, profit, and representation—ancient criticism could never loosen itself for long from the constriction of these three concepts (none of which has much to do with aesthetics) whenever it consid- ered the purpose of art. Since profit was opposed to pleasure and pleasure was not a respectable aim, it followed that literature had somehow to benefit its readers. The critics of course were out of step with their authors. As for representation, no one ever called the literary artist an impersonator (*mimetés*); from the fifth century B.C. on, it called him a maker (*poietés*).

The Platonic attack on poetry, delivered in a style as seductive as any poet's, became one of the best-known parts of his doctrine. Those who knew nothing else about Plato knew that he had ban- ished poets from his ideal community. What was to be their passport for their return from exile? They had to concede that the Muses were no more than a figure of speech. The poetics of inspiration had to give way to the poetics of art. No longer, after Plato, do we hear of claims to special knowledge or insight; that sort of thing was the business of philosophy, and philosophy of the most abstruse kind. Aristotle's discussions of the "practical" parts of philosophy, that is, of ethics and politics, stop well short of any speculations about evil, god, or fate, and so does his *Poetics*. For Aristotle poetry, by which he means tragedy and the epic, ought not to represent to us the confused disorder of real life; that was the business of historians. The true poet—and there were, regrettably, some poets who were really chroniclers in verse—disencumbered our vision and represented an orderly typology of life. In a good epic, like the *Iliad*, Achilles was the sort of man who would talk and act and feel in a certain sort of way; in a bad epic, like the *Cypria* or the *Aethiopis*, he was just a man to whom certain things happened to occur. This view conferred on poetry a degree of intellectual respectability, as Aristotle intended, and it opened the way toward the grammarians' reduction of art to something like a science.

Aristotle was unafraid to pursue theory to its logical conclusion and made the drama into art par excellence; it was the most direct, the most economical, and the most mimetic of the genres. The epic poet could not help but interpose himself as narrator. Most epic poets were nothing but narrators; Homer alone employed a mixed mode, making his characters speak for themselves, as if he were struggling to burst out of an inferior genre. Let the epic poet therefore, Aristotle argued, forget the Trojan War as a whole, or the adventures of Heracles and Theseus: such stories were too big for the comprehension of the reader and were not remarkable for logical coherence. Let him devise a compressed, comprehensible plot that the critic could approach as he would a tragedy, classifying it as simple or complex, pathetic or ethical, and commenting on its parts (structure, characterization, diction, and thought—being recited, as it was in Aristotle's day, the epic could have no elements of music or spectacle).[7] The *Iliad* was simple and pathetic. The plot proceeded smoothly to its climax and was concerned, as was tragedy, with violently destructive and painful acts.[8] The *Odyssey* was complex and ethical. That portion of it, roughly books v–viii and xiii–xxii, which constituted for Aristotle the plot, was full of "recognitions" and changes of fortune; it was ethical not just because it represented the complex character of Odysseus in depth but also because the outcome is in accordance with that character; the good and the wise triumph, and their opposites are confounded.

The Aristotelian contrast of the dramatic and narrative modes is dogmatic. The old singers may have chanted monotonously, their arms encumbered with the lyre, but rhapsodes like Ion were free to gesture like an actor. Nothing could hinder them from miming the hero winding up his body for a spear cast, or crouching behind his shield, or at least modulating their tone of voice in appropriate fashion. Nor for that matter could the tragic poet afford to be ignorant of the arts of narrative. Hardly ever in Greek tragedy is the climactic scene, where the tragic emotions are most deeply engaged, representational at all: it is narrated by a messenger. As in an Iliadic battle scene, the dramatist alternated between the general picture and the telling detail. Similes, more decorative than informative, added color. Direct speech clinched the vital moments. Diction moved up the scale of style to admit epicisms of grammar and vocabulary. In short, Greek drama came close at this regular point to breaking the dramatic illusion. Conversely, the epic poet created a dramatic illusion by appealing to his readers' visual imagination.

To be fair to the epic, it did have certain advantages over the drama. There was no theoretical limit to its length provided it could be comprehended as a whole. As a practical limit Aristotle suggested the length of a trilogy of tragedies, between four thousand and five thousand lines. That is indeed about the extent of the essential plot in the *Iliad* and the *Odyssey*, without the digressive and retarding scenes. For the latter, of course, the epic had a special capacity because a narrative genre could move about in time and place in a way cumbrous if not impossible on the dramatic stage. As G. F. Else has noted, "To the narrator, *just because he is a narrator*, all events lie open and immediately accessible: they are all equally present at the time they are related. If in telling a story I jump back ten years, the time jumps with me; the event I am now relating is just as much present to me and my auditors at this moment as the other one (the later one) was a moment ago. Narrative is a magic carpet which can transport us anywhere in the twinkling of an eye and then take up its course; or it is like a stop-watch which can be halted and re-set and then begins over again exactly as before."[9] Length, the natural consequence of the narrative mode, could itself be an advantage: it lent the epic dignity and variety. Dignity was also the product of the hexameter verse and the special language. Of other verse forms the trochaic foot (long-short) reminded Aristotle of the prancing steps of a dance, and the iambic (short-long) resembled the rhythms of ordinary speech. The characters of epic, the critics said, should be serious (*spoudaîos* in Greek) like those of tragedy and should express themselves in appropriate language. Of the true relation between the hexameter verse and the *Kunstsprache,* and of the origin of the latter in the needs of a preliterate age, Aristotle of course had no inkling.

A final advantage of the narrative mode was the ability of the epic to handle the irrational. What the narrator did not say, the eye of his audience did not see. Whole armies could, as it were, step off stage, as they did at the slaying of Hector (*Il.* xxii). More impressive scenes resulted. It is obvious too that narrative accommodates physical impossibilities even more easily than logical ones: hence talking horses and chimaeras, the Cyclops, the witch Circe, and the rest. Asserting the impossible as fact is a special case of the narrator using his authority as narrator. It became important in the Renaissance theory of the epic, when an element of the miraculous became de rigueur. Aristotle makes no specific mention of this aspect of the epic. He was overly concerned with the faultless structure of plots and probably thought that, like the use of spectacle in tragedy, it was a cheap effect and superfluous to true art.

A careful reading of Aristotle's chapters on the epic (*Poetics* 23–26) suggests that except where he referred explicitly to the *Odyssey,* it was the *Iliad* that he had in mind. He thus reflected the normal critical position, that the *Iliad* was the greater poem, *the* epic. The *Odyssey* was a sort of magnificent sunset, the work of Homer's declining years, as the author of the treatise *On the Sublime* (ch. 9) put it. Essayists quoted the *Iliad* more frequently; commentators gave it more space; the book trade turned out more copies; even Virgil described the Iliadic half of the *Aeneid* as a "greater" work (*Aen.* vii 44); "battles" came close to defining the content of an epic in casual reference. This preference cannot be unconnected with the assimila-tion of the *Iliad* to tragedy and the *Odyssey* to comedy. Comedy did not put on stage characters who were "serious," and indeed the *Odyssey* did give prominence to characters like Eumaeus and Eury-cleia (and to Odysseus in a low social role) to which the *Iliad* had no equivalent. By Aristotle's time there had also been a steep decline in the reputation of Odysseus himself since we left him the darling of the goddess Athene at the end of the *Odyssey.* In tragedy his role is normally that of the villain. Oddly enough, he dragged his comrade Diomedes down with him. After denigration in Virgil (*Aen.* ii 163–64) they ended together in Dante's hell. Achilles, a much less lovable character, tended to rise in critical estimation. Nevertheless, an influence on the course of literary history is not a consequence of critical acclaim, and it is the *Odyssey* that has left the deeper mark on the development of the epic idea.

Translation of the *Poetics* into Latin in A.D. 1498 and 1536 ensured that its influence infected the whole world of learning, with profound effects on composition as well as criticism. The mere name of Aristotle carried a vast prestige in the medieval and Renaissance worlds such as it did not have in antiquity. In its own day the *Poetics* fell on exceedingly deaf ears. The ancient world liked readability, and Aristotle's arid style was meant for serious students, not general readers. The latter, if they ever came across the *Poetics*, would soon have flung aside so perverse a work as did not recognize the supremacy of Homer and his genre. If they persevered, they might reasonably have concluded that Aristotle, in spite of his pose of lecturing an aspirant author, did not offer any criticism of the epic as such but rather commented on the way in which one unusual epic poet had burst out of his genre and practically converted it into something else, drama.

The critics of antiquity scarcely ever devoted their attention to contemporary work; their material was the canon of classical writers. The *Poetics* hardly acknowledged the existence of any fourth-century work; even the wide-ranging author of *On the Sublime* took account of no poet later than Apollonius Rhodius three centuries before. It is useless therefore to expect the critics to confront the problems presented by a revived epic. They would not see that the means and intentions of their contemporaries could not be the same as those of Homer and continued therefore to discuss interminably the excellences of the *Iliad* and the *Odyssey*. Indeed, after the *Poetics* there was retrogression. Neoptolemus (c. 200 B.C.) reiterated the Aristotelian ideas of structure and completeness but lapsed into the old opinion that the ideal poet would mingle utility with pleasure.[10]

The only importance of Neoptolemus is that he seems to have been the mentor of the Roman Horace, whose *Ars Poetica* (c. 14–8 B.C.) was the literary bible of the early Renaissance. In a chatty, tutorial style Horace played again with the old dichotomy of pleasure and profit—both were needed, of course—and went on to comment on another false contrast, that of nature versus art. We had not heard much about inspiration, talent, or genius since the mad poets of the fifth century, but they were in the air again in the Augustan Age.

The poets of Horace's generation had made the disquieting discovery that Ennius, the father of Latin literature, was innocent of art. By art they meant what they had learned from their Hellenistic exemplars, the subtlety, wit, and learning of Callimachus. But there was no denying the force of Ennius' verse. Those who most deplored his lack of art conceded that force and let the old poet emerge as the first example of that familiar figure in literary history, the uncouth genius.

Meanwhile epic poets were seeking to redefine the idea of the epic. Homeric epic had been the product of an illiterate age and a tradition of heroic song. Could it be separated from the social conditions that had created it? Could its ethos be viable in a civilized, bourgeois world whose favorite amusement was the commentary on social manners provided by the New Comedy? Could the form be kept but the essence changed and a new function discovered? What emerged as the dominant idea was that of something grandiose in conception, erudite in style, serious in tone, sound in morality, and set in the Heroic Age—a mythical tale of ancient exploits tricked out in archaic dress but contemporary in its ethos.

This was the image that the Hellenistic commentators on Homer had of their author, and they are embarrassed when he does not seem to live up to it. They commended what we should expect them to; and indeed the literary comment of the scholia, which is derived ultimately from the work of Aristarchus (c. 150 B.C.), is, for a commentary, unusually good.[11] It is their negative remarks that reveal more clearly their concept of the epic poem. What was most desired in Homer, and to their taste most frequently missing, was a consistent elevation in tone. Heroic poetry is hardly ever deliberately low in tone, for it is directly or obliquely praise poetry and therefore avoids the vulgarity that clings to satire and to poetry of blame generally.[12] Unfortunately, there is no absolute standard of unseemliness. Heroic poetry may always have recoiled from crudely scatological or sexual themes, but scenes of blood and wanton cruelty are another matter. In the story of Thebes, when Tydeus, one of the seven champions who attacked the city, lay dying, he seized the severed head of his opponent Melanippus and devoured his brains. He was seeking immortality, say his apologists, but in literature it is simply a scene of horror.[13] The goddess Athene—hardened, one would have thought, to the brutalities of the battlefield—was made to recoil disgusted. There are signs that the Homeric epic already found such motifs repugnant. Heroes make many threats in the *Iliad* that corpses will be thrown out for dogs and vultures, but none is. Achilles promises to bring Patroclus Hector's head, and Hector fancies setting Patroclus' head on a post for all to gaze at—but only in the heat of passion. Tradition had it that Achilles shackled Hector to his chariot and dragged him off alive. Homer allows him to practice the barbarity, but only on a dead body. There is no torture, no abuse of prisoners (if quarter is given), no explicit allusion to rape, and none to the nastier aspects of religion—quite remarkable, if one recalls that the expedition to Troy began and ended with the human sacrifices of Iphigenia and Polyxena.[14]

Much, however, that was offensive remained in Homer. It is easy to understand that the robust attitudes that smiled at the seduction of Zeus by Hera (*Il.* xiv 292–351) and laughed with the gods at the adultery of Ares and Aphrodite (*Od.* viii 266–366) did not commend themselves to the refined taste of the fourth and later centuries B.C. But exception was also taken to the suggestion that the gods might feel fear (*Il.* i 396–406), that they might insult each other (*Il.* xxi 475–77) or bully and threaten (*Il.* vii 35–40, xv 18–31, 212–17) or actually come to blows (*Il.* xxi 385–513). In contemporary philosophy Zeus had become identified with the guiding principle of the universe, as in the great *Hymn to Zeus* of the Stoic Cleanthes, or was consigned with the other gods to a remote existence of eternal calm according to the doctrines of Epicurus. This was not a climate of opinion in which it was possible to attribute natural human feelings to gods, as Homer had done, without seeming to demean them.[15]

Heroes were also expected to elevate their behavior. The great scholar Aristarchus, we are told, "took alarm" at *Il.* ix 458–61, lines in which Phoenix described how, having quarreled with his father, it crossed his mind to murder him.[16] Hardly more acceptable was the language in which Achilles addressed his overlord Agamemnon (*Il.* i 225–33): "Sodden drunk, with eye of dog and heart of deer . . ." That sort of language would have cost a Hellenistic courtier his head. Mean and unworthy thoughts were deprecated, such as Achilles' jealousy of Patroclus' success (*Il.* xvi 89–90) or the imputation to him of mercenary motives (*Il.* xxiv 555–57).

So much seems to have been seriously intended, despite the fact that particular objections may show excessive sensitivity. Critics of all the genres in Hellenistic and Roman times devoted much space to the impalpable concept of decorum, the appropriateness of ideas and language. As the noblest of the genres, the epic was expected to embody the noblest thoughts and diction, just as satirists, at the other end of the scale, were permitted—not to say required—to be vulgar and indecent.

Homer's reputation was rescued by methods that we can readily understand. His commentators argued that a wrong construction was being put on the poet's words, that due allowance was not being made for the primitive manners of the Heroic Age, or that the point of a passage was being misconceived. Thus when we hear Demodocus relating the shocking tale of Ares and Aphrodite, they explain, we must not confuse his characters' voices with the poet's: the Phaeacians and their singer are acting an appropriate part. When all else failed, the Hellenistic commentators concluded that the offending lines could not have been the work of Homer himself and became editors, deleting them from their texts.

To their credit the commentators avoided entirely the practice of forcing allegory on the poet. Intelligent and rational critics among their followers, such as were Cicero, Seneca, and Plutarch, would have nothing to do with it. *Neither did the poets.* During the whole classical period the only considerable allegories composed as such are found in the work of philosophers (e.g. the parable of the cave in Plato, *Republic* 514–17). But so versatile and irrefutable a weapon of criticism as allegory, already ancient in Hellenistic times, was not willingly surrendered. It persisted among certain philosophical sects in order to enlist Homer among their adherents, and in the end it achieved among the Neoplatonist thinkers of the fifth century A.D. an esteem that it did not lose again until the Renaissance.[17] Neoplatonism imposed on Homer its own philosophy, making, for example, the wanderings of Odysseus a symbol of the journey of the soul through life. It is the same exegesis as the Alexandrian Jew Philo and the Christian Fathers applied to the Bible. At the same time, for the fifth century A.D. is the beginning of the Middle Ages, allegory became respectable literature in the hands of the Christian poet Prudentius.

It is significant that in the Hellenistic Age the Homeric poems required commentary. Their archaic language was becoming almost unintelligible without formal education.[18] In the third century B.C.

the comic dramatist Strato introduced a character who found Homeric diction as enigmatic as the riddle of the Sphinx, only to be comprehended with the aid of a dictionary—comic exaggeration, of course, but exaggeration of a real difficulty. Nowadays that would not be important; the world would simply abandon the archaic literature to the scholars. But in the Hellenistic Age and later in Rome a knowledge of literature was a certificate of status. Ambassadors could make political capital out of their acquaintance with ancient poets; a Roman lawyer could pretend he addressed a jury of literary connoisseurs—and gain an acquittal; rich upstarts bought clever slaves to display a vicarious learning.[19] Such a situation was ideal for the sentimental, self-conscious revival of ancient literary forms. The epic did not escape.

There were those, notably the poet-scholar Callimachus in the third century B.C., who thought an attempt to rival Homer presumptuous and held that the course of dignity and prudence would have been to leave the *Iliad* and the *Odyssey* in their splendid isolation.[20] There is no doubt that Callimachus had much reason on his side. When the enjoyment of poetry had become the prerogative of a cultured class, the prettified verse of the poet-scholars could be read with pleasure. It flattered its readers' pretensions to Hellenism and the cultivated mind and did not disturb their moral complacency. At once cerebral and sensual, it seems to us to lack an emotional charge, a shared commitment of poet and reader to a subject that articulated their thoughts. The senses of the Hellenistic Age were attuned to detail, realism, surprise, and a certain sensuality. Two ladies in the fourth mime of Herodas (c. 260 B.C.) admire a painting: a nude boy with hot, hot flesh, so soft it would quiver at a touch; a tinderbox real enough to tempt a thief; a glowering ox, its hook-nosed owner, and his snub-nosed slave. The ladies are amused and excited, not stirred.

It is easier to construct an argument *for* Callimachus than to discover from his fragments his actual train of thought. His clearest comments are stylistic ones and are directed not at an epic but at Antimachus' long elegiac poem *Lyde* and at those who in his opinion confused bulk with achievement. What others saw as "mighty verse" Callimachus diagnosed as mere obesity—his favorite term of criticism is *pakhús*, literally "thick" or "coarse." Yet his talk of "kings and battles" in the context of long poems hints clearly at epic poetry in the Iliadic manner, as if that too was infected by bombastic, sloppy diction. Writing on a smaller scale would certainly invite care and polish, whereas the great epic was apt to be rough hewn; but what as yet remains unclear is whether Callimachus saw a necessary connection between length and morbid style. If he did, then of course he would have to ban the epic from contemporary literature.[21]

Even so, Callimachus could not leave well enough alone. He used, and perhaps invented, a new form in order to epicize without writing an epic. In the epyllion (to give the form its modern name) the poet composed an epic fragment in which he could put the old story into a new setting. He could be ironical or picturesque or romantic and indulge emotions that in the stern world of the heroic epic had to be suppressed. Such crossings of the boundaries of the genres were encouraged by the esteem in which Hesiod was held. The authentic poems of Hesiod begin with epiclike proems apostrophizing the Muses, but the high tone is not kept up. Hesiod denounces the wickedness of corrupt princes and explains how a humble peasant can achieve virtue. From the standpoint of the Hellenistic Age, the *Works and Days* must have looked like a poor man's epic that achieved much of its effect by a crossing of genres.

The model epyllion was the *Hecale* of Callimachus. It is a pity in view of its fame and influence that this poem is not extant, though it is possible to reconstruct at least its outline. Aegeus, king of Athens, kept his son carefully protected, for his life was threatened by the witch Medea's spells. Theseus evaded his guards and set off to tame the bull of Marathon. On the way he was drenched by a rainstorm and took shelter in the cottage of the old woman Hecale. She received him kindly. Theseus went on to subdue the bull and returned to Hecale's cottage to find her dead. He established a deme (a sort of ward or parish) in her name and set up a shrine of Zeus Hecalius.[22]

The *Hecale* is indeed set in the Heroic Age, and its centerpiece is a heroic deed; but the focus of interest is the very unheroic figure of Hecale, and the ostensible point of the poem is a fragment of learned lore, the etymology of an Attic place name. The tone of the meeting between the prince and the peasant can only be guessed at. It recalls the encounter of the hero Odysseus and the swineherd Eumaeus in *Od.* xiv–xv, but it would be strange if Callimachus had not indulged the amused, ironical manner in which the contemporary dramatists of the New Comedy observed society. But not only observation of contemporary mores was involved: the composers of epyllia liked to attribute such mores to the Heroic Age, with humorous effect. When, for example, Erysichthon was cursed with an insatiable hunger, what occurred to Callimachus was that in such a state he would not be presentable in public, quite a problem for the parents of a popular youth:

> For shame they did not send him to the common feast or banquet, and all manner of excuse was devised. There came the sons of Ormenus to call him to the games of Athene: his mother put them off: "He is not home. He went yesterday to Crannon to collect a debt of a hundred oxen." There came Polyxo, the mother of Actorion, who was preparing a wedding feast for her child, inviting Triopas and his son. With a heavy heart the lady wept and answered, "Triopas will come, but Erysichthon was wounded by a boar on Pindus and has lain sick for nine days." Poor mother, what lies did you not tell for love of your child? Someone was giving a feast—"Erysichthon is abroad." Another was being married—"Erysichthon has been struck by a discus," or "He has had a fall from his chariot," or "He is away counting his sheep on Mount Othrys." (*Hymn* vi 72–86)

Hellenistic poets derived a great deal of pleasure from this treatment of mythology, but it is a thousand miles from the spirit that produced the *Iliad*. Some element of moral force is necessary to vitalize the apparatus of gods and battles, similes and funeral games, that epic poets had inherited from Homer. Otherwise the poem cannot have more than an intellectual interest. The point seems obvious enough, even if through its neglect the history of the epic is littered with more disasters than that of any other genre. Yet the urge to write, which should be part of the definition of civilization, drives out caution. Today one writes the great unpublished novel; yesterday one wrote an epic poem. Even Milton in his younger years began, and abandoned, a conventional *Arthuriad*. In spite of all Callimachus' polemics the Hellenistic Age was inundated with a torrent of poetical accounts of Heracles, the Argonauts, and the wondrous adventures of the god Dionysus, a vast production out of which only the *Argonautica* of Apollonius survives. Hellenistic poets were even encouraged by prizes at innumerable arts festivals and with honors and precedence in cities grateful for a passing mention in their poems. In the second century A.D. Roman poets recited enough celebrations of Theseus and the centaurs to constitute a social evil.[23] Such work did not deserve, and perhaps was not intended, to survive, but at least it kept open for that time one of the options of literature.

Practice: Choerilus, Rhianus, and Apollonius

Shame on those who devote themselves so
exclusively to letters that they do not know
how to apply their reading to the profit of their
fellow men.

Cicero

The primary tradition of Greek heroic and epic poetry had faded out by the middle of the fifth century B.C. The first revivals of the form, the first truly literary epics, belong to the last years of the century and the beginning of the fourth. The most interesting and productive as an idea of the epic was the *Persica* of Choerilus of Samos. The most famous in its day, but also the most sterile, was Antimachus' *Thebaid*.[1] These poems, neither of which has survived, represent two branches of the Iliadic tradition in the story of the epic. The *Persica*, the story of the invasion of Greece by Xerxes in 480 B.C., continued the idea of the *Iliad* as history; the *Thebaid*, the story of Oedipus and the Seven against Thebes, reflected the idea of the *Iliad* as mythology and fiction, that is, as literature.

Antimachus was a conscious user of the Homeric idiom, a deliberate artist (no madly inspired poet he), a corrector of the ancients' lapses. An epigram in the *Greek Anthology* (vii 409) describes the impression that a sympathetic reader might form of his work: "Praise the mighty verse of the untiring poet, Antimachus. Worthy it is of the pride of ancient heroes, forged on the anvils of the Muses—if, that is, you have a refined ear and a liking for a serious style and are looking for a path untrodden by others."[2] Antimachus' genius, it seems, was for taking pains. Pains, with refinement and novelty, were the marks of serious poetry for the rest of classical antiquity. Learned in order to be recondite and polished for the sake of brilliance, much Hellenistic verse appeals in forms where an intellectual rather than emotional response is appropriate. Nevertheless the *Thebaid* received many accolades: Plato solicited a copy by special messenger, and when the encyclopedists got to work on literature, it earned its author a place in the canon of epic poets. The emperor Hadrian (A.D. 117–38) is even said to have prized the *Thebaid* above the *Iliad* and the *Odyssey*. Perhaps the alleged gravity and decorum of Antimachus appealed to his sense of Roman discipline; more probably the artistic sense of autocrats is unreliable. The critic Quintilian's professional judgment (c. A.D. 90) put him second to Homer, with the comment that this ranking illustrated what a difference there was between *proximus* "just after," and *secundus,* "second to."[3]

When Homeric battles became remote from the reality of Greek life, they ceased to be a promising medium for civilized poetry. Most likely Antimachus created an excellent reproductive antique. But there was a danger in his subject matter. In the *Iliad* killing is the quest for fame; in a Hellenistic poem what else could it be but the spilling of blood? Indeed, the story of Oedipus and his fratricidal sons was the horror story of the ancient world. It could be powerfully effective on the stage. In narrative form the Roman epic of Statius (another *Thebaid*) shows how its theatricality could be exploited— and how it fell short of epic grandeur. Antimachus pointed the way to a revived genre but his poem, so far as we can see, added nothing to the idea of the epic.

Choerilus, however, saw clearly that the need was not for reproduction but for renovation. In his exordium he blessed the good fortune of his forebears who, as he put it, had labored in the meadow of the Muses when the sward was still uncut. What he meant was that no part of the Heroic Age was left unsung. That being so, his prospects as an epic poet should have been desperate, because epic poetry and the story of the Heroic Age were synonymous. It could hardly have seemed possible to stretch the duration of the age when it was so sharply defined and the special quality of its inhabitants was acknowledged. "Demigods" Hesiod had called them, and in archaic and classical Greece that term was not rhetorical exaggeration. Heroes, many of them heroes of epic poetry, received cult and were conceived as a potent source of aid for those who possessed them. Such a status set them well apart from their descendants.

Yet to this general rule there was a partial exception. Greeks who for centuries had fought no wars save with their neighbors were confronted at the beginning of the fifth century B.C. with the Persian colossus. It used to be fashionable, when hyperbole was an ornament of style, to refer to the conflict as an epic struggle. Such language paid tribute to the intensity of the fight, to the great forces and high stakes, and to the apparent simplicity of the issues: east versus west, Asia versus Europe, autocracy versus freedom. The Persian Wars were a momentous struggle. The Greek miracle of the fifth century B.C. would have been aborted by a Persian victory. Little dramatic sense was needed to universalize this theme and make it into a vehicle to express the hopes and sufferings of all humanity. Later we sense the same feeling of awe in allusions to the Greek stand against Persia as in Homer's attitude toward the Heroic Age, as if a neoheroic age were about to dawn. Nor did the men who fought at Marathon, Salamis, Plataea, and Mycale see the conflict in very different terms. The voice of god, it was believed, was heard above the Greek galleys at Salamis; at Marathon a real hero, disdaining mortal weapons, did savage execution with a ploughshare; and the Athenian dead themselves were heroized and given cult. The Greeks were right: in its scale and issues the Persian War was different from anything the Greek world had known since the legendary days of the war with Troy. There was real heroism, as in the last stand of the Spartans at Thermopylae; but for literature it was not only the facts but also the perception of the facts that was important. Within a few years the Persian Wars had inspired a fine tragedy by Aeschylus and within half a century had, in the work of Herodotus, practically created the genre of historiography, to preserve as the epic had done the memory of great deeds.[4] In their pages we see the beginnings of the process by which events are turned into myth, by which they would be approximated in quality to the stories of the Heroic Age. From the standpoint of the fifth century, if the process went far enough, the Trojan War and a heroized Persian War would not be very different in character. No one doubted that however heroic, Troy, the war, and those who fought in it were historical. As for Schliemann in the nineteenth century, so then did the ruins and tumuli in the Troad and the walls of Mycenae guarantee the veracity of Homer, and in the fifth century B.C. there was more to see. At that time it was possible, if naive, to read the *Iliad* and the Trojan cycle as versified history.

Choerilus accordingly set out to make an epic from the history of the Persian Wars. If we could read it, the *Persica* would be a fascinating document. Homeric in language but contemporary, or nearly contemporary, in subject, it founded the genre of historical epic. Was it a success? References to the *Persica* are few, and none of them report any reasoned judgments. A tradition that made Choerilus a friend of Herodotus probably intended to imply that poet and historian shared a common purpose. That is encouraging, for Herodotus had the breadth and vision of an epic poet. But Herodotus evidently did the job better, and his work survives. Others compared Choerilus unfavorably with Antimachus. That would make him, according to the view taken of Antimachus, either second-rate or abysmal. Perhaps, since classical literary judgments are usually made at this level, Choerilus had not hit on the right style for a literary epic, which for the Greeks came to mean a style that was Homeric without degenerating into a pastiche of Homeric formulas. Choerilus was also sectarian, presenting what had been a national victory as an Athenian triumph.[5]

The real cause of the failure of the *Persica* lay deeper. The Persian Wars were in fact too close in time to be put on the same level as the siege of Troy. Time as well as faith is necessary to make men into heroes, as the Greeks themselves realized. In the *Funeral Oration* attributed to the fourth-century orator Demosthenes the speaker draws a distinction between what he calls mythologized events and those of more recent times. The former—he is listing Athenian legendary acts—included stories of Amazons and the children of Heracles and Oedipus. These the poets had made the subject of their songs. The orator then cites other glories, such as the victory over Persia in 480 B.C., but those events "through being more recent in time have not yet been 'mythologized' and have not been elevated into heroic form" ([Dem.] lx 9). The words may stand as a verdict on Choerilus. The legacy of Homer was a form that could not without absurdity admit any but real heroes from a distant age. If Themistocles was made to speak like Achilles or (more appropriately) like the sly and deceitful Odysseus, if he was made to converse with gods or engage in battle in his own person, too many readers of the *Persica* would recall that Themistocles had been not only the architect of victory but also an unscrupulous politician who had died an exile honored by his country's enemies. The old epic could make a myth out of the Trojan War without incongruence because it transmuted ancient history in a way that singer and audience both accepted.

The new audience, it proved, could not accept the same transmutation of more recent history. For the historical epic, and for any epic with a fragment of history at its foundation, how to make myths out of facts was a problem that would not go away.[6]

Having Theseus and the Amazons, the Athenians did not really need the Persian Wars to legitimize their place in the Greek world. But there was one state that came into existence only in the fourth century B.C. The Messenians had been a colony of Sparta for three hundred years and badly needed an ancient history. The myths of the Homeric Pylos would not do, for it was well known that the descendants of Nestor had fled to Ionia, driven out by the ancestors of the classical Messenians, and the early Dorian kings supplied only a genealogical list enlivened by notices of murder and disinheritance. Moreover, Messenian identity resided in their long resistance to Sparta; Messenian myths had to be anti-Spartan myths. The need of course was fulfilled, and it provided the occasion for the one Greek historico-heroic epic of which we have more than a modicum of information.

What we know of Rhianus' *Messeniaca* is preserved in the historical notes that Pausanias incorporated into his *Guide to Greece* in the second century A.D.[7] It was a strange choice of authority, for the imaginative nature of Rhianus' material is only too evident. He took as his subject the struggle historians of Sparta call the Second Messenian War and date to the seventh century B.C., and he made of it at least six books.

Even with the good fortune that incorporated the *Messeniaca* into Pausanias' guidebook it is idle to attempt a reconstruction of the poem, but some points can be made. The Messenian War was so distant that it was hardly more than a name. There was no need to mythologize a history that did not exist, and Rhianus inevitably adopted the contents as well as the conventions of the old epic. He thus avoided the trap into which Choerilus had fallen. Would his fictions, however, clothe a theme strong enough to support them? Rhianus knew his Homer well—he prepared an edition of the *Iliad* and the *Odyssey*—and did not see himself as a chronicler any more than Homer did. He began in medias res—that much is certain—in the third year of the war with the Battle of the Great Trench. But since Pausanias relates incidents from the first and second years of the war, it is clear that somehow Rhianus must have included them, just as Homer did not begin the *Iliad* with the outbreak of the Trojan War but contrived to allude to all its major incidents.

The Messenian Achilles was one Aristomenes, a brave and resourceful soldier but in Rhianus prone to traditional epic adventures. Like Patroclus, he was warned not to pass a certain mark and did so. As Odysseus and Diomedes penetrated Troy to filch the Palladium, so Aristomenes slipped into Sparta to dedicate a trophy in the enemy's own temple. Like Odysseus and Diomedes again, who slaughtered the sleeping troops of Rhesus in *Il.* x, he massacred the Spartans in the disguise of Castor and Pollux. There were un-Homeric triumphs too. Hurled over a precipice in his armor, he glided gently to safety beneath his shield and then escaped from the chasm by following a marauding fox. How ever could such a hero have suffered defeat? Only by treachery. Forced to retreat to the hilltop castle of Ira, Aristomenes and his men stood siege for ten years, like the Trojans. In the final scene, when the Spartans forced entry to the citadel, Aristomenes fought in the manner of the trapped heroes of Germanic epic. Rhianus' analog was the last fight of Troy. We know how that could be related from the pathetic and impassioned narrative in book ii of Virgil's *Aeneid;* Rhianus would have known the story from the jejune lines of the cyclic epic the *Iliupersis.* He turned them into a stirring fight. One feels the power of Rhianus' verse even in Pausanias' prose. Like Aeneas, Aristomenes escaped, but no great destiny awaited him. Rhianus was a Hellenistic poet, and his great epic suddenly contracted to the dimensions of an *aition* (*aitia* are stories that explain the origin of a rite, name, or custom): Aristomenes went off to Rhodes to become the ancestor of an aristocratic family.

Whether the Messenians were grateful for Rhianus' literary offering we do not know. Other Hellenistic poets who were adroit enough in their flattery received golden crowns and honorary decrees from their cultured audiences. Such a public was more interested in detail, which it was trained to appreciate, than in the whole of an epic poem, which might propound serious questions. People read Homer for particular excellences, as Horace recommended Homer to the young Lollius as a better moral philosopher than the best Stoics (*Epistles* i 2); or they would become ecstatic over beauties of language and style, as did the author of *On the Sublime.* But after Aristotle, whose interest in form was narrow enough, few ancient readers seem to have attempted to view an epic as a whole or to have theorized about what it might be that would hold together a string of adorn-ments. Such readers would appreciate in turn the succession of brilliant adventures in Rhianus' poem without realizing that by com-parison with the Panhellenism of Homer, its theme was parochial. However well finished its writing, however successful its heroization of an ancient war, the *Messeniaca* was irrelevant to the world at large.

Distance in time allowed Aristomenes to be mythologized; meta-phorical distance could do the same for kings. When Alexander the Great allowed himself to be proclaimed a second Achilles and then a son of Zeus, no less, had he not mythologized himself in his own lifetime sufficiently to achieve that distance from present reality that the heroic epic required? What from the practical viewpoint could be more relevant, more apposite to the needs and aspirations of the age, than poetical panegyrics on its brilliant and beneficent rulers? These were the literary equivalents of the sacrifices and temples their grateful subjects offered to Hellenistic kings. It is depressing that the epic genre should have been put to such purposes, and no one regrets that the fragments of Hellenistic historical epic are fewer than the remnants of its architecture. The kings got what they deserved—ex-cept perhaps Alexander himself, for whom it was sheer bad luck that his poetical adulator should have been another Choerilus, Choerilus of Iasus, whose lack of skill and genius became proverbial.[8]

When Portuguese explorers and Spanish conquistadores of the fifteenth and sixteenth centuries expanded medieval Europe, they released vast stores of intellectual energy. We tend to look at Alex-ander's conquest of Asia in a similar light, as a channel for the energies of a nation. Even as a general statement, this needs more qualification than most. By a doubtful decision of the stewards of the Olympic Games the Macedonian royal house was allowed to be Greek, but the same indulgence was not extended to its subjects. More ethnic Greeks fought for Darius than for Alexander, and to say that the Greek cities were reluctant allies in his Asiatic adventure does not do justice to the assiduity with which their politicians sought to free themselves from his tutelage. The conquest of Asia had been urged on Alexander's father by the Athenian Isocrates as a means of relieving the economic depression of Greece. It was not a national crusade. No pent-up energy was released, no impetus cre-ated; nothing therefore comparable to Camões' *Os Lusiadas*, Tasso's

Gerusalemme Liberata, or even Ercilla's *La Araucana* was inspired, for the Greeks could not see the fall of Persia in heroic terms.

From the literary standpoint Alexander even overdid it. His exploits were too close to the contagion of romance for their artistic health. The Iliadic tradition would have coped with the spear fight at Issus and the Persian chariots at Gaugamela, but Porus' elephants were, so to speak, straight out of the wanderings of Odysseus. And what was the *Odyssey* to the Hellenistic reader? An adventure story certainly, full of marvels. How much more, it is hard to say. For one of the less happy results of the arrangement of subject matter in the *Odyssey* is the prominence into which it throws the hero's wanderings in books ix–xii. For speed and brilliance of narrative style there is nothing to match Odysseus' story of his adventures until the bow is brought out for the final massacre in book xxii. If Hellenistic readers read the *Odyssey* for the wanderings, they were not the last. But these books have little to do with heroic epic. Blown past Cape Malea, Odysseus sailed into a world of fantasy: the Lotus-Eaters, who lived in blissful oblivion; the Cyclops; the island of Aeolus, god of the winds, and his family of incestuous children; the cannibal Laestrygonians; the witch Circe; the land of the dead; then the Sirens, Charybdis, the Cattle of the Sun, and, for a touch of realism, the final shipwreck. All this is folkloric. However, it was not in the nature of the Hellenistic world to frighten itself with such terrors; a sentimental revival of the Odyssean epic would be romantic in spirit and depict a world that was strange and exciting but over which the hero would safely triumph. Alexander's invasion of India inspired many accounts of the adventures of Heracles and Bacchus beyond the limits of the known world. The mythological epic Antimachus had revived was thereby diverted into productive channels. In this tradition is the one major epic poem of the Hellenistic age that is fully extant, the *Argonautica* of Apollonius Rhodius.

Were it not extant, the *Argonautica* would still claim an honorable mention in literary history: it is the first epic that we know of in which the heroic element is not dominant. The setting of the poem in the Heroic Age conceals this step, yet it was decisive. The old heroic deed compelling awe and admiration, which could survive in mythologized history, receded into the background; in its place Apollonius, Virgil, Lucan, and their Renaissance followers put their romantic, philosophical, and religious concerns. There was a risk in the latent conflict between the concerns of the poets and the paradigms of epic poetry bequeathed by Homer: Apollonius, Lucan, and Milton have not always been accepted as epic poets without reserve.

The tale of the Argonauts, the quest for the Golden Fleece, perfectly suited a taste for the exotic. It was a long way from Iolcus in Thessaly, where the Argo's voyage began, to Colchis, where the fleece was guarded. There were many lands and peoples to visit on the way, and the voyage out was matched by the voyage home along a different and more exotic route. Apollonius devoted seven thousand lines to this tale. It is recorded (without explanation) that its first publication was a disaster and that Apollonius devoted his years of exile in Rhodes to careful revision. Nevertheless, until the 1950s critical opinion, when not downright hostile, had been condescending. E. M. W. Tillyard wrote:

> Over the whole is an air of delicate refinement; and what we remember most are the prettily described scenes, the Argonauts telling one another tales; all the gods watching them set forth, with Chiron the Centaur going down to the shore to wave them off, Aphrodite seeking Eros and finding him playing dice with Ganymede. Like the painting of the Hellenistic age, Apollonius' poetry was the work of a sensitive and sophisticated professional done for the amusement of a coarser set of patrons: it was not like the art of earlier Greece, the work of one citizen written to interpret the feelings of other citizens.[9]

Apollonius *is* a difficult author for the modern reader precisely because of his sophistication, which is of course the sophistication of his own Hellenistic culture. "Professional" too is correct both as a fact and as a judgment. Apollonius was a scholar in the pay of the second Ptolemy at Alexandria and ended his career as curator of the great library. The combination of poet and scholar was a common one, for the Hellenistic age valued skill and learning more than it deplored aridity and pedantry. But the professional competence of Apollonius, as noted in *On the Sublime* (chap. 23), was such as avoided faults. Whatever the impulse to write, it did not impart to him vigor. His verse is elegant and musical; his diction, for an epic poet, is restrained; he constantly echoes Homer but seldom steals a phrase unchanged. At this level, then, he is a careful and workmanlike author, fortunate in his time of writing. Callimachus had banished the sloppiness of Antimachus, and Hellenistic verse writing had not yet surrendered to the love of virtuosity for its own sake. Apollonius would not have thought it a fault if a certain predilection for rare words were noted. Only satirists and comedians, after all, were supposed to use normal diction; epic poets had to presume a readership steeped in Homer and familiar with Homeric scholarship. However much classical authors might flatter themselves with thoughts of their originality, they were always conscious of the tradition of their genre. Apollonius introduced Homeric characters —Sirens, Circe, Arete, and Alcinous. He Homericized his diction, but he did not compose in formulas, and in consequence his writing is more intricate and less additive than that of the old epic. Hence the style does not convey the Homeric sense of effortless pace and leaves the art more nakedly exposed.

There is another and more significant way in which the styles of the old and the new epic differ. Careful readers of Homer have noted that he deploys two languages: a strictly objective language for the narrative and an emotionally loaded one for the direct speech of the characters. Direct speech is necessarily emotionally committed in most contexts, so that the striking thing is the emotional neutrality of the Homeric narrative. This neutrality is in sharp contrast with the style of the narrative lyric poets. Pindar and Bacchylides did not work to withdraw their personalities from sight. Nor in his own way did Apollonius. He invoked the Muse as if he were a traditional epic singer, but the fiction was transparent and hardly worth maintaining. So Apollonius readily moved between the heroic world (where Homer always remained) and his own. In accordance with Hellenistic taste he worked in familiar and realistic detail, as when Eros is portrayed as a sulky child (iii 111–66).[10] The *aitia*, which are concerned with rituals, names, and monuments of Apollonius' day, are frankly set in Hellenistic time. Apollonius did not shrink from authorial comment, often in the form of an apology for the nature of his material;[11] nor could he, writing as he was for a learned readership, conceal the fact that by choosing one version out of many he was composing fiction, not relating definitive history, as Homer had pretended. Henceforth an epic always has two authors—the implied author, who articulates the general voice of his time and place (or sometimes the general voice of another time and place), and the real author, whose personal voice is ever louder. There goes with this duality a style that adumbrates the subjective manner of Virgil. When, for example, Aietes saw the self-destruction of the warriors who sprang from the dragon's teeth, his heart sank like that of a farmer contemplating the effects of a storm; *ouloon*, "deadly" anguish, seized his heart. The epithet is used in Homer to describe demonic agents; transferred to the pain they cause, it is no longer formulaic but injects the feeling and judgment of the author. [12]

The story of the Argonauts is simple enough. Pelias, king of Thessaly, sends Jason on an "impossible" quest for the Golden Fleece; the heroes pass through a series of adventures, arrive at Colchis where the fleece is kept, gain possession of it, and return home and to vengeance. This matter could easily be arranged in the same way as Homer arranged the *Odyssey*: begin with the arrival of the Argonauts at Colchis, let Jason tell his previous adventures to the Colchians, and end with the discomfiture of the wicked Pelias. It would be easy, but unoriginal, and worse, a direct challenge to Homer. Instead Apollonius chose a simple linear narrative whose paratactic arrangement seems to fly in the face of everything that Aristotle had said about the proper structure of a plot. So much the worse, then, for Aristotle: unity is not a straightforward idea, although it often plays a critical role in the evaluation of literature. [13] It is not necessary that every epic story should carry the hero inexorably to his doom; a goal is required, and then it is enough if the sequence of scenes is perceived to be moving in its direction.

The *Argonautica*: Synopsis

Book i	1–330	Catalog of the Argonauts.
	331–579	Election of Jason. Launch and sailing of the Argo.
	580–909	The Lemnian women. Jason and Hypsipyle.
	910–1152	Samothrace. Cyzicus. The Doliones.
	1153–1362	Loss of Hylas and Heracles.
Book ii	1–163	Amycus and Polydeuces.
	164–447	Phineus and the Harpies.
	448–1283	Aristaeus. Mariandyni. Amazons. Chalybes. Tibareni. Mossynoeci.
Book iii	1–209	Jason's plans.
	210–438	Jason at Aeetes' place. Medea in love. The ordeals announced.

Apollonius may isolate each of the Argonauts' adventures from its neighbors; he may digress into etiology (there are more than thirty *aitia* in the *Argonautica*); but the stories cohere well enough so long as the Argonauts are on their way *to* Colchis. It is when they are returning, their goal achieved, that the additive manner of telling their far-fetched and disconnected adventures threatens to become irksome. As a goal to be achieved, the mere return to Greece cannot compare with the capture of the Golden Fleece. The climax of the old legend was Jason's and Medea's gruesome revenge on Pelias, an ignoble act of cruelty. (His daughters were tricked, by the hope of restoring his youth, into boiling their father alive in a cauldron.) Apollonius cut that part out. It was incompatible with the civilized Hellenistic taste that infuses his poem. So, with a sense of anticlimax, we leave the Argonauts as they approach the shores of Thessaly.

Some of the dissatisfaction when the paratactic form of a narrative is criticized is likely to arise from a feeling that the narration is monotonous as well as additive. The scene may be different, the names may be changed, but the pattern repeats itself. In *Argonautica*, books i–ii, the pattern is that the heroes overcome a series of obstacles by means of their heroic resources. The monotony is broken by digressions and then removed retrospectively, as it were, by the thematic contrast of the third book. Heroes dominate books i and ii; a heroine takes over in book iii. In book iv courage and cunning are set in opposition. The technique was not entirely new (Homer had contrasted the worlds and aims of men and gods); what was new was the manipulation of thematic contrast as an organizing principle.

The careful attention to detail that Apollonius gave to his work does not touch a deeper problem. Can an epic be civilized if it is set in the Heroic Age? Can the cult of prowess and personal honor be reconciled with justice and order? The classical world found it hard to imagine any opposite to the barbarous violence of the heroes except inglorious nonviolence. Therefore Homer's Phaeacians, the only people in either of his epics who lived wholly at peace, were seen as hedonists and voluptuaries. The problem dogged all the classical writers of mythological epics, and none worked out a solution immune from criticism. By confronting it, Virgil gave an uneasy depth to his epic, and by ignoring it, Statius showed how repulsive savagery could be.

At first sight the learned and unmilitary Apollonius may seem too civilized for an epic poet. We look at his Jason, expecting to find an Achilles or an Odysseus, and find a weak and colorless figure, at best a supple diplomat, overshadowed as a character by Medea. Even his courage is without conviction, for it will never do merely to assert that the hero is brave; his bravery must be demonstrated in action. But in the end, when Jason faces his ordeals in Colchis, he relies on the unheroic aids of folktale, Medea's spells. Other Argonauts had their unheroic aids built in, so to speak: the winged sons of the North Wind; Euphemus so fleet of foot that he ran over the water without sinking; Lynceus with his penetrating sight; Heracles with his supernatural strength; Polydeuces (Pollux) with his murderous punch; and Orpheus inseparable from his lyre. Like gods who cannot die, these are heroes who cannot be defeated; neither gods nor heroes, therefore, are capable of true heroic grandeur.[14] There is not much grandeur in Apollonius, and not in the expected places. The Golden Fleece itself is not an idea for which men should strive, not a Holy Grail precious in itself and symbolic of something even more precious. It is simply a goal set by Pelias for Jason in the hope that he would not return from the quest. Anything else would have served Pelias' purpose. For the old heroes, of course, the nature of the goal did not matter so much as the fact that it was there. But what passes in a heroic lay can look very slender when raised to the dimensions of an epic poem.

Homer could pretend that he and his progenitors were mere entertainers, but we know better. Neither heroic lays nor folktales are ever entirely frivolous, and what has been said of Greek tragedy may be said of epic: "Within these limits [i.e. the parameters of myth] the tragedy may be grave, terrible, exciting, witty, inventive; it may end happily (though only after troubling vicissitudes) or in catastrophe, the issues at stake may vary greatly in profundity but there must *be* issues at stake, and something must emerge, however darkly, fitfully, or enigmatically, about the dealings of gods with men."[15] By that standard it is easy to find the *Argonautica* wanting, as if it were no better than an upscale version of the wild stories of love and adventure that the authors of the prose novella (the most significant contribution of the Hellenistic age to literature) were creating.

However, to talk of grandeur and gravity betrays the prejudice of those for whom the parameters of the epic genre have been drawn exclusively by Homer, Virgil, Tasso, and Milton. Since the mid-twentieth century criticism has been kinder to Apollonius. The *Argonautica* was certainly a sentimental reuse of the Homeric form, but it did not make a corresponding sentimental reuse of heroic attitudes, as Rhianus' poem seems to have done. Therein lies its value as a poem and its interest as a mutation in the evolution of the epic genre.[16] Apollonius shifted the focus of the epic away from the heroic machismo of Homer and replaced it with something expressive of the ideals of his own age. The relics of the Heroic Age, Idas and Heracles, are dismissed or drop out. Aphrodite is the patron goddess of the Argonauts (ii 420), a deity whom Homer had banished from the battlefield. The new man, Jason, does not dominate because he is not intended to dominate; he personifies no virtue or principle because he is one of the first examples in literature of what has become the "hero" of the novel—a person, not a paragon. The *Argonautica,* like the novel, displays its creator's private vision of the world. Yet it embodies the spirit of the Hellenistic age too deeply not to have some echoes of the public voice of the epic. Jason makes his way by charm and diplomacy. He succeeds or fails by fortune, that Fortune whom the historian Polybius saw as the real arbiter of the world.

The archaic age in Greece tended to look at personal relations in terms of obligation and advantage. Passion, *eros,* was thought to be destructive, perverting those it seized from the path of duty. Perhaps only Homer conceived and described personal relations that were unselfish, uncalculating, mutually supportive, and long enduring.

From the fifth century B.C., however, there was more and more opportunity to meet with the literary manifestations of romantic love. Sophocles dedicated a fine ode to the power of *eros* (*Antigone* 781–99); Euripides shocked and fascinated audiences with his portrayals of Stheneboea and Phaedra; and when Plato in his *Symposium* had subjected the concept to the analysis of the Socratic dialectic, the youth of Athens certainly knew what emotions nature was supposed to have prepared for them. For the audiences of the New Comedy in the late fourth century it was axiomatic that young persons were in love. In such an atmosphere ancient myths were seen in a new light, all the more readily when the decline in piety was turning myths into fairy tales. It is therefore understandable that Apollonius should introduce a love interest into his epic.

At first he does so tentatively, making what his characters feel subordinate to what they do and suffer. He suggests obliquely one instance of homosexual love, that of Heracles and Hylas. Yet there is an odd reticence about Apollonius' treatment. Neither when Hylas is introduced (i 131–32), nor in the story of his loss and of Heracles' despair (i 1187–1283), does Apollonius actually say that Heracles was Hylas' lover. Perhaps he remembered the discretion (as his age would have seen it) with which Homer had handled the relations of Achilles and Patroclus. The time was not yet when epic heroes could decently swoon for love. So Jason's first encounter with a queen is an amour. He is received by Hypsipyle, queen of Lemnos, whose island she and her female subjects have just purged of its male inhabitants. Hypsipyle proves to be as deceitful as Odysseus, and since Jason must abandon her, so does the poet. Medea's role could not leave *her* portrait so half-complete.

The active women of the old heroic poetry had simply assumed the masculine role: Atalanta hunted the boar, and Penthesileia fought with shield and spear. Apollonius' Medea is indeed a witch and murderess, but she enters the epic as a Hellenistic woman and for long so remains. That identity limited what Medea could do even when she is the focus of the narrative in the third book, but Apollonius' exploration of her mind makes her easily the most sharply drawn character in the poem.

Medea is struck to the heart by Eros' arrow. In other words (for no one takes these gods seriously), she falls in love at the first sight of Jason. The symptoms are classic: if Apollonius had not observed them—and he was an observant man, as more than seventy Homeric-style similes show—he could have read them in the lyric poetry of Sappho. Medea was tongue-tied; she glances furtively but compulsively at Jason; she turns pale and blushes; every detail of his appearance is implanted in her mind. Nor is Apollonius an observer only; he has a certain empathy with his heroine. She tries to banish the stranger from her mind. She is terrified for him when the ordeals are announced. She cannot sleep for tears and palpitation. But her agonies can have only one issue: duty, modesty, and reputation are flung aside; still petrified and speechless, she joins the Argonauts and lends her indispensable aid to Jason. Such is Medea the woman as Apollonius conceived her, and she is his permanent contribution to the content of the epic genre. Virgil's Dido and the amorous witches of Tasso are her descendants.

The heart of the *Argonautica,* the third book, is by any standard a fine poem. It has cohesion, movement, and denouement. But it is only too clear that the focus of interest, the "hero," of this poem is not Jason but Medea. Even in heroic poetry there were heroines who played a middle role between that of uncomplaining wife and that of Amazon queen: Clytaimnestra and Kriemhild, in the Germanic epic, were women driven by wounded honor to great and terrible deeds. Neither did Medea's poem end amid the rosy clouds of romance. She sails into the sunset, scattering the severed limbs of her murdered brother in her wake to frustrate pursuit.

IV

Roman Historical Epic

The matter of poetry should be like the matter of
history and resemble it, but it ought not to be
the same.

Castelvetro, on chapter 1 of Aristotle's *Poetics*

Q. Ennius, the earliest nondramatic poet of the Latin language
whom later ages thought worthy of respect, was born in 239 B.C. His
productive life spanned most of the fifty-three years (220–168 B.C.)
during which, according to the historian Polybius, the Roman republic made itself the master of the world. Polybius meant political
mastery. The tide of cultural imperialism ran the other way and in
Ennius almost swamped whatever there might have been of a genuine Italian literary tradition.

The Romans, of course, had sung heroic lays. They composed
them in the (to later ears) clumsy meter called Saturnian. (Saturn
was the god of a mythical ancient golden age.) The example of Greek
literature was needed to turn Saturnian song into an epic poem.
Livius Andronicus' translation of the *Odyssey* in the mid-third century B.C. provided the model. Just as important was the Romans'
increasing knowledge of that prestigious intellectual activity called
literature as it was practiced among contemporary Greeks. It was all
very well for Romans of the ancient mold to say *rem tene: verba
sequentur*, "stick to the point; the words will follow"; that was not art
and not how Greeks extolled the achievements of their kings. That
the historical epic in Greece had led to no great successes was

certainly not apparent to the Romans. It is hard for contemporaries to judge their own art; as for those who have no art, even bad art seems marvelous. The Romans were a people who revered their ancestors, and the panegyrics of historical epic were something they could immediately understand.

Rhianus, the two Choerili, and their emulators pointed the way. The heroic age of Roman expansion called for an epic that was also a record. The result was a verse chronicle, the *Punic War* (i.e. the First Punic War, 264–241 B.C., not Hannibal's war) of the poet Naevius. Little enough is known about it, and were it extant it would probably be praised as a bold experiment. Ennius, in Roman fashion, was more direct; it was, he said, "the poetry of Fauns and soothsayers."

Naevius' poem was important in one respect, however. It claimed for the epic genre the designation "national." Many peoples nowadays have "national epics," but few of the poems were composed as such: the status was imposed on them by later generations. No Greek of the classical period, supposing the *Iliad* had not existed, would have chosen the distant exploit of an extinct tribe to create a literary expression of national consciousness. The *Iliad* was not composed as national epic, the literary expression of national consciousness and pride; it *became* one. Naevius and then Ennius consciously set out to create the Roman equivalent.

Annales was the title of Ennius' poem, the story of the Roman people from the fall of Troy to the poet's own day.[1] Many Romans were irked by Greek cultural superiority and consoled themselves with convenient myths: the Greeks were morally inferior, slippery, mercurial, congenitally incapable of understanding the nature of an oath, and nonstarters in the arts of government and war.[2] That was a comforting belief, provided it was not examined too closely, but it did little to erode the fact that Greece had a rich historical record of more than a thousand years and Rome nothing more than the scrappy chronicle of the Pontifex Maximus (not much more, it was said, than the state of the weather and the fluctuations in the price of bread). The deficiency mattered in a world where a history was an asset, and Roman imaginations were soon busy creating their past. The most brilliant stroke—and on what foundations it rested no one knows—was to annex the illustrious survivor of the Trojan War, Aeneas. He fled to Italy, it was proclaimed, to found the Roman race. He brought with him a whole mythology, a divine ancestry, a moral justification for Roman aggression against Greece, and a venerable antiquity: in short, he was the Roman passport to membership in the civilized world. Naturally, Ennius began with Aeneas. He then raced ahead. As it is reported to us, the *Annales* was in eighteen books, i–iii covering the time of the kings of Rome, iv–vi the conquest of Italy by the republic, vii–ix the wars with Carthage, especially the Second or Hannibalic War (218–202 B.C.), x–xii the wars in Macedonia and Greece, xiii–xv the defeat of Antiochus and the triumph of Ennius' patron, Fulvius Nobilior; xvi–xviii seem to have been a sort of continuation, telling of the wars that followed almost to the poet's death in 169 B.C.

To see the rise of Rome over so many centuries as the fulfillment of the destiny of a nation was no mean vision. Competent critics like Cicero and Lucretius agreed that Ennius was one of the great epic poets, better than his crude language and imperfect verse would allow. In the second century B.C. those defects did not matter. It was Ennius who set the standard and for a hundred years he reigned unchallenged. He was fortunate in living when he did: a generation earlier and it would not have been clear where the destiny of Rome was leading, to empire or to a minor role as an underdeveloped country on the fringes of the Hellenistic world. That question was answered decisively by the Second Punic War, one of the great turning points in history. What was important for literature was that the long struggle and final victory created a unity of purpose and sense of invincibility that lasted more than half a century. It could not last forever, and Roman historians later theorized that the final capture of Carthage and the simultaneous destruction of Corinth in 146 B.C. marked the moment when the ancient morality and concord gave way to dissension and corruption. Epics are not written about decline nor, except in special cases, about civil wars. But when Ennius died, all that lay ahead. He could survey the rise of Rome and see it (for poets are not bound by the strict rules of history) as a continuous process taking the city under the ordinances of heaven from nothing to absolute supremacy and power. The hero of this story could not be one person. Ennius, it is true, did not recoil from the duties of patronage and admitted both panegyric and polemic. It was a bad precedent, but the taint affected only the later books of the *Annales* and the narrative of contemporary affairs. The real hero of the epic is the Roman people itself. *Moribus antiquis res stat*

Romana virisque, "By ancient ways and by her men the Roman state stands firm," was one of Ennius' most famous lines, and justly so. It encapsulates the vision that carried him through the daunting difficulties that the almost total lack of traditional artistic competence set before him.

Ennius began with the usual salute to the goddesses of song. He called them the Muses. That appellation itself was significant. The goddesses invoked by Livius and Naevius had been the native Italian Camenae, a thin disguise, it must be admitted, for the Greek Muses (the Camenae seem really to have been water nymphs). But in Ennius the Muses are unashamedly Greek, and they dwell on Mount Olympus. Such Muses were simultaneously a confession and a boast —a boast that the Romans were taking over where the Greeks had left off, and a confession that there was no Italian literature and, despite the efforts of Naevius, no foundation on which an Italian literature could be built. Literature for the Romans would be Greek literature composed in Latin. Three hundred years after Ennius the critic Quintilian dared claim Italian originality for only one genre, satire.[3] Elsewhere literature consciously rested on the Greek tradition: Horace was the first (he said) to produce a Latin version of the lyric poetry of Alcaeus and Sappho and of the bitter iambics of Archilochus; Propertius was the Roman Callimachus and thought the *Aeneid* a second and superior *Iliad;* Virgil sang the Syracusan song, that is, the pastoral of Theocritus, and introduced the didactic poetry of Hesiod.[4] Ennius was the Roman Homer—quite literally, he suggested, for the specter of Homer had appeared to him in a dream to reveal that his spirit, after several intermediate incarnations, now dwelt in the breast of Ennius. It is an interesting slant on the concept of literary ancestry. There is such a thing as honest pride, but he might, one editor suggests, have been seeking to preempt the criticism of the Callimachean school: Ennius could legitimately attempt a Homeric epic because he *was* Homer.[5]

The reincarnated Homer brought with him the long traditional apparatus of the Greek epic. Later poets decided that some of it was a mistake—his language for example. The arcane, polysyllabic diction of the Greek epic was a splendid tool. The most banal and prosaic thought would sound poetic in Homeric dress. Such diction, however, had taken centuries to perfect and could not be reproduced in a day, *mutatis mutandis,* in another language. In fact it could not be reproduced at all, for the special features of the epic language rest on certain features of the Greek language, on its patterns of syllabification and word formation. It sounds right in Greek to say *hypsipetēs*, "high-flying," of a Homeric eagle, but Latin *altivolans* merely sounds clumsy. Ennius even resurrected ancient grammatical forms: the "king of Alba Longa" is *rex Albai Longai* (for *Albae Longae*). Some he actually invented, as *Mettoeoque Fufetioeo* (for *Metti Fufetii*). Later ages laughed at these aberrations and called their author shaggy and unkempt. But such language and diction was not a dominant aspect of Ennius' style. In a fragment of twenty lines on the augury of Romulus and Remus that Cicero preserves (*De Divinatione* i 48) there is one compounded epithet, one archaism, and one poeticism, no more.[6] Ennius does not reproduce Homer; he hints at him, allusively. This approach is much more subtle than the frankly Homericizing style of Hellenistic epic, but it rests on the same assumptions, that the reader draws on a certain literary background and will interpret the language as poetical because of the echoes of Homer perceived in it.

It is difficult even from honest motives to pervert language in an acceptable way. If it was Ennius' intuitive wish that his readers would feel there was a great language in the background and the spirit of a great poet, not many of his means to that end survived him. Yet the problem of a language for the epic to match its matter persisted. Virgil rejected almost all Ennius' archaisms in his normal grammar and adopted a new means: to echo Homer's matter rather than his language, compounded by allusions to Ennius' more successful turns of phrase. Later Romans, such as Silius, Statius, and Valerius Flaccus, in their turn echoed the language of Virgil; and as every reader of Milton is made aware, modern classicizing epic poets have not been slow to use similar means to proclaim their literary allegiances.

Ennius left a deeper mark on Latin poetry by his choice of meter: the second Homer used the first Homer's hexameter and consigned the Saturnian verse forever to the dustbin. No doubt this was another example of cultural deference, a Greek meter for the Grecizing language of a Greek genre, but it proved to be one of the soundest decisions that any pioneering writer has ever taken. The character of Latin was changing. The heavy initial stress and reduced medial vowels of Old Latin were giving way to the classical penultimate accent in which, if Latin grammarians correctly described it, pitch was an important component. In consequence Latin could be versified in a manner approximating that in which Greek was versified. Ennius sometimes applied the rules mechanically, with hideous results; more often he achieved a kind of ponderous dignity. Solemnity was the virtue of the Latin hexameter, heaviness its vice, and Latin poets soon learned that a careful attention to the balance of word accent and verse accent was the way to achieve the one and avoid the other. Another way was through rhetoric. Having Homer in the background, Greek narrative style is notably free from rant. Stripped of its adjectival decoration, it becomes the "plain style" of the oratorical handbooks.

Ennius could write at length in this fashion:

> Exin candida se radiis dedit icta foras lux;
> et simul ex alto longe pulcherrima praepes
> laeva volavit avis, simul aureus exoritur sol.
> Cedunt de caelo ter quattuor corpora sancta
> avium, praepetibus sese pulchrisque locis dant.
>
> 85–89 Skutsch

> (Then with its rays a light shone brightly forth;
> And from on high a bird flew toward the left,
> Luckiest of winged omens, at the same time as the golden sun arose.
> There came from heaven three times four holy shapes of
> Birds and took themselves to lucky and well-omened places.)
>
> [*author's translation*]

Never mind the bumpy metrics: this is plain without being spare. (Note the redundancy or weak force of *ex alto, longe, de caelo,* and *pulchris locis.*) Latin, which has a natural affinity for the rhetoric of the honest man of few words, could do better. Here is King Pyrrhus addressing Roman ambassadors:

> Nec mi aurum posco nec mi pretium dederitis,
> nec cauponantes bellum sed belligerantes,
> ferro non auro vitam cernamus utrique:
> vosne velit an me regnare era quidve ferat Fors,
> virtute experiamur.
>
> 183–87 Skutsch

> (Gold I ask not, nor shall you pay a price.
> No traders' war but warriors' war be ours;
> With steel and not with gold our lives be tried.

What Chance may bring, if by her will you
   rule
Or I, let strength and valor be our test.)
                                    [*author's translation*]

And Ennius could rise to real eloquence:

Incedunt arbusta per alta, securibus caedunt,
percellunt magnas quercus, exciditur ilex,
fraxinus frangitur atque abies consternitur alta
pinus proceras pervortunt, omne sonabat
arbustum fremitu silvai frondosai.

                                    175–79 Skutsch

(Then strode they through deep thicket woods and hewed
With hatchets; mighty oaks they overset,
Down crashed the holm and shivered ash outhacked;
Felled was the stately fir; they wrenched right down
The lofty pines; and all the thickest wood
Of frondent forest rang and roared.)

                                    Warmington

In the Latin all the verbs but the last are in the present tense. It was a trick that Ennius had learned from the old Saturnian poets, for no Greek epic poet had enlisted the so-called historic present to give immediacy to his narrative style. As a trick of style it is wondrously simple yet effective. Ostensibly the poet remains in the background, as a follower of Homer should, yet the present tense prods the reader's slow imagination into life. To say "All the wood resounded" is to state a fact, but with a certain intellectual reserve, as if it were a proposition in logic; to keep the tense of the Latin and say "In they stride and hack down the wood" is to say something that can hardly be apprehended without the visual imagination. The device had been well known to orators since the fifth century B.C., when they presented their versions of events to Athenian juries. They realized that their audience would not visualize the event without feeling some empathy with the participants. This present tense may stand as the Latin contribution to poetic narrative style. Homer had gained empathy by similes, but it was a great advantage to extend the effect throughout the whole narrative. Literary epic has almost universally adopted it.

For those with minds to understand, Ennius had drawn the outline of Roman epic and provided the tools for achieving it. It was to be a national poetry in its inspiration but Greek in meter and Homeric in its apparatus. Few serious poets quarreled with this prescription. But had Ennius hit on the right means? The *Annales* must have suffered, like the *Argonautica*, from too much incident related in simple paratactic sequence, and the closer Ennius came to his own time the more he would meet with the troubles of Choerilus in handling "unmythological" material. It is not conclusive evidence that the Romans themselves appear to have found nothing to criticize. They were confronting a new phenomenon in literature, an epic poem in their own language. They were amazed that it could be done at all and so did not ask whether it was well done; and having been done, the *Annales* set a precedent and created a tradition. That was especially true of the later books, in which Ennius had eulogized the Greek campaigns of his noble patron, Fulvius Nobilior.

The political prejudice of the present day does not make it easy to believe that to extol imperialism and war could produce great literature; and the dismal record of the Roman historical epic after Ennius only confirms the feeling. For a century and a half Roman epic meant the versified account of contemporary wars: hence a *Bellum Histrium*, a *Bellum Sequanicum*, a *Bellum Gallicum*, and similar sublime titles. The genre persisted even to the end of antiquity; there was a *Bellum Africum* as late as the sixth century A.D.

Many of these chronicles doubtless had no aim beyond their immediate target, the patronage of the victorious general, and were odious in their adulation. Worse still, to our way of thinking, were the self-panegyrics of politicians such as Cicero who found no professional poets equal to praising their achievements. Epic poetry was debased to the level of a political tract and composed according to a set prescription. "For instance, anyone who attempts the vast theme of the Civil War," wrote the satirist Petronius in the first century A.D., "will sink under the burden unless he is full of literature. It is not a question of recording actual events in verse; historians can do that far better. The free spirit of genius must plunge headlong into allusions and divine interpositions and rack itself for epigrams colored by mythology, so that what results seems rather the prophecies of an inspired seer than the exactitude of an oath before witnesses" (*Satyricon* 118). Behind the satirist's mockery is the damning verdict: the historical epic had become no more than a vehicle for virtuosity.

At that humble level the writer who poeticized the punitive expeditions of Roman legions against barbarians seemed assured of literary success. When his friend Caninius announced a project on the subject of the emperor Trajan's Dacian War (c. A.D. 105), the Younger Pliny, no discriminating critic, was ecstatic:

> Where could you have found so topical a subject, so full of material, so extensive and poetical, so wondrous and yet so perfectly true? You will tell of rivers diverted or bridged for the first time, of camps pitched on mountain crags, of a king ever resolute driven from his palace and even out of life itself and of two triumphs, one over a nation till then unconquered, the other over its final subjugation. . . . Come then, exercise the right of poets and invoke the gods—and among them that hero [i.e. the emperor Trajan] whose deeds and counsels you are going to celebrate—let loose your cordage, spread your sails, give your genius free rein! (*Epistulae* viii 4)

The only problem, thought Pliny with staggering superficiality, would be reducing all those barbarian names to the dactylic hexameter. In fact, what he describes is not epic poetry and is scarcely even narrative: it is a string of set pieces.[7] To quote Petronius again, "People who are tired out with forensic oratory often take refuge in the calm of poetry as in some happier haven, supposing that a poem is easier to construct than a declamation adorned with quivering epigrams" (*Satyricon* 118). Cicero's fury at the suggestion would have been sincere and eloquent, but the cap already fitted him perfectly. Discredited in politics, he had written his memoirs in verse.

Cicero thought of himself as a connoisseur, but on closer inspection his attitude toward literature turns out to be patronizing. Since he was exceptionally well read and liberal-minded, his attitude is important for the history of Latin literature, and the statement needs explanation and defense. Cicero's apology for literature forms the central panel of his speech for the poet Archias, delivered in 62 B.C. The circumstances of the trial—it was a question of Archias' entitlement to Roman citizenship—virtually compelled Archias' counsel to argue that poets were useful citizens, Archias in particular because he was engaged in extolling Cicero's suppression of Catiline's conspiracy. But the views expressed in *Pro Archia* are so widely echoed in Cicero's extensive writings as well as in those of other Roman authors of his class that they cannot be thought to represent a stance adopted for the occasion.

First, argued Cicero, the Roman is a scholar, but a practical scholar. "Do you think that I could find inspiration for my daily speeches on a manifold variety of topics did I not cultivate my mind with study, or that my mind could endure so great a strain did not study too provide it with relaxation? I am a votary of literature and make the confession unashamed. Shame belongs rather to the bookish recluse who knows not how to apply his reading to the good of his fellows or to manifest its fruits in the eyes of all" (*Pro Archia* 12). The Roman is a public man—preferably a soldier, Cicero had to admit, but if not a soldier, then an orator. Literature was his refreshment.

Second, literature is the teacher of sound morality. "Had I not persuaded myself from my youth up, thanks to the moral lessons derived from a wide reading, that nothing is to be greatly sought after in this life save glory and honor, and that in their quest all bodily pains and dangers of death or exile"—prophetic words— "should be lightly accounted, I should never have borne for the safety of you all the brunt of so many a bitter encounter or bared my breast to the daily onsets of abandoned persons [i.e. Catiline's supporters]. All literature, all philosophy, all history abounds with incentives to noble action" (*Pro Archia* 14).

Third, there is something admirable about poetry. It rests on an inborn faculty. Poets, as the great Ennius had said, were holy, as if recommended by the benign favor of heaven (*Pro Archia* 18). We expect a claim like that of Pindar, to be a mouthpiece of the Muses, or at least something like the Platonic irony that compared the inspiration of the poet to demonic possession. But no, Cicero's divine poet is an entertainer. He was astonished, he said (no doubt recalling intellectual soirees at his Tusculan villa), at the facility with which Archias improvised verses on contemporary affairs.

Fourth, poetry perpetuates one's memory more effectively than statues, an important point to members of the Roman aristocracy. Cicero cites the literary patronage of the great Romans from Scipio Africanus to Pompey the Great (*Pro Archia* 19–22). "Deep in every noble heart," he concludes, "dwells a power which plies night and day the goad of glory, and bids us see to it that the remembrance of our names should not pass away with life but should endure coeval with all the ages of the future" (*Pro Archia* 29).

Enjoyable, instructive, admirable, and useful, these are the parameters of Cicero's criticism—and a sorry list they are, at least for those who dare to think that poetry may be valuable, that it may awake the imagination and free the mind. What we know of Cicero's own poetical essays confirms the picture. In 54 B.C., for instance, seeking some needful goodwill, he prompted his brother Quintus to compose an epic on Julius Caesar's conquest of Gaul; but Quintus knew his limits and suggested that Cicero should do the job himself. Cicero hesitated; he was too occupied with more serious business but might take it in hand next vacation (*Ad Quintum Fratrem* ii 15, iii 8). One is not surprised to learn from this same exchange of letters that Caesar had found the first book of Cicero's own epic, *De Temporibus Meis* (My Times), something of a curate's egg, good in parts but rather sloppily put together. Obviously this quarter of the Roman literary scene did not have the imagination to rejuvenate the creaking machinery of Ennius' historical epic.[8]

However, when Cicero delivered *Pro Archia*, he was in his middle forties; it was not long before he was complaining of the behavior of the rising generation of young Romans. They were indifferent to the honor and glory of public life, and those with literary gifts were reacting sharply to the traditional forms of Latin literature. It had taken time, but Greek ideas, and ideals, were at last being taken seriously by a significant number of Romans. The career of a notable literary opportunist, Terentius Varro Atacinus (fl. 60–50 B.C.) is instructive. His *Bellum Sequanicum* of 58 B.C., an account of Caesar's first campaign in Gaul, was a historical epic in the ancient mold. But Varro soon learned that the literary avant-garde had a low opinion of that sort of writing.[9] High poetry called for learning and scholarship. Varro's next work was still an epic, but the subject was mythological —the Argonauts again. Next, he abandoned epic altogether and threw off two didactic poems in the Callimachean manner. Finally, he fancied himself in love and wrote elegies to one Leucadia, a real or imaginary mistress. Varro's fickle genius, it is clear, responded to every shift in the winds of literary fashion. Those who set the pace were the New Poets, a group whose leading lights included Catullus. Nowadays Catullus is best known for his occasional verse, what tongue in cheek he called his "trifles"; in his lifetime he and his friends were the advocates of the more extreme forms of Hellenistic taste. The theory was that of the austere Callimachus, the practice that of the decadent Euphorion (c. 250 B.C.). The offspring of such literary parentage were epyllia on obscure and sometimes morbid themes. They included Catullus' own *Wedding of Peleus and Thetis* (no. 64), Calvus' *Io,* Valerius Cato's *Dictynna,* Cornificius' *Glaucus,* Caecilius' *Magna Mater,* and Cinna's famous *Smyrna,* which Catullus extolled with the sort of praise that revealed its faults: "My friend Cinna's *Smyrna* is out at last after nine summers and as many winters while Hortensius has been tossing off fifty thousand verses. . . . My pleasure is in the slender memorials of my friend; let the crowd delight in Antimachus' bombast" (no. 95).

The *Smyrna* was overwrought and gave employment to commentators. Extreme Alexandrianism, as practiced by the New Poets, would have led nowhere. It was fortunate that their successors had the taste to look to better models than Euphorion. But it was the New Poets who made the literature of the Augustan Age (say 40 B.C. onward) possible. They passed on their respect for everything Greek, especially their regard for Greek mythology as a means of poetical expression and their passion for art and learning; but their most valuable legacy was to restore to poetry its self-respect. No longer could amateurs like Cicero flippantly promise to compose an epic in the holidays; serious poets sweated blood for years, to the exclusion of all other activity, and their writing began to sound a new note of authority. As Romans should, they meant their work to last.

V

Virgil

The Long Road to the Aeneid

> This theme will suit but ill my playful lyre.
> Whither, Muse, are you setting forth? Cease
> willfully to recount the words of gods or demean
> great deeds with your humble strains.
>
> Horace

Julius Caesar's attempts to impose stability on the Roman state were cut short by his assassination in 44 B.C. More disorders followed until the surviving warlord, the crafty, unmilitary Octavian, Caesar's nephew and adopted son, returned to Rome in 28 B.C. to face the political problems that had beset the state for three generations. There was much to be forgotten, and much to be rewritten. "When I was nineteen years old," he recalled near the end of his long life, "I recruited an army at my own expense and restored the state to liberty when it was oppressed under the tyranny of a faction. . . . The whole of Italy of its own accord swore allegiance to me and insisted that I lead the army in the war I won at Actium. . . . In my sixth and seventh consulships [28 and 27 B.C.], when I had brought the civil wars to an end, I transferred the state from my own power to that of the senate and people of Rome." He declined, he said, all unconstitutional honors and exercised no more power than his colleagues in office.[1]

No one is deceived by these self-serving declarations. From a perspective of two centuries the historian Cassius Dio saw what had happened only too well: the free republic had died, and as for its vaunted resuscitation in 28 B.C., that was the moment when the Roman empire had become an autocracy.[2]

What did these political changes mean for literature? Augustus (as Octavian became in 27 B.C.) was, for an autocrat, tolerant and benign. Not until his last years were the works of the satirists Cassius Severus and T. Labienus publicly burned and a poet, Ovid, exiled because his taste was not the same as the emperor's. In his early years the purest feeling in the minds of most Romans was doubtless relief. For the first time in their lives conflict was not present or imminent. One of Augustus' first acts after triumphing over Mark Antony was to have the temple of Janus closed: that act symbolized—and Augustus was an expert at political symbolism—that the entire empire was at peace. Little political expertise was needed to see that Augustus was the price of peace. There is a deep sincerity in the prayer with which Virgil concluded the first *Georgic:*

> Gods of my country, this young prince at least do not hinder from succoring a shattered world. Enough has our blood for long atoned for Laomedon's crime; for long has Heaven envied us your presence, Augustus, and complained that you care for triumphs on an earth where right and wrong are turned upside down, where the plough meets with no honor, the wasted fields are robbed of their tillers, and the sickle is forged into the sword. Unholy war rages through the world; even as when the gates are opened and the chariots burst forth and speed away, and the driver tugs vainly at the reins as he is borne along and the car heeds no restraint! (*Georgics* i 498–519)

Augustus, it seemed, had brought the world back from the abyss. For the moment few cared to inquire into his methods or question the legitimacy of his rule. As early as 40 B.C. Virgil had obliquely conferred divinity on him, for poets were permitted to use such hyperboles, and in 29 B.C. in the prologue to the first *Georgic* he speaks openly of his posthumous deification. Horace speculated what divine title would suit him best. But Augustus was too wise to rely on so transient a feeling as gratitude and too cunning to rest his power, which he never actually relinquished, solely on force. Politicians must keep moving. Augustus followed up peace with regeneration. He wanted the settlement of 28–27 B.C. to seem like a second foundation of Rome, and for a moment he was tempted to add the name of the first founder, Romulus, to his titles.[3] The new Rome was to be defended by its ancient virtues. Historians disputed when the state had become corrupt, but they did not doubt its corruption. It had sunk into the depths; now the cycle of history would carry it up again. The practical effects, of course, were slight: temples were refaced in marble, and laws were enacted to force the upper classes into fruitful marriages.

What would the regenerated Rome have been like? The emperor's virtues were proclaimed by his decorations: a golden shield was presented to him by the senate and people in gratitude for his firmness of spirit, his sense of justice, his clemency, and his piety. Subjects did not have the same opportunities to display those praiseworthy talents, but among them, as Horace affirmed in his role of poet laureate, "Faith, peace and honor, ancient chastity and long-neglected virtue dared to reappear" (*Carmen Saeculare* 57). These were the ancient ways by which the state was supposed to stand. No one could disagree. Neither could anyone disagree with the restoration of the forms of religion. But ancient virtue had more disputable elements. The old Romans had been tough and martial, making a virtue out of their ignorance of the arts at which the Greeks excelled. The new Romans were to take pride in their bellicose ancestors, whose statues Augustus erected around his new forum, and were to welcome their imperial destiny. They were not required to cultivate the mind.

As gratitude for the Augustan peace faded, the real character of the Roman revolution revealed itself—autocratic, militaristic, and philistine. As the truth sank in, there were those who capitulated; hence the cold panegyrics of Horace's fourth book of odes or the sixth elegy of Propertius' fourth book. Others reacted with disdain. The pleasure-loving youth of whom Cicero complained had no use for politics, nor had their spiritual descendants under Augustus. The hypocrisies that sickened true republicans they merely found amusing. Ovid was their spokesman. He alleged that the magnificent buildings with which the emperor had adorned his capital were excellent places—for meeting girls. The shows and games that ornamented his triumphs were even better, and who cared whether the Britons or the Parthians were represented? Augustus had problems recruiting for the army, and Ovid suggested he take a tip from the first Romulus, who offered his troops a special bonus in the shape of the Sabine women. As for the cult of ancient virtue, Ovid shuddered at those unkempt ages: "Now is the golden age of Rome. . . . All is elegance without a trace of ancient boorishness."[4] Such men needed to be taught a lesson; even before his exile Ovid had learned to turn to historical themes and blatant eulogy.

In the next generation disdain turned into resentment sharp enough to inspire an epic poem, Lucan's highly original *Bellum Civile*. It was a denunciation of Caesarism shot through with anger and despair, and it cost the author his life. Such futile gestures were soon abandoned to philosophers, and under the Flavian emperors (A.D. 70–96) literature played it safe. What exception could be taken to a historical epic on the Second Punic War, fought and won three centuries before, or to the antediluvian adventures of the Argonauts (again!) and the Seven against Thebes?

In Virgil's youth and prime all that lay in the future. During the 30s B.C. Octavian seemed to promise peace and order; in the 20s, as Augustus, he seemed to have delivered them. A keen eye may see signs of doubt and anxiety in Virgil's works, but there is no disdain, resentment, or withdrawal. The poet loved his country, but his patriotism (unlike that of Cicero, for example) had nothing to do with the factions of Roman politics; and if he was unhappy, his unhappiness was with the world at large. The line he wrote of his hero Aeneas, *sunt lacrimae rerum et mentem mortalia tangunt*, "tears for the nature of things, a heart touched by mortal miseries," many have thought applicable also to the poet.

Two epyllia, called *Culex* and *Ciris*, now usually judged to be spurious, were at one time attributed to the juvenile Virgil. It would not have been odd if he had followed the taste of the New Poets before his own was formed. He himself would have us believe that his early ambitions even turned to the grand epic in the historical mode. "When I was singing of kings and battles," he wrote in the sixth *Eclogue*, "Apollo plucked my ear and gave me warning, 'The shepherd should feed fat his sheep, but sing a fine-spun song.' There will be others, Varus, to sing your praises and put grim war into verse." The language is straight out of the prologue to Callimachus' *Aitia*:

pinguis, "fat," is the Greek *pakhýs*, Callimachus' term for the bloated, pretentious style of Antimachus; *deductus*, "finely drawn out," translates *leptáleos*, "refined, slender." Poets are not on oath, and the lines should be taken as evidence of what Varus, a patron who was also a soldier, was believed to want in the late 40s B.C.—not that Virgil actually followed in the footsteps of Varro and Volusius. It is more likely that Virgil's early thoughts of a great poem are described in Silenus' song in the same *Eclogue:* a cosmogony, translated into contemporary philosophical language, but moving thence into mythology. That was the kind of thing literary people had taught themselves to admire. Apollonius had already put Orpheus' song into the *Argonautica* (i 496–511), and Virgil was to use the same idea for the songs of Clymene (*Georgics* iv 345–47) and Iopas (*Aen.* i 740–46). Propertius had similar thoughts (iii 5, 25–46), and Ovid's *Metamorphoses* was a grandiose realization of the form. These ideas reflect the influence of Lucretius' didactic poem *De Rerum Natura*, with an important difference. As a committed Epicurean, Lucretius had been obliged to reject mythology for scientific reasons. Verse, he thought, would be sufficient to shed the Muses' charm over rational argument.[5] It wasn't, not in an age when poetry and mythology were thought to go hand in hand. Silenus' cosmogony therefore slipped from philosophy into the poetical world of myth. He even incorporated a digression, in the manner of Hellenistic epyllia, on the poet Gallus receiving on the slopes of Mount Helicon the gift of the pipes of Hesiod from the Muses. The song of Silenus is thus a revealing whimsy: philosophy had to be mythologized to make it poetry.[6] How to mythologize Roman history was the Latin epic's problem, and it was not to be solved by a crude mingling of Homeric divinities and contemporary chronicle.

Virgil had met Varus and another early patron, Asinius Pollio, in unhappy circumstances. After their victory over Brutus and Cassius, Octavian and Antony had to demobilize their armies. The Roman solution to this social problem was to discharge the men with a land grant as gratuity. The matter was urgent. To obtain the land, the triumvirs resorted to confiscation, and Varus and Pollio, their officers in Cisalpine Gaul, could not afford to distinguish too carefully between the disloyal, the suspect, and the neutral. Whether Virgil saved or recovered his property near Mantua is uncertain, but he soon left his home town and seems never to have returned. Inevitably he went to Rome, where he met the subtle and devious Maecenas. No one knows what to make of Maecenas: his dress and personal habits, it was said, were disgusting, his morals a scandal, and his literary style pathologically corrupt, yet his sinister presence guided Octavian through the political quagmires of two decades.

Maecenas was a great patron. In anyone else that role would be commended: in Maecenas it has been suspect. Could he have sought the society of poets because he enjoyed their conversation or was gratified to receive their dedications? Historians have refused to believe that his motives could have been innocent. Surely his design was to control what we now call the media, to organize opinion and teach citizens to love despotism. Such a systematic use of the higher genres of literature for political ends would have been unprecedented. Propaganda is not so indirect. When Romans wished to denigrate enemies, they composed invectives; when they wished to reinterpret history, they wrote more history. But poets who accepted patronage accepted also the obligation to please, and patrons for their part had the duty to encourage and warn.[7] What sort of thing, when Horace recoiled from the hostile criticism of his satires, would Maecenas have suggested as certain to please the world (or Augustus)? What we are told of the taste and literary outlook of both patron and master is not encouraging: "In reading the writers of both tongues [Latin and Greek] there was nothing for which Augustus looked so carefully as for precepts and examples instructive to the public or to individuals" (Suetonius, *Divus Augustus* 89). That is the utilitarian view of literature in its crudest form. Not surprisingly, then, there is abundant evidence that Maecenas hinted to his protégés that an epic account of Augustus' wars was certain to meet with a warm response in the right quarter. Already in the mid-30s B.C. one Cornelius Siculus versified the defeat of Sextus Pompeius. "Versified" is Quintilian's word (*Institutio Oratoria* x 1, 89), and it puts the finger on the defect of the whole corpus of Latin epic at the time: it just wasn't poetry. As for old Ennius, wrote Quintilian, he was like an ancient monument, for which one felt "religion" rather than genuine admiration. Moreover, the *Annales* had petered out a century and a half before the heroic rise of Augustus. It needed little knowledge of literature to see the gap in the writings of the Roman people.

Maecenas hinted; Horace and Propertius demurred and Varius

Rufus succumbed.[8] Virgil thought round and round the problem of the epic poem in a sophisticated age. Before he met Maecenas, he had dismissed it (*Eclogue* vi 3); now he wondered. At the beginning of the third *Georgic* he allegorizes: he will build a temple to Caesar (i.e. Augustus), that is, he will glorify him in his next and greater work. Virgil's ideas at that time (c. 29 B.C.) were still imprecise, and the allegory has not helped commentators clarify them. This much seems secure: Virgil was moved by the legitimate hope of fame (*Georgics* iii 8). Since he had made his contribution to the pastoral and didactic genres, the epic must now be in his sights—but not uncritically. Pure mythology was hackneyed (3–8); it might amuse vacant minds, but how could it engage the emotional commitment of the poet? The *Georgics* had shown that such commitment was essential to Virgil and made all the difference between his own didactic poetry and that of Hellenistic virtuosi like Aratus and Nicander. The alternative to the mythological epic was the historical: Virgil therefore would sing of the past and future triumphs of Augustus. It would have been tactless to have said at this point that a hundred and fifty years of Roman literary history had shown such an enterprise to be impossible. But there is a hint: the poetical temple would immortalize also the Trojan and divine ancestors of the Julian house. Mythology, being almost synonymous with poetry since the days of the New Poets, was not to be excluded, but it was to be a relevant mythology that could symbolize the poet's feelings toward his historical theme.

What Virgil describes in the preface to the third *Georgic* is far from being an *Aeneid*. The elements have not fallen into place nor assumed their right proportions, but they are there. Nor should another aspect be overlooked. The temple would be thronged by Greeks, who would abandon their country to join in Augustus' triumph. It is doubtful that Augustus cared a jot for literal Greek plaudits, but to imply that Greeks would abandon their literary monuments to gape in admiration at Virgil's poetical temple was an extraordinary claim. It controverted what had been a fundamental clause in the credo of the artistic world, that in all intellectual matters the Greeks were the leaders and the masters. Virgil was going to outdo them. Perhaps it would not have seemed a hopeless task to surpass the tepid products of the Hellenistic age, but a poem that included Trojan heroes in its cast of characters was implicitly making a bid for higher fame, a challenge to Homer himself.[9]

Virgil completed the *Georgics* in 29 B.C. and recited them to Augustus on his return to Italy. "He listened with patience and courtesy to authors reciting their works" is as far as his biographer, Suetonius, will go (*Divus Augustus* 99) in commending the emperor as a patron of letters; but no doubt Maecenas had told him that here was his greatest catch, a poet both able and willing to create a monument worthy of the New Rome.

The Aeneid

> A spirit within sustains heaven and earth, the
> oceans, the sun, and the gleaming orb of the
> moon, and Mind, pervading all its parts, directs
> the mass of the universe and mingles with its
> mighty frame.
>
> Virgil

In book vi of the *Aeneid* (724–27) Virgil makes Anchises give his son Aeneas a lecture in Stoic astrophysics, but he might well have thought that the lines expressed quite neatly the magnitude of the task Maecenas so lightly set his literary friends. Any one of them could have thrown off a few thousand verses on the rout of the eastern hordes of Antony at the battle of Actium and would have been ashamed to have composed something so devoid of poetic feeling. How then could the great mass of an epic poem be made to speak, and what should it say? Precedent and patronage insisted on a public voice. It would praise Augustus, of course, but a great epic would have to sound a deeper note than the strident tones of propaganda. It would express the Romans' vision of themselves as they looked back on the road to empire and forward to the new age. This was the voice of Ennius, but it would speak in a mature poetical idiom. Nothing less would carry poet and reader through ten thousand verses.

Virgil's epic would therefore be a national epic. That meant, in the circumstances of the first century B.C., that it had to be a nationalist and imperialist epic, for nationalism and imperialism were then honorable principles. It was the right and duty of the

Romans to rule others. In Virgil's time this assertion called for no argument; it needed only to be stated, provided that the emphasis was not on the profits of empire but on the duty of Romans to take up their burden of bringing order to the barbarism and chaos of the world:

> Tu regere imperio populos, Romane, memento
> (hae tibi erunt artes), pacique imponere morem,
> parcere subiectis et debellare superbos.
>
> (*Aen.* vi 851–53)
>
> (Remember thou, O Roman, to rule the nations with thy sway (these shall be thine arts), to crown peace with order, to spare the humble and to tame in war the proud.)[1]

The ambiguity here in the second-person singular (is *tu*—Aeneas— the personified Roman people or a particular Roman?) would have been acutely felt when Virgil recited this part of the *Aeneid* before Augustus himself in 23 B.C. It reminds us that the destiny of Aeneas (to whom Augustus is unobtrusively assimilated) is a subtle affirmation of the values of monarchical rule.

Later, elaborate political and philosophical arguments were invented to demonstrate that the Roman empire was right, just, and advantageous. They may be read in the *Hymn to Rome* of the sophist Aelius Aristides or in the second chapter of Gibbon's *Decline and Fall of the Roman Empire*. It must be said that there is not much of that attitude in the *Aeneid*. In Aristides the whole world, implicitly including Italy, was subject to its emperor; in Virgil the world is subject to Italy, and Virgil is proud of it. The Romans had *imposed* peace on the squabbling Greeks and coarse barbarians of the west and north. That they had been able to was because some metaphysical power had so ordained, as thoughtful men were prepared to believe. It is not unnatural that they did so even in an age notably lacking in religiosity. History often seems to be a sequence of events having a sort of dynamism of its own. Virgil calls this intuition fate or personifies it as the god Jupiter; others have called it providence, God's obvious design, manifest destiny, or the march of history. What these terms mean is that we feel borne along by forces we are helpless to stop or deflect.

But something could go wrong. Men might be unworthy of their destiny or might actually reject it. The collapse of the republic in civil war left the collective consciousness of Rome seared with guilt. The right relation between the state and whatever power presided over it had broken down. In the traditional form of religion this relation was called *pax deorum*, the compact with the gods. However much Romans might philosophize and rationalize, they felt that the outward form of religion had to be kept up and were uneasy if it was not. Augustus did not reinstate cults and temples merely for ostentation; he was visibly restoring the special relationship between Rome and whatever it was that guided her affairs. This restitution was a vital part of his policy. The national epic therefore would have to be a religious poem, religious at a deeper level than that implied by picturesque myths about the divine parentage of Aeneas and Romulus. Someone could be skeptical about such fables while feeling the symbolic truth within them.

Fate, however, was on the side of the moral heavyweights. Neither the mercurial brilliance of the Greeks nor the wild passions of Gauls and Germans was to inherit the earth. The national epic would depict the eclipse of such vices by solid Roman virtues. Even as Virgil marshaled his thoughts, the historian Livy was rewriting the history of Rome as a series of tableaux exemplifying the qualities that had made the city great.[2] First, there was *pietas*, "piety," that respect for religion, and the actions and attitudes prescribed by religion, that constituted the *pax deorum*. *Pietas* was closely connected to *fides*, "good faith," the respect for obligations solemnly entered into that stood in such sharp contrast to the duplicity that seemed to characterize Rome's enemies, whether Carthaginian or Greek. Then there was respect for authority, *disciplina*, and its concomitant, concord. And among the private virtues were frugality, foresight, and reason, together with chastity and steadfastness. In short, Romans took a very serious view of life, *gravitas*. They would have been shocked if an impertinent Greek had said that this view was not only self-delusion but insofar as it was true described a ruthless, self-centered, and philistine people.

Did Virgil, a most retiring and literary person, believe this picture of the Romans? Probably, after a thoughtful pause, his reply would have been affirmative. In all his work Virgil revealed a determination to Latinize Greek attainments while showing his respect for them. He set Theocritean idylls in northern Italy; the hero of the *Georgics* is a Roman farmer; the Homeric Aineias became the Roman

Aeneas. Clearly he loved Italy, he loved the Latin language, he admired what the Romans had achieved, and he refused to surrender to the allure of Hellenism; but he recoiled at what had been done to Italy by war and exploitation and shrank from the collectivist mentality that had made the Romans irresistible. Such thoughts, however, could not be deliberately expressed nor perhaps consciously entertained. If they had been, the poet would not have spent ten years of his life on the composition of an intentionally national epic.

The theme of the *Aeneid*, then, is the genius of the Roman people. To embody it, the poet required an exemplar to do for him what Achilles and Odysseus had done for Homer. His first thought was the obvious one—Augustus himself. But the courtly language of the dedication of the third *Georgic* conceals what must have been a quick rejection. No follower of the New Poets and their Hellenistic mentors could have pursued the same trail as the two Choerili. That left the formula of Rhianus: the great exemplar could be historical but remote enough to be mythologized. Historians had been hard at work heroizing the aristocratic P. Cornelius Scipio Africanus, the victor of the Second Punic War. A millennium after Virgil this Scipio was made the hero of Petrarch's Latin epic *Africa*, so well had Livy, for example, done his work. Yet however ideal Scipio may have appeared from the moral standpoint, he could not serve Virgil's broader purposes. Stating what is obvious to every reader, the poet's biographer described these as to compose "as it were a mirror of both poems of Homer, to treat Greek and Latin affairs and characters together, and to give at the same time an account of the origins of Rome and, which was the poet's special aim, of Augustus also" (Suetonius, *Life of Virgil* 21). That meant the *exemplar virtutis* would have to be found in the mythological age of the Greek heroic epic.

Here the ideal candidate was Hercules. In Greek myth Heracles (Hercules in Latin) was *the* example of virtue, a mortal who by his toils achieved immortality among the gods. The Roman senate could not immortalize Augustus to honor his toils in the service of the state, but it could, and did, confer on him deification. Moreover, Heracles had journeyed to the west, he had passed through Italy, and he had performed a minor labor on the site of Rome itself. As the divinity of success—Hercules Victor as the Romans called him—he presided over one of the most widespread and popular cults of the time.[3] If he was not numbered among the supposed ancestors of

Augustus, that minor obstacle could easily be circumvented by some convenient figment. Yet Virgil rejected Hercules. It was a hackneyed theme, he said. Perhaps there was another reason: Hercules was indeed the supposed ancestor of a noble Roman house—the Antonii. His biographer, Plutarch, draws a diverting picture of Mark Antony's public relations: "The breadth of his forehead, his shapely beard and aquiline nose were thought to show the masculine qualities special to the pictures and statues of Hercules. The tradition [that the Antonii descended from Hercules] Antony imagined he bore out both by his appearance and his dress. For when he was going to appear in public he always wore his tunic hitched up to his thigh, with a huge sword hanging at his side and a heavy cloak draped over his shoulder" (*Life of Antony* 3.1–2). So Hercules is allowed to enter Virgil's epic only to sanctify an ancient Roman cult.

Accordingly, the mythology had to center on the Trojan ancestors of Augustus. The gentile name of the Julii Caesares was derived from the name of Iulus, son of Aeneas. The story of Aeneas' coming to Italy was no hackneyed theme. Apart from a cursory relation in the poems of Naevius and Ennius it was apparently unknown to literature. There is no mention of it, for example, in all the voluminous writings of Cicero.[4] In itself this feature was attractive, for educated taste ran to what was novel, and there were manifold possibilities. The story would be balm to Roman feelings of inferiority and would assert the Romans' antiquity and worth against the Greeks. It left the poet's imagination largely untrammeled: Aeneas could go where he wanted, be what he wanted, feel what he wanted. And on the literary front it declared war on Homer. In this Trojan War the Trojans would win, and the chronicle of their victory would be a single epic in Latin that achieved all that the Greek Homer had achieved in two. This was Virgil's private battle—he had no allies at the time and few before or afterwards—but it was a battle he fought on behalf of the public and on behalf of Latin literature.

Homer determined the architecture of the *Aeneid*. It was nowhere said openly, but the feeling seems to have been abroad that the *Iliad* and the *Odyssey* were too long. Not until Nonnus' monstrous *Dionysiaca* (c. A.D. 400) did anyone dare to write at Homeric length. The *Aeneid* therefore was shorter, less than ten thousand verses divided into twelve books. Six of these would mirror the *Odyssey*, six the *Iliad*. Like Homer Virgil would begin in the middle, a good half way along Aeneas' quest for Italy; then like Odysseus before Alcinous he could narrate, with all the emotive power of a first-person narrative, his previous adventures. the battles of the final books would be organized on Iliadic lines. In one respect Virgil disagreed with the Homeric design: he cut out the coda that in both Greek epics follows the climactic point. Yet the *Aeneid* is not left incomplete, as the *Iliad* and the *Odyssey* would be if they were shorn of their last two books. The duel of Aeneas and Turnus with which the *Aeneid* closes does indeed correspond to the slayings of Hector and of Penelope's suitors, but only superficially is the death of Turnus the event at which the story of the *Aeneid* culminates. If a producer of Shakespeare were to ring down the curtain at the moment Macbeth falls and cut out the platitudes of the anemic Malcolm and his English allies, the effect would be similar. We know that Macbeth is doomed when the messenger reports that Birnam Wood is in motion; and when Macduff reveals the details of his birth, we can sit back and enjoy the swordplay. Turnus also is abandoned by his gods before he turns at bay; the details of his death are unimportant. The *Aeneid*, the epic of the Roman people, culminates a little earlier when the gods of Olympus determine what the course of history shall be in Italy. The mere story of Aeneas is nowhere as important as the "spirit within that sustains and directs its mighty frame."

Homer likewise determined the apparatus and, with a major exception, the principal episodes of the *Aeneid*. Gods were inescapable, and funeral games, descents to Hades, catalogs of tribes and heroes, ornamented shields, night raids, *aristeiai*, and duels were hardly less so. The exception is the Hellenistic contribution to the epic: Aeneas must love, or at least be loved.[5] The result was the tragedy of Dido (*Aeneid* iv) and the most agonizing of Aeneas' trials. Virgil took a certain risk, not the risk that a Roman readership would condemn Aeneas—Dido had for them a complex significance and evoked the real and imaginary dangers of Carthage and Cleopatra—but the risk of breaking the homogeneity of his material. The surface of the *Aeneid* is carefully archaized, so that everything belongs to the same genre, Homeric heroic epic. For example, whatever view we take of Homeric gods we can also take in the first instance of Virgilian gods: we can judge Turnus as we would Achilles or Hector. Dido detains Aeneas as Calypso detained Odysseus; Dido, however, is more like Apollonius' Medea than the pale nymph Calypso, and the fact that Virgil could put her into his reconstruction of the heroic world is evidence of his respect for the epic of Apollonius. And like Medea, Dido is focus of the story of her love affair.

But what makes the *Aeneid* unique in the epic tradition is the extent and detail of the Homeric material used at every level from phrase to plot, so densely that contemporary detractors accused Virgil of plagiarism. His retort is on record: "It is easier to steal his club from Hercules than a line from Homer!" (Suetonius, *Life of Virgil* 46). Homer's Greek would not translate word for word into Latin without destroying its Homeric quality. What Virgil created was a careful mosaic of Homeric elements, mingled, adapted, and transformed.[6] The extent to which Virgil treated Ennius' work in the same way is only now being appreciated.

Here is a broad outline of what emerged:

Book i   The Trojans are wrecked on the coast of Africa and are welcomed by Dido, queen of Carthage (cf. parts of *Il.* xiv, *Od.* i, v–vii, xiv).

Book ii   Aeneas relates to Dido the story of the sack of Troy (cf. the cyclic epic *Iliupersis*).

Book iii   Aeneas describes his wanderings through Thrace, Crete, Epirus, and Sicily (cf. for structure, but not for content, *Od.* ix–xii).

Book iv   Dido falls in love with Aeneas. He deserts her to fulfill his mission. She kills herself in despair (not Homeric except for some details; cf. Apollonius, *Argonautica* iii).

Book v   Aeneas celebrates the funeral games of Anchises (cf. *Il.* xxiii).

Book vi   Aeneas descends to Hades (cf. *Od.* xi).

Book vii   War breaks out between the Trojans, now in Latium, and the Latins, led by Turnus. Catalog of the Latin forces (cf. *Il.* ii).

Book viii Aeneas lands at the site of Rome, is welcomed by Evander (cf. *Od.* iii), and receives new armor (cf. *Il.* xviii).

Book ix   Nisus and Euryalus make a night raid on the Latin camp (cf. *Il.* x).

Book x   *Aristeia* and death of Pallas (cf. *Il.* xvi). Mezentius and Lausus are slain by Aeneas (cf. various Iliadic *aristeia* and duels).

Book xi   Funeral of Pallas (cf. *Il.* xxiii). A truce is made and broken

(cf. *Il.* iii–iv). Exploits and death of Camilla (cf. the Amazon Penthesileia in the *Aethiopis*).

Book xii   Aeneas is wounded and healed by Venus (cf. Diomedes'
            healing in *Il.* v). He finally meets Turnus and kills him in
            vengeance for Pallas (cf. *Il.* xxii).

Overall the plan is Odyssean: the plunge in medias res, the
first-person narrative, the arrival of the hero at his (new) home, and
his struggle there to assert his rights. But from the beginning of the
seventh book the material is almost all Iliadic.[7] The plan is also
Aristotelian in its time span, economy, and coherence. In fact
Horace, in his role as critic, gives an excellent appraisal of the
structure of the *Aeneid* while purporting to summarize the peripatetic
view of the epic (*Ars Poetica* 128–52; it is there the slogan *in medias
res* is first attested). One may speculate whether Virgil knew or cared
about Aristotle, but the great critic would have been gratified that
the great poet was, if anything, more Aristotelian than Homer. The
brisk start of the *Odyssey* soon degenerated into the futile wanderings
of Telemachus and ground to a halt while Odysseus and Eumaeus
exchanged pleasant and irrelevant stories. The *Aeneid* has its pauses
and digressions, but if it is borne in mind that the story is secondary
to the presentation of the Roman people's destiny, the construction
will appear tight. Virgil possessed a well-developed sense of drama—
witness the tale of the sack of Troy and the tragedies of Dido,
Camilla, and the lovers Nisus and Euryalus—but the complex purposes of the *Aeneid* obstruct its narrative interest. The digressions
(books v, vi, ix) are too long, the preparations (books vii and viii)
extended, and the narrative goal—not to defeat Turnus but to "found
a city and bring his gods to Italy" (i 5–6)—too negative. But emotional interest is strong (or was, for Romans), and the story does its
job, which is to accommodate Virgil's historical and philosophical
perspectives and endow the epic tradition with a Roman hero.

The design of the *Aeneid* selects and condenses the best Homeric
scenes and avoids the repetitions. Some scenes that stick in the
mind of the reader of Homer, such as the set duels between Paris and
Menelaus and between Ajax and Hector, the archery of Teucer, the
fighting on the ships, or the rescue of Patroclus' body by Ajax and
Menelaus, are passed over. In other cases Virgil may well have been
influenced by the doctrines of literary decorum preached by Helle-

nistic critics. He did not employ the quarrel scene with which the *Iliad* opens nor any of the less decorous Olympian episodes. Where Virgil did adapt a scene in which the critics had discovered difficulties, he conformed to critical taste.[8] But since the objections preserved by the Homeric scholiasts are as often cavils as criticisms, these "improvements" on Homer are mostly of little importance to modern readers of the *Aeneid*. In sum, however, they help to give the *Aeneid* its elevated and dignified tone and set a standard for the style of epic.

Sometimes in their search for difficulties Hellenistic scholars had a real insight. Near the beginning of *Il.* xiii there is a simile comparing Hector's charge to a great boulder broken from a cliff that goes thundering downhill, smashing all before it. If Homer had used a common word for "boulder" it is unlikely that the commentators would have seen more in the simile than an illustration of the irresistible force of Hector's attack; but he used an archaism that left the Hellenistic Greeks wondering if there were something special about this boulder. They decided that it signaled the barbaric and irrational nature of Hector's charge. The comparison of Hector to lion, leopard, or wild boar provoked similar inferences about inner states of mind. Virgil's method of description is more direct. His Turnus follows inexorably in Hector's footsteps as he prepares to meet Aeneas in the last lines of the *Aeneid*: "Within that mighty breast seethed mighty shame and madness mixed with grief, and consciousness of heroism and passion stung by fury" (xii 684–90). Then comes the simile of the boulder, its details sharpened to make them more apposite to their context. (That is Virgil's practice.) Turnus is branded irrational and barbaric, a hero in the Homeric style, the antithesis of Aeneas. Readers of Homer can call on their historical sense and stomach a battle scene as a monument to an irrational and barbaric age, but the poet of a rational and civilized age (as it saw itself) could not hold up a hero of the Homeric sort as a paradigm of all that was admirable. His hero must show virtues of a quieter, more cooperative kind.[9] Since most of us have a sneaking regard for Cossacks, Indian chiefs, and Zulu kings, if not for Genghis Khan and Tamerlane, civilized heroes like Jason and Aeneas are apt to seem negative and colorless. But what is civilized behavior if not restraint on self-assertion? Aeneas therefore does not drive across the battlefield with severed heads swinging from his chariot rail, as Turnus does. He surrenders without ransom the corpse of Lausus. He does not enjoy killing or rush headlong into battle without in Roman fashion first seeking allies to share the burden. He does not take umbrage at the simple hospitality of Evander.

Much critical cogitation would have been saved if Virgil had had a word for this aspect of Aeneas' presentation. The obvious Latin word, *humanitas*, does not accommodate itself to the Latin hexameter, and it seems that *pietas*, "due respect for gods and men," which is the virtue of Aeneas, expresses also his humanity. But *pietas* may require a person to be stern. When Turnus lay wounded at his feet, it crossed Aeneas' mind to spare him. That, said the ancient commentator Servius, showed his *pietas*, his humanity. But Aeneas' eyes then fell on the trophy Turnus had torn from the body of Pallas, and in vengeance he drove home the sword. That too, said the commentator, showed *pietas*. Duty imposed vengeance, but not the ruthless, insatiable vengeance of Achilles.

Even so, devotion to duty is an ambiguous virtue, for the sacrifices it entails are not necessarily those of duty's devotee. Many readers of the *Aeneid* feel this ambiguity most strongly in the fourth book, in the tragic story of Dido's love and desertion. Duty imposed on Aeneas a heartless role, and he himself seems heartless. But his creator has made him in this episode, as everywhere, the incarnation of destiny and of Roman and epic values, and he therefore cannot permit his character to express feelings appropriate to a real human being in such circumstances. The focus of the narrative accordingly swings away from Aeneas to Dido and the story is told very much from her viewpoint. It is a way, much in evidence in Virgil, by which the narrator balances the epic and national values with others that readers intuitively identify as Virgil's own. Read by itself, the fourth book is superb; within the *Aeneid* it offers an obstacle to comprehending Virgil's Aeneas. At other places in the poem the latent conflict is surmounted. The pitiful death of Lausus (x 802) falls into place when Aeneas comes to the forefront of the narrative and delivers his praises of the youth he has slain. But in a literary tradition in which tragedy held so esteemed a place, and in which women could now play major parts, Dido had to have her hour. She could not be treated as her distant literary forebear, Calypso, had been treated—pushed offstage and forgotten.

Turnus, the paradigm of all that Aeneas is not, was more easily characterized: he was the victim of *furor*, "madness," a kind of

barbaric irrationality. *Furor* was a prominent part of Cicero's vituper-
ation when he denounced the irresponsibility of self-seeking politicians, the sort of men of whom the historian Sallust wrote in a
famous passage that "the people turned their freedom, the nobility
their rank, into self-gratification and seized, looted and pillaged for
their own benefit, so that everything was divided between two
parties and the commonwealth that lay in the middle was torn
apart. . . . Greed with power but without limit or restraint was everywhere, polluting and destroying, holding nothing sacred or of value,
until it brought ruin on itself" (*Bellum Jugurthinum* 41). *Furor* is the
driving force of this anarchic society, under whose impulsion Julius
Caesar had thought civil war a reasonable alternative to a diminu-
tion of his "dignity." Nothing could be more different from the public
morality of a restored Augustan Rome.

Turnus has his moments; his heroic leap into the Tiber when he
escapes from the Trojan camp was that of a real Roman hero,
Horatius Cocles. But he cannot submit to fate—that is his primary
madness. Therefore he makes war on Aeneas. Personal happiness—
not in plentiful supply in Virgil's world—lies in cooperation with
Fate, and Turnus ends his career by an act of virtual suicide. Dido,
whose passion is also characterized as furious, ends in the same way,
mouthing words of malevolent hate. Since *furor* is thus a sort of
cosmic principle, and since Virgil employs the Homeric divine apparatus, it is natural for *furor* to have an Olympian personification,
namely Juno.

When they were not fighting on the plain of Troy, Homer's gods
would watch the battle from some handy mountain peak. We see the
action through their eyes, but we do not see very far. If Zeus had
some grand design, it did not extend for centuries into the future.
How could it when the Trojan War spanned one decade? Ennius' epic
covered seven or eight centuries, and his gods could take a longer
view. In the fragments of the *Annales* there are half a dozen Olympian scenes, and they are all in some way concerned with destiny.
Jupiter comments on the action at its decisive moments, unlike the
gods of Homer, who participate in it on trivial occasions. There is
much to be said for handling in this way an apparatus that the
evolution of religious belief had turned into literary ornament. The
gods could symbolize the struggles and success of a nation, not just
the fortune of a hero.

Hera, the Greek Juno, was motivated to aid the Greeks by a thoroughly Homeric impulse, personal pique at her humiliation in the Judgment of Paris. Such moral anthropomorphism would not do in an age when traditional theology had to contend with the refined speculations of philosophers, and Virgil will have none of it. The Juno of the *Aeneid* is not a personality but a personification of opposition—opposition to the course of destiny, opposition to order, and specifically opposition to Rome. Why Juno? Carthage, a colony of the Semitic Phoenicians, worshiped one of the queens of heaven. To the Romans, therefore, it seemed that their enemies bowed down to Juno, the greatest of their goddesses. Already in Ennius she was the patroness of Carthage and only yielded to Jupiter on the defeat of Hannibal. Virgil's Juno does not wait for defeat to make her submission, and she drives a hard bargain: let Rome prevail, but let every trace of Troy and the Trojans be extinguished.

In his youth Virgil had been an Epicurean, and the Epicureans affected disbelief in any divine concern or influence in the world. Like most Romans, Virgil lacked total conviction in his philosophy. After praising Epicurean science, he wistfully commended the theological innocence of the Italian peasant. *Fortunatus et ille deos qui novit agrestes,* "Happy the man who knows the gods of the countryside" (*Georgics* ii 490): that line probably represents Virgil's truest sentiment, though it tells us little about his personal faith. His Epicureanism would not have prevented him using gods as poetical symbols.[10] Olympus had to be more than poetical ornament if the poet was not to lose more in pretension and incongruity than he gained in diversion and fantasy. The question was how to achieve a consistent pattern of poetical symbolism. The philosophy of the Stoics happened to be that which was most concerned with the idea of fate. Hence it suited Virgil for the sake of his poem to adopt a view of the world that behind its Homeric facade was more or less Stoic.

In their weightiest role, therefore, Virgil's gods are an allegory of his historical determinism. Jupiter (most noticeably at i 257 and xii 830) discourses as if he were the mouthpiece of Fate, and when Aeneas seems unmindful in Dido's palace of the glory to which he is called, it is Jupiter who causes him to be put in mind of duty. He does not do so directly but sends Mercury, for the Homeric color of the divine apparatus must be maintained. The minor gods have only such minor roles in the *Aeneid*: Aeolus raises a storm, and Neptune pacifies it; Vulcan fashions new weapons for Aeneas. Or the gods are made to intervene so as to bring into play feelings that are already immanent in the human characters: Amata's hostility to the Trojans is intensified by Allecto, and Dido half loves Aeneas before Cupid works on her feelings.

These gods have a limited vision. "Aeneas will never reach Italy," wails Venus (i 229), to which Jupiter replies from a superior vantage point, "Fate stands immovable": Aeneas shall reach Italy and shall conquer. But Jupiter's speech is more than an adumbration of the last books of the epic, as it would have been in Homer. The divine vision reaches the poet's own day, touching lightly along the way on some salient points of Roman history, which is thus revealed as providentially leading to the role of Augustus—and beyond, for Jupiter has given the Romans empire without end. This grand assertion of the political destiny of Rome is balanced by Jupiter's final discourse in the twelfth book, where the god proclaims the Trojans' cultural and religious destiny, to adopt the cults and customs of the Italians and to maintain above all other peoples the *pax deorum,* in a land of peculiar sanctity. That prediction, however, is not addressed to Aeneas at all but to Virgil's readers. The determinism of this epic, the preordination of the Roman empire, becomes a means by which the historical, national, Ennian epic is inserted into the mythological, literary, Homeric form.

The national theme, however, needed something more specific than Jupiter's vague prognostications and something more formal than sporadic historical and etiological digressions. Virgil is liberal enough with these: Iulus is ancestor of the gens Julia, Clausus of the Claudii, and by some ingenious etymologies Mnestheus of the Memmii, Sergestus of the Sergii, and Cloanthus of the Cluentii; Dido prays for an avenger; Hercules established the priesthoods of the Potitii and Pinarii; the *Lusus Troiae,* the showpiece of the imperial Secular Games, was instituted at the obsequies of Anchises. In many cases Virgil permits himself no more than a passing reference: it would have been an ignorant Roman indeed who did not know that Dido's avenger was the terrible Hannibal. In emotional terms the poet can say as much in a few lines as a historian can in as many chapters. Nor is it only persons who are listed in this allusive and suggestive fashion. Aeneas was a wanderer and visited many cities.

These places are no more than sonorous sounds to us unless we have steeped ourselves in Roman history. Place names share the emotional force of the events that happened there. When Virgil used the simple devices of Aeneas' tour of the site of Rome (viii 306–69) or a catalog of Turnus' allies (vii 647–817), we may be sure no Roman had a soul so dead that it did not respond to the recital of those hallowed spots. Many were literally hallowed and were mentioned for that reason. The longest entry in the catalog (vii 761–82) concerns the sacred grove of Diana at Aricia, the most numinous spot in the whole of Italy;[11] and when Aeneas lands at the site of Rome, what should he find on the banks of the Tiber but the Great Altar of Hercules, reputedly the most ancient of Roman cults. In this way the *Aeneid* stresses the sanctity of Italian soil and its special relationship with the divine powers.

Virgil's history is careful to avoid the appearance of system. The most comprehensive historical passage (vi 756–892) adapts a Platonic eschatological fantasy in order to parade before Aeneas in the underworld the unborn heroes of the Roman state from Aeneas' immediate descendants to those of the poet's own time. Virgil lingers, as is fitting, over the two founders, Romulus and Augustus, and sheds a tear over the young Marcellus, whose early death in 23 B.C. destroyed Augustus' first hopes of founding a dynasty.

In Cicero's time such a list of famous names would have been closely scrutinized for its party political bias. Was the great conservative Aemilius Scaurus included, or C. Marius, the people's consul? (Virgil has neither.) The Metelli or the Gracchi? Horace (*Odes* i 12) has a briefer list but gives it a conservative color by including Scaurus and that pillar of republicanism, the Younger Cato.[12] Horace knew the meaning of such details; Virgil gives the impression of supreme indifference to the niceties of party political argument. He mentions the revolutionary Gracchi—their motives could be considered pure— but has no other figures of controversy. A national epic, of course, should not be partisan.

There are two other extensive allusions to Roman history, the Latin catalog (vii 647–817) and the shield of Aeneas (viii 626–728). The catalog is an indirect device, but it should not pass without notice that the ethnography is extensively coincidental with the personnel of Livy's first five books (i.e. with the first century of the Roman republic, more or less). Since the shield is a description of

the engraved decoration of armor, it turns into a series of short
anecdotes mostly concerned with the regal period of Rome (753–510
B.C.). Virgil had covered the great days of the republic in book vi and
passed over them here to picture Catiline, the "conspirator" of 63
B.C. and one of the most libeled figures in history, suffering the
torments of Tantalus in hell while the priggish Cato dispenses justice
to the righteous. The effect is curiously topical, like that of many
entries in Dante's *Inferno;* but in the early years of Augustus' rule as
emperor, when his political stance was notably reactionary, Virgil's
sentiments were conventional enough. The last panel of the shield
depicts the battle of Actium and the triumph of Augustus. Truth is
not to be expected at this point. It will be found, if anywhere, in the
sober narrative of Cassius Dio (l 31–35). Augustus' achievement was
not so much his victory, cheaply gained, as his skillful presentation
of a sordid conflict between two warlords as a great patriotic struggle
against the barbarian hordes of the east. No protégé of Maecenas
would deviate from that presentation; but where Propertius, for
example, was stilted and frigid (iv 6), Virgil contrived a restrained
rhetoric and even a certain warmth:

> Hinc Augustus agens Italos in proelia Caesar
> cum patribus populoque, penatibus et magnis dis,
> stans celsa in puppi, geminas cui tempora flammas
> laeta vomunt, patriumque aperitur vertice sidus.
>
> > (*Aen.* viii 678–81)

(On one side was Caesar Augustus leading the Italians to battle
with senate and people beside him, and the Penates and the
Great Gods, standing on his lofty vessel, from whose joyful brow
flames blazed forth and above whose head appears his father's
star.) [*author's translation*]

The courtly style, beside which Homer seems quite earthy, is typical of
Virgil's taste and magisterial manner. In an age possessed of an acute
feeling for language it ensured immediate acclaim for the *Aeneid*.

The language of the *Aeneid*, by general consent, marks the apogee
of Latin verse style. According to Cicero, a public speaker ought to
be master of every stylistic register, whether plain or impassioned,
barbed or tranquil. He was right: the attention span of an audience is
brief, and any sustained manner of speaking soon loses its effect.
Readers are a little kinder to their authors, but not much; and in

Virgil's time a change was coming over the nature of literary publication that brought poets out of their study and confronted them with
the problems of the public orator. It was the historian Asinius Pollio,
it was said, who first gave public recitations of his works. We know
that Virgil recited the *Georgics* and parts of the *Aeneid* to the
imperial family. The ultimate results of this practice were pernicious,
for it encouraged authors to put a premium on immediate, superficial
effects, to mistake debating points for thought, and to impress rather
than move. The *Aeneid* has its moments of intense rhetoric: Dido's
addresses to Aeneas, the horrors of the descent to hell, the description of the Fury Allecto, and the battle of Hercules and Cacus. But
these are moments. The tone changes rapidly, for example, from the
Gorgons and Harpies that guard the gates of Hades to the pathos of
the untimely dead waiting to cross the river Styx; from the ironical
characterizations of Juno and Aeolus in the first book to the vigorous
description of the storm at sea. One does not suppose that Virgil
required advice on the value of variety in a long poem, but variety
(*poikilía*) was one of the virtues discerned in Homer by those Hellenistic commentators for whose views Virgil had respect.

Virgil's diction is complex. The parameters of an Augustan style
are easy to describe: it must have weight, dignity, and a recognizable
poetic quality. Ennius had defined this problem for Latin, but he had
not solved it. And if the historical epicists had shown how the Latin
hexameter could be exploited, they had not improved their diction
to the same degree. They were happy to use words with prosaic and
neutral connotations. That practice, in the opinion of Greek and
Roman critics, was no bar to nobility of thought and expression, but
it did not help evoke the atmosphere of a heroic, mythical world.
Evocation was all that was necessary, a reminder that the *Aeneid* is a
fantasy, not a history. Archaism in moderation is effective, but not
just any archaism will do. When Sallust revived the language of the
Elder Cato, his readers were reminded of his predecessor's reputation
for fearless honesty. Virgil's archaisms echo Ennius, just as his
Grecisms echo Homer. They stake his claim to stand in the grandest
epic tradition.[13] It is therefore not the archaism or Grecism as such
that is important but the literary provenance of this part of Virgil's
language.

Ennius and Lucretius thought in prose and forced meter onto their
language: "hammered into verse" is a cliché of their critics. The

verse of a narrative poem must not give that impression, but it must not be too facile either, or it will appear clever, like that of Ovid, and lose dignity. The pace of Virgil's verse is therefore slow—stately was Tennyson's description—with much elision of heavy syllables, many spondees, and a frequently involved syntax. The quality of Ovid's writing seems to lie on the surface and invites imitation; Virgil's, by contrast, is dense or deep—the metaphors are unavoidable—and defies imitation as absolutely as it defies translation.

For example, compare the descriptions of the Furies Allecto (*Aen.* vii 324) and Tisiphone (Ovid, *Met.* iv 481). Ovid is pictorial:

> At once the fell Tisiphone snatched up
> A robe all drenched in gore, and seized a torch—
> It dripped with blood—and wound a writhing snake
> About her. As she started forth there went
> Beside her Grief and Terror, Madness too
> And Dread...

It is a pleasure to frighten ourselves with this bogie, for her terrors are entirely superficial. Virgil is altogether more suggestive. Juno descends to hell

> To rouse Allecto from the infernal seat
> Of her dire sisters and their dark retreat.
> This Fury, fit for her intent, she chose;
> One who delights in wars and human woes.
> Even Pluto hates his own mis-shapen race;
> Her sister Furies fly her hideous face;
> So frightful are the forms the monster takes,
> So fierce the hissings of her speckled snakes.[14]

Until we reach the speckled snakes (without which no Fury is properly dressed), there is nothing visible in this description; everything else is indeterminate and therefore powerfully suggestive. To work on the imagination of readers, to involve them, is the purpose of what a distinguished critic has called Virgil's subjective style.[15] The authors of literary epic cannot be literally anonymous, nor can they suppress their personalities like the craftsman-poets of the old heroic poems. Apollonius moves in and out of his narrative; Virgil, the real author behind the narrator, is there almost all the time.

One may ask how far the presence of the poet and his private feelings were compatible with his public voice, in which the shared attitudes of many were given expression. In short, is the public voice forced? Enthusiasm and Roman pride had acclaimed the *Aeneid* as something greater than the *Iliad;* as a historical epic and the charter myth of the Roman state the *Aeneid* had made Ennius a literary curiosity. Yet something rankled in the poet's mind. In 20 B.C. the poem was almost finished, but Virgil announced his intention to devote three more years to its revision and attempted to arrange for its destruction if he could not complete it. Perfectionists have been known to commit such crimes, and there is nothing inherently unlikely if Virgil's unhappiness lay in matters of detail. He did not work methodically but "so that there should be nothing to hold back his inspiration he left some passages incomplete, others propped up, as it were, with very tenuous lines" (Donatus, *Life* 22). No doubt his design evolved; no doubt he sometimes forgot what he had already composed. The poet's account of the death of Palinurus (v 833) cannot be reconciled with that of Palinurus' ghost (vi 337). The narrative of the third book has a detached quality, more appropriate to the persona of a storyteller than to that of a participant; the emotionalism of the second book is in strong contrast. Could the third book have been the first of an earlier draft and cast in the third person?[16]

Such details are not of a kind to fill an author with despair; it would be more depressing if he felt a conflict among his various aims or between his aims and methods. Virgil's means is the world of Homer, one of jealous gods and self-willed heroes; his end is a literary monument to Rome, where Rome represents not only a glorious destiny but also a sense of the cost and effort of pursuing that destiny. *Tantae molis erat Romanam condere gentem,* "so great a toil it was to found the Roman race" (i 33): this famous line seems to epitomize much of the feeling that created the *Aeneid.* Their traditional virtues equipped the Romans for a hard, unglamorous life in pursuit of the general good. That is a great part of the meaning Virgil wished to impart, but he leads up to it by a classic statement of the Homeric wrath-of-a-god motif. Juno loathed Troy, and Aeneas was a Trojan. What, one may ask, has Ganymedes and the Judgment of Paris (i 27) to do with the efforts of will that wore down Pyrrhus and Hannibal and humbled Hellenistic kings? The passage is an instance of the way in which Virgil makes a fantasy, the Homeric Olympus, stand for something real, the Roman sense of history.

At the highest level these devices work; but as we come down to the particular events of Aeneas' wars and travels, the viewpoints of the Homeric and Augustan ages are reconciled with increasing difficulty. Virgil's characters seem to represent pieces in a grim game played out by selfish gods, not heroes struggling with circumstances and their own weakness. The very first scene of the *Aeneid,* where Juno crudely bribes Aeolus to wreck Aeneas' ships, shows these gods at their moral nadir. [17] If Virgil had consistently maintained this tone, there would have been nothing to distinguish these divinities from the crude apparatus of the historical epicists except the dignity of Virgilian verse.

Aeneas' task was a *moles,* a mountain to be moved not only by faith but stone by stone, day after day, with no thanks at the end. Homer may hint that heroic *kudos* is vanity but he does not deny its fascination or the zest with which the heroes pursue and defend it. Aeneas has no such zest at all; he is tired of wandering, tired of war, tired (at his first appearance, i 94) of life itself. Homeric zest for a good killing is assigned to Turnus and called *furor.* However, such zest is sympathetic; we like heroes to be men of spirit, and it is a liking that easily overrides revulsion at their moral turpitude. The Iliadic books of the *Aeneid* are no less a fantasy than the Odyssean, and this would have been appreciated by the Roman reader; the fighting is unreal, as unreal as the unarmed combat of Hercules and Cacus (viii 190–267). But the Homeric mode of Virgil's narrative can seduce the reader into a historical fallacy and invest Turnus, the symbol of all that is not Roman, with too much reality. With reality comes sympathy and a sense of injustice, as if Turnus were innocent, a good man misled by Juno, flawed only by his impetuosity, and courageous to the end. [18]

The danger is nowhere more evident than in the criticism of the final scene of the *Aeneid.* If Aeneas represents a primitive Roman who even in Homeric surroundings practices his nation's virtue of clemency, how is it that he slays Turnus deliberately (Turnus is helpless) and "in hot fury" (*furiis accensus*)? Virgil has done all that can reasonably be expected, in comments and asides, to condemn the arrogance and barbarity of Aeneas' victim and adumbrate his death. Yet if we nevertheless recoil from the manner of his execution, it is not the only point in the *Aeneid* where the editorial comments of the poet are overridden by the intuitive sympathy for his characters that Virgil plants in the reader's mind. When Dido dies, do we recall that her love was a *culpa* (iv 172), that is, blameworthy? Do we believe it? Did Virgil believe it? It is rare indeed for him to take a resolute moral stance. Catiline's condemnation (viii 668) is an instance, but then Catiline was supposed to have plotted to burn the city and massacre the men of substance. More characteristic is the verdict on the first Brutus (vi 817–23): he was *infelix* (something like "to be pitied for his misfortune"). This Brutus enjoyed fame not only as a liberator who had freed Rome from the tyranny of the Etruscan kings but, more mysteriously, as one of those noble Romans who passed sentence of death on their own sons. No illustration of the triumph of duty over affection could be more vivid. Yet Virgil does not react here or elsewhere with conventional praise or genuine indignation; rather, he reveals a kind of sad recognition that life, or at least the life of the true Roman, was unmercifully hard. It is in keeping with this feeling that all the *Aeneid*'s laudations of imperialism are made indirectly, put into the mouths of Jupiter or Anchises or attributed to the craft of Vulcan; Virgil's private voice will not sound the note of triumph. Too much can be inferred from this reticence—for instance, that the poet was secretly hostile to the program of his emperor.[19] There are moments when Virgil rises above the interests of Rome and regards the world, as the gods in Homer did, as a spectacle to be viewed impartially. But whereas the gods in Homer found the strife of the heroes a pleasure to behold, Virgil's pervasive emotion is sorrow. The whole world is *infelix*, from the stag pursued by hunters to the lovelorn queen of Carthage in her palace. That Justice had fled from the earth, that the present age was an age of iron, and that the dispensation of Jove was harsh had been stated many times since the days of Hesiod, but Virgil alone not only said it but manifestly felt it. If he had not, the *Aeneid* would have remained a national epic, an elegant Ennius, the tale of a tribe that grew smaller and smaller in the perspective of history. As it is, the *mortalia* that touched the heart of Aeneas are made universal. It is a quality to which the literary epic, to be worthy of its place as the first of the genres, must at least aspire.[20]

After Virgil

Et tamen ille tuae felix Aeneidos auctor
   contulit in Tyrios arma virumque toros,
nec legitur pars ulla magis de corpore toto
   quam non legitimo foedere iunctus amor.

(The blessed poet of your Aeneid
Put Arms and Man in hapless Dido's bed;
And of the queen by sinful love oppress'd
All haste to read, and then forget the rest.)

Ovid

Most of Virgil's readers had long outgrown the ancient habits of frugal piety that his epic celebrated.[1] From comfortable villas in choice surroundings they acclaimed the *Aeneid*, but their literary darling was Ovid, twenty-four years old when Virgil died. Ovid, the disappointing firstfruits of the Augustan peace, came from the shadow of the Gran Sasso in the central Apennines, from precisely that background for which the emperor looked in the young men he helped along the conventional paths to status and renown. Those were the army and the law, and both required a long apprenticeship and a modicum of application. But Ovid had two talents by which to circumvent those inconveniences: an elegant wit and a ready knack for versification. For twenty years he poured out a stream of clever, lighthearted verse that made him the favorite of Roman high society. "If it's fame you are seeking," he told the pale scriveners and sun-burned soldiers, citing a string of examples from Homer to Virgil, "better be a poet. Then your glory will last forever."[2]

Romans were used to wild behavior on the part of privileged young men. They were prepared to admit, when it suited them, that the wilder a man's youth, the sounder his character might be in maturity. There were even those, like Mark Antony, who combined a spectac-ularly dissolute style with outstanding energy in the public service.[3] But on the whole a man was expected to grow up, and this applied to poets as well as young noblemen. Could light, witty, outrageous, ironical lines really be immortal verse? Modern readers of Catullus or Ovid may well say yes, because the informality of such poems makes them seem spontaneous and heartfelt; their authors called them trivia and pretended to have higher things in mind.[4] Nor did Ovid fail to feel the insidious social pressure. While at work on the *Amores* (Love Poems) he actually began a *Gigantomachy*, the battle of Zeus with the Titans. The subject had fascinated minor epic poets since the Greek archaic age and continued to do so until the very end of pagan antiquity. (Claudian, the last exponent of the Roman classical

tradition, began his career with a *Gigantomachy*.) As a subject, its
horrendous thunderbolts and monstrous cast of characters had a fatal
appeal to minds imbued with rhetoric and the aims of rhetoric.
Ovid's mistress, he tells us (*Amores* ii 1, 11–22), was unimpressed;
she closed the door on him but relented when he returned to elegy.
Not till the poet was almost fifty did he finally succumb to conventional ideas of literary value.

Ovid's attempt at higher things was two-pronged: a didactic poem
constructed around the Roman calendar, the *Fasti,* and a vast narrative poem, the *Metamorphoses.* The genre of the *Fasti* was well
entrenched, so well that Ovid had been able to exploit the form in a
brilliant social satire and literary squib, the *Ars Amatoria* (Art of
Love); the *Metamorphoses* had a new form, if indeed it had a form at
all, for Ovid strains the traditional ideas of genre well past breaking
point. Its novelty does not help the critic, who is at a loss what to
expect or what critical criteria to apply. Let us begin by trying to
define Ovid's problem. He was a man of taste, and from whatever
angle he looked at the *Aeneid* it must have seemed to him that Virgil
had brought the epic genre in Latin to perfection, in other words,
that he had killed it. Ennius, Apollonius, even Homer, could all be
seen as pointing the way to the *Aeneid;* but the *Aeneid* was the
end—it did not point forward. Yet could a poet be a great poet if he
could not write an epic? Callimachus had suffered from that innu-
endo, and a poet as conscious of his genius as Ovid was must have
felt its pressure. Could then the public be deceived into applauding
something that looked like an epic but was not a pale ghost of the
Aeneid, something that would proclaim Ovid's genius as surely as
the *Aeneid* had done Virgil's?

The *Metamorphoses* is a collection of about two hundred and fifty
stories from mythology. Ovid was not the first to make such verse
anthologies or find fascination in the topic. As subject it was Hellenistic par excellence; but in the literary tradition of that age such
anthologies were associated with the example of Hesiod, not Homer;
that is, they belonged, as we should say, to the didactic, not the epic,
genre. The prestigious exemplar was Callimachus' *Aitia.* The prologue
to the *Aitia* is extant, and in it Callimachus disavows any intention to
compose a "single continuous song." When Ovid wrote *di . . . ad mea
perpetuum deducite tempora carmen,* "Spin finely, gods, my song's
unbroken thread" (*Met.* i 2–4), the allusion was plain to every reader.

Here was Ovid, the essence of all that was Alexandrian and neoteric, cocking a snook at the grand master himself. But then impudence had always been one of Ovid's most endearing (or infuriating) traits. The opening lines of the poem are not just a joke; they pose a question. How could the gods spin finely (*deducere*) a continuous (*perpetuus*) poem? To call a poem *perpetuum* was to proclaim an epic allegiance, to summon the gods of poetry to *deducere* the theme was to use the language of the antiepic Callimachean school, the language the early Virgil had used in the sixth *Eclogue*. Ovid contrives to spin the thread fine by mingling elegiac attitudes with epic pretensions. The creation story with which the *Metamorphoses* begins was an epic theme. Something like it was sung before Aeneas at Dido's court (*Aen.* i 740–46). But the Lucretian echoes of Ovid's prologue give way to a very Roman divine council before the episode concludes with an *Aeneid*-like tale of Python and Apollo. The story of Apollo continues but takes us directly into the world of Ovid's elegiac verse. Cupid smites Apollo with love of Daphne.[5] Not till the closing lines of the story, when Daphne has become a laurel, does the epic color return:

> With thee [the laurel] shall Roman generals wreathe their
>   brows,
> When shouts of joy acclaim triumphal shows
> And long processions mount the Capitol.
> Trusty thou shalt Augustus' portal shade
> With leaves that like my godhead never fade.
> (*Met.* i 560–63)

And so it is throughout the poem.

Another question is what sort of continuity unites the episodes of a story into a story? Is the *Metamorphoses* one poem or an anthology? Continuity and interconnection are relative matters, and Ovid's continuity, it turns out, is less like the logic of a Sophoclean tragedy than like the transparent artifice that distributes the tales of Boccaccio's *Decameron* into ten sets. Ovid has a temporal continuity: he begins with the creation of the world and proceeds through time to the empire of Augustus. He has also, even if it is a by-product of his chronological scheme, a certain thematic unity at any stage. Stories about gods are followed by stories about Greek heroes, and they by tales of ancient Rome. Links between episodes, however, are often triumphantly inconsequential: Apollo pursued Daphne, daughter of the river god Peneus; the other river gods come to console Peneus *except Inachus,* for Inachus had lost his own daughter Io, pursued by Jupiter; Io's son was Epaphus; now his companion was Phaëthon; and so on. This is but the illusion of a continuous narrative.

The effect of maintaining the illusion of continuity is that it gives the *Metamorphoses* the spurious appearance of a poem of epic length. Nor is that all. Ovid persistently nudges the reader with epic suggestions. Everything that he had written before (save his tragedy, the lost *Medea*) had been in elegiac meter; the *Metamorphoses* uses the epic verse, the hexameter. But it is an elegist's hexameter, not Virgil's. The latter's verse is slow of pace, conscious of its dignity; Ovid's dactylic verse is skittish and flippant, ideal for the pleasing fictions he relates.[6] He avoids archaism and deliberate echoes of Ennius and Homer. It is the same with narrative style: Ovid affects often enough the impersonal manner of the epic; he emphasizes the more violent, that is, more "heroic" emotions; he involves gods and even the march of history. But the grand manner is not supported by grand conceptions. Ovid has at all times a fixed temporal standpoint, his own day, and therefore recognizes that his mythical subject matter has a ludicrous side. The epic gods are humanized so thoroughly that the stories about them turn into episodes of social comedy.[7] His similes (for similes are obligatory in epic) are contemporary. Above all his personages are polite inhabitants of the villas and palaces of Augustan Rome, profoundly unheroic.

Ovid uses some pieces of the epic apparatus. In the first book Jupiter convenes a divine council; but the divine senate is oddly like its earthly equivalent:

> High in the firmament with lustrous ray
> Shines heaven's bright thoroughfare, the Milky Way.
> And there the palace lies; on either hand
> The crowded doors of courted nobles stand.
> Elsewhere (to speak so bold) the suburbs lie,
> Where dwell the common people of the sky.
> But here where powers and princes make their home,
> Heaven has its social summit, much like Rome.
> Now when the gods of rank were seated all
> Within the marble rondure of the hall,
> And Jove, in high authority and place,
> Presided...
>
> (*Met.* i 167–78, trans. Otis)

When Jove speaks, his words are such as to raise a suspicion that the senatorial manner of Augustus had provided the model.[8]

Nor are we spared the traditional epic horrors: a descent to Hades (iv 432) complete with Furies who, like well-bred girls, comb the snakes *out* of their hair; an excitingly chilly personification of Hunger (viii 788), all skin, bone, and swollen ankles, like Phineus in Apollonius (*Arg.* ii 197–205). Ovid has the same fun when he moves into indisputably epic territory—the hunt for the Calydonian boar, Hercules, Troy, Aeneas, and the apotheosis of Julius Caesar: the youthful Nestor is treed by the boar, and Hercules confutes the logic of Achelous with his fists. Only in the last books do these touches of comedy become sparse, and only there, in long rhetorical and philosophical discourses, does the poem approach something like the gravity of literary epic.

Is, then, the *Metamorphoses* a mock epic, like Pope's *Rape of the Lock?*[9] Ovid had earlier exploited the sustained parody of a literary genre in his pseudodidactic masterpiece, the *Ars Amatoria*. He is well aware of the ludicrous aspects of his subject matter in the *Metamorphoses*. But the mock-epic element is not kept up; it is subordinate to an aspect that was immediately evident to Ovid's Roman readers—a tendency, as Quintilian put it (iv 1, 77), to *lascivire*, "show off." What holds the reader to the *Metamorphoses* is sometimes the poet's literary impudence, sometimes his social or political bravado, but always the anticipation of the unexpected. The poem is a singularly sophisticated variety of the narrative art with an interest that lies not in what happens in these familiar tales but in what Ovid will make happen.

The *Metamorphoses* therefore stands by itself, its author's ultimate literary intention elusive. Inevitably a writer who is half-serious, half-flippant, will be overestimated or underestimated according to the seriousness or flippancy of the reader. But the impulse of the *Aeneid* cannot be set aside. Ovid wrote with Virgil's ghost at his shoulder. He is aiming higher than he did with the *Ars Amatoria*: he must constantly suggest, pretend even, that an epic poem has come into his reader's hands, but he must never provoke a direct comparison with Virgil and make a real (i.e. conventional) epic out of his poem.[10] In this case a refusal to imitate was the sincerest flattery.

Whether a poem is or is not an epic is not so important as the expectations raised by its being thought of in those terms. If it is an epic, it should have a plan, and the plan should be the means of expressing something neither trivial nor ephemeral; the epic poet has something to get off his chest. Yet even when Ovid approaches the climax of his poem and gives a long speech to the philosopher Pythagoras (xv 75–478) in which change is erected into a principle of nature, he puts it into a context that prevents any serious interpretation: Pythagoras' theme is the moral wickedness of eating meat since, in view of the universal metamorphosis of nature, we may inadvertently devour our reincarnated ancestors![11] Neither has the *Metamorphoses* any plan in the sense required. It is a series of word pictures, and like painted pictures they are arranged into groups: a major tale is flanked by minor episodes, and hero tales are balanced against comic and pastoral scenes.[12] The reader is drawn along but without any sense of direction. We look in vain for a general theme.[13] We strain to catch the sound of the poet's public voice, but all we hear is the voice of Ovid—brilliant, clever, and not a little narcissistic. "And now my work is done," Ovid writes in his last lines, "which neither the wrath of Jove, nor fire, nor sword, nor the gnawing tooth of time shall ever undo. Be it when it will, let that day come which has no power save over my mortal body and end the span of my uncertain years. Still in my better part shall I be borne immortal far beyond the stars and have undying fame" (*Met.* xv 871–79). No epic poet would dare to hector his readers with such a boast any more than he would condescend to chat with them as Ovid does in a thousand asides and comments on his stories.

The *Metamorphoses* is not to be categorized without being misconceived.[14] Parts are heroic, parts tragic, pastoral, and romantic, but there is no word to characterize the whole. Ovid plays with all the genres in turn and especially with the epic.[15] The *Metamorphoses* is always promising to become an epic poem but breaks off with a laugh whenever that consummation is seriously threatened. Ovid had seen the problem and proposed his own ingenious solution. The Roman epic had culminated in the *Aeneid*. No one was going to beat it on its own ground, and to join the ranks of its imitators was an obvious mistake. To gain a new lease on life at Rome, the epic would have to achieve a metamorphosis of its own. It had passed already from heroic to historical, romantic, and national forms: what next?

VI

Lucan and the Flavian Epic

The Bellum Civile

Lucan is impassioned, spirited, full of lively
thoughts; indeed, to be frank, a better model for
orators than poets.

Quintilian

Thus Lucan has not deserved to be counted
among the poets, because he appears to have
composed a history, not a poem.

Servius

Lucan has seldom been considered on his merits.

Morford

Ovid's literary good sense was not widely shared, and in the decades after the *Aeneid* many epics were written according to formula. There is a list of them to c. A.D. 15 in Ovid's farewell to the world of literature (*Ex Ponto* iv 16).[1] That was about the time when, for those who stood about the throne, the empire began to go wrong. To work a system in which subjects were supposed to be equals, from a vantage point of power legalized but barely constitutional, required a suppleness of mind rarely cultivated among a people who prided themselves on plain speaking. Yet when the princess Agrippina married Claudius in A.D. 49, optimists had cause for hope. She brought with her a son of impressionable age and appointed as his tutor the foremost *litterateur* of the day, the younger Annaeus Seneca. His name, after Claudius had been induced to adopt him, was Nero.

Politically nothing had changed. When his pupil became emperor at the age of sixteen in the fall of A.D. 54, Seneca addressed to him a treatise, *On Clemency*. It begins with the following remarkable passage: "Have I of all mortals found favor with Heaven"—it is Nero communing with his soul—"and been chosen to serve on earth as vicar of the gods? I am indeed arbiter of life and death for nations; it is in my power what each man's lot shall be; by my lips Fortune declares what gift she will bestow on each man; from my pronouncements peoples and cities have reason for rejoicing." Or not rejoicing, for he proceeds: "Without my favor and grace no part of the world prospers; all those thousands of swords my peace restrains will be drawn at my nod; which nations shall be utterly destroyed . . . which kings shall become slaves . . . which cities shall fall . . . this it is mine to decree."

It is as if the world were on trial, with the imperial displeasure the penalty for failing the test. The victims of these autocrats were mostly among those who played politics, but in Rome writers and public figures were one and the same group. Authors had been banished by the aged Augustus to remote and insalubrious places; his successors executed them outright. Literature oscillated between panegyric of living emperors and defamation of the deceased or was carefully unpolitical.

Defeat, if not shameful, can be stimulating; fueled by resentment, it has produced some of the best heroic epics. Was there not room for an epic poem that took a view of Roman destiny opposite to that of the *Aeneid?* The difficulty was that few Romans saw the defeat of the republic in heroic terms. The old political order had fallen, so its historians taught, because it was incapable of controlling the corruption of the state. It had been destroyed by civil war. Civil wars were never seen by Romans as a praiseworthy purgation of the state, as a revolution in the modern sense; civil war was fratricide, and the overwhelming feeling it aroused was that of guilt. The best literature of the Silver Age, the latter half of the first century A.D., is introspective. Satirists expressed their private disgusts and historians their despair. The epic writers of the time, Silius, Flaccus, and Statius, had no relevant public voice; they chose instead to write of Thebes, the Argonauts, and Hannibal. Such themes may have been poetically bankrupt, but at least they were safe.[2] Only in their worst moments did emperors detect treason in the guise of Greek mythology.[3]

The exception, but a partial one, was Lucan. The first five years of Nero's rule (A.D. 54–59) were a period of genuine liberalization, and the new emperor's devotion to the arts in all their forms was real and survived his small talent for any of them. Lucan's uncle Seneca was for the time being Nero's chief minister. In this atmosphere of light the poet began the composition of the *Bellum Civile* (called *Pharsalia* by older critics) concerning the civil war of Caesar against Pompey and the senate, 49–47 B.C. Nothing about its early books or its evident design upset Nero until A.D. 64, when the emperor forbade Lucan to recite in public; in effect he banned publication.[4] He was motivated, it was alleged, not by alarm at the subversive message of the epic but by envy of Lucan's superior poetical talents. Soon afterward the poet was implicated in Piso's conspiracy against Nero, and after interrogation he committed suicide.

The theme of the *Bellum Civile* is the demise of the free republic and the loss of liberty. That is why the conflict between Caesar and Pompey was "more than a civil war" (*Bell. Civ.* i 1). It was not the defeat of one overpowerful general by another, as the struggle of Marius and Sulla had been, but the destruction of the old order by Julius Caesar. Caesar therefore personifies tyranny, and Cato, his last and noble opponent, liberty and virtue. It is the possession of this theme that raises the *Bellum Civile* out of the ruck of historical epic poems, just as it is the intensity of the passion it aroused in Lucan that turns his declamatory style into poetry. But certain questions remain. If literary works of permanent value come in time to exist in a kind of vacuum, they once had roots in the situation that created them. How then does Nero relate to Caesar and Cato? When Nero turned against Lucan, Lucan's retort was to turn against Nero. There is a sharpening of tone in the later books of the *Bellum Civile* and a generalization of the triumph of tyranny: "The wound the world suffered from that battle was too deep to heal in one generation. More was lost than life and safety. We are laid low till the end of time. Every generation born to slavery was crushed by that conflict. What did the descendants of the defeated do to deserve to be born under despotism?" (*Bell. Civ.* vii 638–43). The empire, the regime of the Caesars, and by implication the rule of Nero, had come to be synonymous with tyranny. But was it always so?

Lucan follows the announcement of his theme with the sort of dedication that Virgil used to decorate the introductions to his didactic poems, a laudation of the patron:

> If Fate could find no other way [than civil war] for the advent of Nero, if an everlasting kingdom costs even the gods dear . . . then we complain no more, ye Powers above. Even such crimes and such guilt are not too high a price to pay. Let Pharsalia heap her awful plains with dead, let the shade of Hannibal be glutted with carnage . . . yet Rome owes much to civil war, since what was done was done, Nero, for your sake. When your watch on earth is over and you seek the stars at last, the celestial palace you prefer will welcome you. . . . But choose not your seat either in the northern region or where the sultry sky of the south sinks down; from these quarters your light would shine aslant upon your Rome. Should you lean on any part of the boundless universe, the axis of the sphere will be weighed down. Remain at the center, maintain the equilibrium of the world. . . . To me you are divine already. (*Bell. Civ.* i 33–63)

No one supposes that Lucan meant a word of this, and some have thought the flattery so gross that it could only be understood as sarcasm.[5] Flattery is insulting in an egalitarian age, but when emperors wielded the power of gods it was courtesy, protocol even. Tacitus noted without surprise or censure that when a consular senator feared he might have offended Tiberius (a modest emperor at the time), he offered his apologies on his knees.[6] There was no insincerity in his abasement. Like Lucan's praise of Nero it was the correct form of address.

No emperors began as tyrants or saw themselves in that light; most were happy to hear their predecessors denounced. When Lucan began to write, his ideological onslaught on Caesarism need not have been taken to include the government of Nero among its targets; when he died reciting verses from the *Bellum Civile*, it is clear that he intended that every line he had written about freedom and tyranny should apply to all emperors without exception and to Nero in particular.

The *Bellum Civile* is unfinished. The ten books would presumably
have become twelve, the canonical length of a Roman epic, but the
end point is obscure. The death of Caesar would have satisfied a
taste for poetic justice, but historically it solved nothing and would
have blurred the theme of the *Bellum Civile* that tyranny was trium-
phant. Probably the epic ended with the suicide of Cato, the final act
that turned the incorruptible Stoic into a republican myth. That
ending would permit the epic to fall into three blocks of four books,
dominated in turn by the figures of Pompey, Caesar, and Cato.
Historical epic cannot assume that its span will be short enough and
its action coherent enough for its structure to be built around a single
heroic figure; and to the figure from whose standpoint one might
have viewed the whole civil war, Caesar, Lucan is implacably hostile.
Other epic poets of Lucan's generation (though they wrote later
under a different emperor) were faced with the same problem. Silius
Italicus cannot keep Hannibal from the foreground of his poem no
matter how pro-Roman his sentiments; Statius cannot sympathize
with Eteocles nor make a central figure out of one of the Seven who
attacked Thebes. But Silius and Statius thought of the epic poem in
terms of the *Aeneid,* believing (quite rightly) that it was a great thing
to stand in the shadow of Virgil. Lucan lacked the humility that
comes with age; he wrote, it is astonishing to realize, in his early
twenties, and his way with the *Aeneid* is to repudiate it. He will have
none of its symbolic mythology, none of its allusive style, none of the
complexities and uncertainties of its central figure. He is happy to
have no central figure at all. His poem is about issues, and since to
Lucan the issues are perfectly clear, there is no need to approach
them indirectly through the tormented soul of an Aeneas. The
Bellum Civile is therefore an epic built about a theme; its unity is its
issue.

When heroic poems such as the *Chanson de Roland* or the Serbian
songs of the Kosovo cycle celebrated a defeat, they confronted the
task of making defeat glorious, something of which their audience
might, paradoxically, be proud. Such is not the intention of Lucan in
the *Bellum Civile.* There is no hint of the universal excuse for failure,
betrayal; the struggle for liberty was lost in a fair fight, and the
struggle will stay lost. Lucan's instinct is to present this wretched
prospect in the starkest possible light. Nothing is mythologized or
heroized. The Romans usually fight in Lucan as they did in the field,

with the *pilum* (javelin) and the *gladius* (sword), rarely with their poetical equivalents. When they die it is *mors* (death), not "doom" or "fate," and it is a *cadaver* (corpse) that lies on the ground. Nor does Lucan avoid, as the writers in the higher genres tended to do, the technical terms for the panoply of war.[7] Such direct diction commended itself to the fashionable Stoic philosophy of the day. "Speech that addresses itself to the truth should be simple and unadorned," Seneca had written (*Epistulae* 40.4). Rhetorically, if not logically, the proposition could be inverted and blunt straight-forwardness made the badge of truth. That suited Lucan's literary purposes. He had a stark and brutal subject, whose horror he was by no means anxious to minimize, and he favors the stark and brutal word.

The direct language is molded into an unsubtle meter. It is no way to treat the variety possible within the hexameter, but the declaimer is not concerned to be subtle. His art is to hammer home a point. The heavy, insistent metrics suits the staccato sequence of short sentences. Such a style was much admired in an age when connois-seurs like Lucan's grandfather, the elder Seneca, made scrapbooks of the choicest phrases of the oratorical virtuosi. Vehemence and decla-mation go together, but with every shock the mind's response dimin-ishes; a long declamation defeats itself. What then shall be said of the *Bellum Civile*, which for 8060 lines allows its reader not a moment of repose? One critic could not get beyond the opening lines without protest:

> Of war I sing, strife worse than civil war,
> Of crime made justice and our empire's might
> Victorious turned on its own vitals; how
> Kin fought with kin, and how the shattered world
> Strove to make felons out of all mankind:
> How standards clashed with standards, spears with spears,
> Eagles with eagles, friend and foe the same.
>
> (*Bell. Civ.* i 1–7)

"Wilt never have done, Annaeus!" complained Fronto.[8] The insist-ent hectoring of the reader dims the brilliance with which Lucan throws out the string of lapidary summations of his thought. It is these thoughts (*sententiae*) that catch the eye of every reader. Thick and fast they come, supplanting argument as the rhetorician's primary means of persuasion. A typical concatenation is found at *Bell. Civ.* v 240–99, the mutiny of Caesar's troops:

Scit non esse ducis strictos sed militis enses   254
(The sword, he realizes, once drawn belongs to the soldier not
the general)

Quidquid multis peccatur inultum est   260
(The crimes of thousands go unpunished)

Toto exercitus orbe / te vincente perit   266–67
(Everywhere *you* are victorious—and your soldiers die)

Manibus ferroque nocentes / paupertate pii   272–73
(Our hands and swords are guilty, our poverty absolves us)

Facinus, quos inquinat, aequat   290
Crime makes equal those it stains)

Quidquid gerimus fortuna vocatur   292
(Our achievements are called your luck)

Irato milite, Caesar, / pax erit   294–95
(When the soldiers rebel, Caesar, then there will be peace)

Together with the poetical words and Virgilian rhythms Lucan discarded the poetical ornaments. His learning has a scientific color, culled from textbooks of geography and zoology, and he is sparing in his evocation of the romantic world of myth. Some myths, of course, could provide fitting images in the context of civil war. What other conflict could equal the battle of Pharsalus but the conflict of Jupiter and the giants (*Bell. Civ.* i 34–37)? There is a straightforward *aition*, Hercules and Antaeus (*Bell. Civ.* iv 593–660), a challenge to the grand manner of Virgil's Hercules and Cacus (*Aen.* viii 184–279); but for ornament Lucan prefers to darken a somber story with historical allusions or an excursus on the atrocities of Marius and Sulla, the grimmest period of the civil wars (*Bell. Civ.* ii 68–232). All things in Lucan serve the turn of emphasis. His similes occur with about the same frequency as Virgil's;[9] but whereas one of the traditional functions of the extended simile lay in its contrast with the narrative—the world of peace against the world of war—in Lucan the simile is typically another example, emotionally intensified, of the violence and horror of the main text. Scaeva is pierced through and through "as the Libyan elephant, attacked by a throng of assailants, breaks all their missiles that rebound off his horny hide and twitches his skin to shake off the spears sticking in his body; his vitals lie hidden within and the weapons planted in him stick fast and draw no blood. A thousand darts and a thousand arrows are too few to bring about one death" (*Bell. Civ.* vi 207–12; cf. the pathos of Virgil's wounded stag, *Aen.* iv 69–73). Lucan's metaphors, often drawn from the gladiatorial shows and the gory practices of ancient medicine, echo this repulsive taste. The hyperbole can be effective, as in Lucan's first simile, where the fall of the republic is likened to the cataclysmic end of the Stoic universe (*Bell. Civ.* i 72–80). The hyperbole of Lucan's similes sometimes falls short of the hyperbole of his narrative: the mangled limbs of the victims when a building has collapsed are scarcely equal to the horrid end of Marius Gratidianus: "His arms, wrenched from his shoulders, fell to the ground; his tongue, cut out, quivered and beat the empty air with dumb motion; one cut off his ears, another his nostrils, a third pushed his eyeballs from their sockets when they had witnessed the fate of his limbs and scooped them out. Few," Lucan modestly continues, "will believe such an atrocity" (*Bell. Civ.* ii 181–86).

However, it was not the inclusion of sadism on such a scale that offended the hardened susceptibilities of the Neronian age but Lucan's omission of the tired yet graceful apparatus of the Olympian gods. His disdain for the hackneyed frigidities that disfigured the historical epics of Cicero and Silius should have been commended, but tradition was too strong. Even Lucan's contemporary Petronius, whose taste was famous, wanted epic gods. It seems that an epic poem cannot dispense with a supernatural apparatus altogether; there must be some direction to events. Mere chance is not a satisfactory explanation for the course of history. Chance personified —especially that Chance that is not quite random, Luck or Fortune —is more likely to deceive the mind that the world is not out of control, and Fortune is the goddess that presides over the *Bellum Civile*. [10] She downgrades the old gods into curiosities of anthropology and an opportunity for Lucan to show off his youthful erudition: Isis, Osiris, Apis, Jehovah (ii 592), the Gallic demons Tentates, Hesus, and Taranis—these are mentioned alongside deified Roman emperors (an especial object of the poet's scorn). Lucan's is a god-abandoned world, and when he mentions gods, as he does often enough, it is as a rhetorical figure to give edge to his protests at the triumph of evil. As for their moral creditworthiness, it is less than that of a good man (*victrix causa deis placuit sed victa Catoni*, "the gods voted for the cause that won, Cato for that which lost") and no better than that of the decayed and vacillating Pompey.[11]

To speak of Fortune is one way—the way of its victims—of expressing the Stoic view of history. There was no personal god in Stoicism but the ineluctable principle of Fate. Cause and effect brought off Caesar's victory, and since the nexus of cause and effect has no moral connotation, it confers no moral blessing on his success. Fate carried him from crime to crime; Fate ordained his assassination. Lucan's rhetorical imagination saw a link: Caesar was preserved by Fate from a sordid death in order to perish by Brutus' virtuous hand.

The baroque manner of declamatory rhetoric was ideally fitted for denunciation. Lucan rants; but if there are degrees of excellence in rant, he must be given the prize. In an epic, however, rant has a salient defect: it is not a good medium for narrative. It does nothing to induce the orator to be objective and simple, everything to lead him into hyperbole and comment. He wants to be noticed and in control. He will hector and bully. No readers are left in doubt anywhere in the *Bellum Civile* as to what they are supposed to feel, but they must often be content with a short general statement of events, not the loving analysis of action into its separate stages that is typical of Homer. Lucan composes by scenes of fifty to sixty lines and leaps from one scene to the next. Sometimes the leaps are sideways, for the *Bellum Civile* has a remarkable number of digressions: geographical excurses (Gaul, i 392–465; Italy, ii 399–438; Thessaly, vi 333–412; the Syrtes, ix 303–318; Libya, ix 411–97; the Nile, x 192–331), historical analogs (Marius and Sulla, ii 67–233; Alexander the Great, x 20–52), myths (Antaeus, iv 593–660; Medusa, ix 619–99), and topicalities (Delphic oracle, v 65–236; witches and necromancy, vi 438–568; snakes and snakebites, ix 700–838). The seventh and eighth books do not appear on this list, for they are the narrative core of the poem, the battle of Pharsalus and its aftermath.

Res ipsa loquitur, Cicero would say, but only after a tendentious presentation of his case, for a rhetorician cannot allow the plain facts to speak for themselves to untutored minds. The history of epic narration, which began with the precise and detailed objectivity of Homer, is the history of the intrusion of the narrating poet; tentative in Apollonius, discreet in Virgil, in Lucan it is everywhere and blatant. Homer would split a battle into the *aristeiai* of competing heroes, the *aristeiai* into separate duels, the duels into spear casts and sword thrusts; unless he has a choice incident of unusual horror to relate, Lucan paints a general description with lurid, moralistic strokes. This was the method of the "tragical" school of Hellenistic historiography to which (or to its Roman imitators) Lucan seems to owe more as a stylist than to the epic tradition itself.

His telling of the battle of Pharsalus (Book vii) begins indeed with some scenes that would not be inconceivable in the Iliadic *Aeneid*. The sun is unwilling to rise on the dreadful day; Pompey dreams of happier times; his soldiers clamor for action; a deluded counselor (Cicero, not in fact present in Pompey's camp) is made to urge him on; he recognizes that Fate has decreed his doom; the troops don their armor (vii 1–150). Yet even here Lucan cannot remain in the wings but must rush onstage to apostrophize the sleeping Pompey and enlarge on the irony of his blissful dreams, to comment on the frenzy of the troops ("We rush upon our ruin and clamor for the arms that will destroy us" [vii 60]), and to stress again that the day would settle for good the fate of Rome and the world ("Use up in one day, Pompey, all means of future triumphs by shedding the blood of all mankind!" [vii 233–34]).

The day was presaged by horrendous omens ("How great were these men to whose destiny all heaven was attentive!" [vii 205–6]). That had always been the case in Roman history. The opposing generals, as any reader of ancient history knows, then harangued their men in long, well-constructed speeches arguing opposite conclusions from similar premises (vii 235–384). Their sentiments, of course, and their language are the purest Lucan—and the purest rhetoric. "Your crime"—Caesar means that of beginning the civil war—"can only be expiated by a greater crime," that of triumphing over their compatriots. That is the verdict of the poet, not the confession of the general. Pompey preferred more conventional appeals to wives, children, and the natural justice of his cause (vii 347–82). He sounds like a beaten man, and when he alludes to the hopes of generations yet unborn, no knowledge of history is needed to recognize the tragic irony of his words. The armies charge, but before they meet, the poet claims the historian's privilege to reflect again on the significance of the great event (vii 387–459). It decimated the human race, set limits to the empire, made mockery of the interlude of republican government, disproved the existence of god, and left free spirits for their cold comfort only the farce of emperor worship—a fair summary of the message of the *Bellum Civile*.

And so to arms. There are many ways to describe a battle.[12] For the military historian generalship is a skill, and battles are reduced to dispositions, lines of advance and communication, weapons, and supplies; and no one below the rank of divisional commander must be mentioned by name. But war is not like that: there is no feeling in a *Kriegspiel*, and that lack mattered even to some historians. What was it like to have taken part? In Homer the moral element is to the fore. Battle is heroic exploit, so no time is wasted on dispositions and very little on general descriptions. Individual action dominates. In Virgil the method is the same but the emphasis is different: for Aeneas war is a mistake, a futile hiccup in the march of destiny. Battle therefore is tragedy and waste. But historians, if their intention is to present battle as well as, or instead of, analyzing it, have a particular difficulty. They are like landscape painters who must also be cartographers. This is where the pseudohistorian, the historical novelist, scores most heavily. To cite a celebrated example, mere history, that is, at the level of generalship, is not the strongest feature of Tolstoy's description of the battle of Borodino in *War and Peace*, but it may rank as one of the finest representations in literature of the internal aspect of battle. Such a representation must be neither overdrawn nor oversimplified. Lucan, inevitably, is guilty of both faults. His account of Pharsalus is a heady, impressionistic ferment. It is true that sometimes he speaks of the cavalry, of Pompey's auxiliary troops, or of the wings and the center, but the confusion is of morals rather than battle. Fratricide, frenzy, massacre, and pillage delineate Pharsalus, a hyperbole exceeded only by the hyperbole of Caesar's characterization, if such it may be called, for Caesar is reduced to the mere embodiment of sanguinary passion.[13]

In short, it is easy to find faults in the work of Lucan the poet—the melodramatic pessimism, the simplification of issues, and the crude bias and overwrought style. The same faults were counted to the credit of a declamatory rhetorician and ensured that Lucan continued to be read and to influence for centuries the style in which Latin hexameter narrative was expressed. His contribution to the idea of the epic at that level is a significant one. In other respects the contribution of the *Bellum Civile* has been slight. Lucan's experiment stripped the epic of so many of its formal features that in the common view (such as that of Servius in the chapter epigraph) it ceased to be recognizable as an epic.[14] His successors were quick to follow the advice of Petronius and welcomed back the gods. But the deepest flaw in the *Bellum Civile* is its narrowness. When Homer speaks of the human race we believe him; but the human race in Lucan means the Romans, and by Romans he means the interests of a self-centered class. The *Bellum Civile* is a stunning, baroque monument in the history of literature but not a universal hymn to liberty.

After Lucan

> During the whole month of April scarce a day
> has passed when we have not been entertained
> with the recital of some poem.
>
> Pliny

> Shall I never retaliate for all that I have suffered
> from Cordus' *Theseid?*
>
> Juvenal

Lucan's concept of a political epic was the last significant development of the genre made in antiquity, for the classical world survived the hardening of all the arteries of its culture by three or four centuries. Eight centuries of continuous literary history had preceded Lucan, exhausting the traditional forms of thought and expression. Reactions to this impasse varied. To the satirists the tedious predictability of the higher genres was an object of derision: they forgot to say what ought to be done. Thoughtful critics pondered the decline of literature: it had something to do, they decided, with the loss of political freedom and the stimulus it had given to active minds. The arts had lost their public voice, and nowhere more so than in poetry. In Tacitus' *Dialogue on Oratory* poetry is derided as the passion of the recluse. Jason and Agamemnon (and who should come to mind but they!) may be made to declaim with the tongues of angels, but they will bring the poet neither fame nor riches. Let him enjoy the peaceful solitude to which his profession has condemned him; at least he will escape the perils and corruption of public life.

There were others, of course, who did not recognize the predicament of literature. Pliny, through complacency or obtuseness, rejoiced in the deceptive fecundity of the age, for literature flourished with seeming vigor under the Flavian emperors (A.D. 70–96) and beyond. It is hard to see why. The emperors were not notable for sensibility or generous patronage; their subjects had lost their sense of destiny, even their capacity for resentment. It was an age lacking in energy. Yet that may be the clue. Just as the Hellenistic Age in Greek literature stood in awe of the classical achievements, so the Silver Age of Latin literature fed on the masterpieces of the Augustans. A lack of originality in his pupils did not trouble Quintilian, the first salaried professor of rhetoric at Rome; he maintained that in every branch of art there is a standard set by the artists of merit toward which it is the duty of every rising talent to aspire. That aspiration was sufficiently general and canonical to be assigned a technical term, *imitatio. Imitatio* with *variatio* was the literary law for anyone with respect for genre.

Quintilian was a thoughtful man and saw *imitatio* as a first step with which no writer should rest content, but it was an essential first step. And most writers—Quintilian speaks with long experience of the schoolroom—would do well to keep their exempla before their eyes. With becoming modesty he practices his own doctrine: "Would I could always imitate Cicero successfully," he cries, yet it would not be wrong sometimes to borrow the vigor of Caesar, the vehemence of Calvus, the precision of Pollio, and so on. Epic poets did not have that range of choice: the *Aeneid* had obliterated all rivals. Quintilian's faint praises of his long list of narrative poets makes amusing reading—"by no means to be despised," "worth reading," "portions merit our praises," "remarkable in one so young," "to be studied by those who have the time." As for Lucan, he sinned against the first commandment of the classicist's creed and confused the genres; he wrote like an orator, not like a poet.[1] Nothing exposes the weakness of Quintilian's standpoint so well as that famous dictum. For all that he urged his pupils to exercise their faculty of judgment, his program locked them into set forms and set styles. He preached imitation and then complained about Ciceronian tags and unending periods. His efforts had made imitation easy at that level, and it was the same with hexameter verse. It was not a difficult trick to turn Latin into meter, and it was easy for those who had mastered it to mistake the result for poetry. Cornelius Severus and Silius Italicus are named by extant sources for their labored verse. In Silius' case the verdict was justified, for we have his verse to test it by, but it was his misfortune to be singled out from the herd of conventional versifiers. Mass production is always the same—competent and dull.

Parody is one reaction to dullness. When in the eighteenth century the trick was turning English into heroic couplets, parody was used with great effect by Pope in the *Rape of the Lock* and the *Dunciad*. But there was no mock epic in the first century A.D. Such a work would have seemed like mockery of Virgil, and one does not make fun of holy writ. Lucan's frenetic rhetoric was another reaction, and at least Lucan's style was substantial enough to be worth denouncing. The usual pitfall in the way of classicist writers is mannerism. They wish to write in accordance with the rules, but to go one better. When commentators condemn artificial and affected expression, straining for effect, and brilliance in preference to clarity, they are condemning mannerism. These aspects of classicism (except for the parodist's reaction) are represented by the three extant epic writers of the last quarter of the first century: Silius is dull, Valerius Flaccus is correct, and Statius is mannered.

Silius (c. A.D. 35–100), his friends allowed, had less inspiration than enthusiasm.[2] He tells a short story well enough in unpretentious style: five passages in the seventeen completed books are singled out by J. D. Duff, the Loeb translator: the wounding of Mago, v 344–75; Hannibal's escape from Fabius, vii 282–376; the friends Marius and Caper, who in death were not divided, ix 401–10; the god Pan, xiii 326–47; and Scipio and Syphax, xvi 229–76. It is a meager result for so deep a trawl. But Silius was not a poet by choice, like Flaccus and Statius. His behavior under Nero had tainted his reputation, and verse was the pastime of his retirement. The *Punica* (Punic War), both in its genre and its subject, is a reminiscence of Ennius. The old poet receives a respectful reference (xii 408–13), but it was not yet time (it came in the second century A.D.) when one could actually admire Ennius; it was as much as Quintilian could do to be polite. Yet Hannibal and Scipio, dead for three centuries and without the perils of political relevance, begged to be mythologized, and Ennius' verse clamored for polish. If Silius thought to endow his age with the

best of Ennius raised to Virgilian standards of taste, he would have
been responding to the same instinct as was felt by seventeenth-century English dramatists who rewrote Shakespeare according to the
civilized sensibilities of their own time. It was a process that extinguished the vital spark. For a truly epic story of heroic leaders and a
resolute nation united in the face of awful odds the reader had better
turn to Livy's prose epic of the Roman people.

As a follower of Apollonius, Valerius Flaccus had little scope for
originality, at least in that part of the Argonauts' journey that he
completed (the poem breaks off in the eighth book); and if it were
extant, no doubt the same verdict would be passed on his use of the
Argonautae of Varro Atacinus. Quintilian approved his efforts. Varro
was distant enough to be uncouth but not distant enough for his
antiquity to be a virtue. He would stand rewriting. With these
sources Valerius blended *imitatio* of Virgil: Juno is again the goddess
of opposition, this time incensed by Hercules' embarcation on the
Argo; and Dido's struggle with conscience is the model for a very
Roman Medea torn between passion and *pietas*. It was a pity that the
romantic color of the story did not commend itself to an age that fed
its imagination on violence and terror. What was wanted for instant
success and lasting fame was a "lurid, frenzied, blood-sodden poem
. . . a series of violent episodes, empty of moral or historical meaning,
alternating with deliberative episodes tending to hysteria."[3] What
else would serve but the tale of Thebes and the house of Oedipus?
Statius felt its primitive horrors would stand amplification: horses'
hooves trample the dying and become entangled in their entrails
(*Thebaid* vii 760, x 476), and men, speared through the mouth, gush
blood and vomit (*Theb.* ii 624, x 320). Whether the effort has
seemed worth eleven years of Statius' life has depended on the age in
which the critic lived. Posterity long took the justified admission
with which Statius ends the *Thebaid,* that he was second to Virgil,
for a justified assertion that he was second only to Virgil and, not
unreasonably, to be mentioned beside him. Yet a poem that was
cited with respect by Dante and Chaucer has undergone total critical
eclipse, at least from the inception of the the Romantic movement.
The fate of literature is as unjust and capricious as other kinds of
fate. Statius is no hack writer, but his fate is the clearest warning
that in an epic poem the idea is paramount, whether it be a certain
idea of heroism or something more cosmic. The gift of conceiving

such an idea has nothing to do with fluency of style, subtle depiction of character, balance of plot, evocation of atmosphere, or anything else that comes with study. But it does not all depend on the poet; great epic poems are composed at a time when the poet's public voice is given something important to say.

After Apollonius Greek epic slipped calmly into the doldrums from which Callimachus thought it should never have been rescued. Hellenism, respect for the art and language of Homer, kept up the idea of narrative poetry for a period of six centuries from which only the flat verses of Quintus of Smyrna's *Aftermath of Homer* have for some reason been preserved. Quintus was faithful to the tradition of the cyclic epics, too faithful to accept the florid style and erotic sensuality of later Greek verse writing. Even when dead, the great genres of literature are capable of twitching. What the Greek epic, and the Latin epic after Lucan, were waiting for was new society with new ideals to express. But empires are conservative, and the Roman empire resisted cultural change to the last. Its literature did not progress; it revived from time to time the traditional forms.

One such period of revival was the fourth century A.D. It produced on the Latin side the short historical epics of Claudian and on the Greek side the monstrous *Dionysiaca* (Story of Dionysus) of Nonnus, in forty-eight books.[4] Religion had failed to produce an epic poem in classical times, and in Nonnus' age the old religion survived only among intellectuals and peasants. The *Dionysiaca* is not a religious poem; it is a romance. Nonnus in fact was probably a Christian. It is true that among the love scenes and exotic landscapes there is some fighting; but it is not heroic fighting, for Dionysus is a god, and his array of frenzied maenads cannot be defeated as long as he is present to inspire them. Heroism requires at least the possibility of tragedy. The style of the *Dionysiaca* is the extreme example of Hellenistic verbal mannerism.[5] It brings to life some sensuous episodes—the story of Actaeon (v 301–69), Morrheus gazing in rapture at, or through, the diaphanous tunic of Chalcomede (xxxiv 269–340, cf. xlii 441–85), the lady wrestler Pallene (xlviii 106–71)—yet the lush verbiage turns all but the strongest stomachs.

The success of Nonnus and Claudian in reproducing antique forms and styles obscures the fact the forms *were* antique and relied for their comprehension, not to say their intelligibility, on the classical education of readers. The models were good, and to follow them was a good recipe for good writing, as the uncertain steps of their contemporary Prudentius show. Prudentius was an allegorist and a Christian, and allegory and Christianity were not yet comfortable in hexameters.[6] Good writing, however, is not the same as great writing, and it was with Christian writers and Christian forms that the future lay. In the meantime whenever learning—which means a knowledge of Classical literature—revived, the attempt was made in Latin to emulate antique forms. The Paderborn epic (A.D. 799) imitates Virgil to praise Charlemagne.[7] In the twelfth century Walter of Châtillon imitated Lucan to execute a competent and at the time much-admired *Alexandreis*. The bookish poet of *Beowulf* may have owed the very idea of turning heroic poetry into an epic poem to his acquaintance with the *Aeneid*.[8] But generally the vernacular epic of the Middle Ages was quite innocent of these classical pretensions. In the evolution of the genre it stood in much the same place as Homer or the predecessors of Homer, and in *Beowulf*, *El Cid*, the *Chansons de Geste*, and the *Nibelungenlied* we hear again the simple note of heroic action without the trills and descants of funeral games and Olympian gods. It was a note, however, to which the intellectual life of the Middle Ages was deaf, for it had imprisoned itself in Latin.[9] Latin could express the life of medieval men and women in exciting new forms of lyric verse. But in the classical tradition lyric verse was seldom taken seriously. Serious and would-be serious poetical thoughts fixed themselves on the eternal models of poetic form, Virgil and Lucan.

VII

The Form of Epic

Re-forming the Epic

> Just as I do not blame a daring that is guided by
> reason, so I do not praise a boldness that is
> without reflection, for I think it an insanity that
> anyone should want to create an art from chance.
>
> Tasso

In the practice of classical poets genre was as much a matter of tone and scale as it was of form. Satirists affected to be bitter, elegists to be in love, comedians to be realistic, and epic poets to sing in lofty strains of kings and battles, mythological or real. But if poets deigned to take advice, they were told to read the old masters—good advice, no doubt, but the only advice possible when the masters of criticism, like Quintilian, classified poetry by meter and grouped Homer with Hesiod and Virgil with Lucretius. The genres consequently were discussed by the critics in terms of their supposed primary exemplars. Hellenistic epic poets were would-be Homers; Aratus, a didactic poet, as we should say, had the sense to follow Hesiod; and so on. Even Aristotle describes Homer in order to define "representation in narrative and in meter" (*Poetics* 23.1459a).

138

However, these names were not ciphers. The ancestor stood for his descendants, for the literary kind that together they ostensively defined. That sort of definition left room for variation. Conventional claims to true and legitimate literary descent were compatible (as the examples of Ennius and Virgil show) with highly original conceptions of the genre. It is easily forgotten, for example, that the Romans did not see Greek literature as a corpus that could be assembled in the confines of a single library, the dross for the most part sifted out by time. They saw the outlines of Homer with difficulty when Choerilus and Antimachus obscured the view. So there was nothing pure about the descent of the *Aeneid* from the poems of Homer. The genes were mingled most obviously with those of Apollonius and Ennius but also with many others. The *Aeneid*, of course, was a fortunate mutation. The consequence of hybrid ancestry is often something vigorous but ill defined, like the *Metamorphoses*. Yet Ovid was alive to the genres with which he played. During those postclassical ages conventionally called dark, the literary tradition was attenuated; and as it contracted, so the possibility of creative crossing diminished. When even an intuitive perception of the literary kinds was lost—when Dante could call his narrative poem a comedy and the *Iliad* a tragedy, when Lucan was thought to be a historian—the poet who composed in Latin was seeking to grasp a shapeless ghost.

Nor was the form of the epic rendered more palpable when the Renaissance enlarged the horizons of literature.[1] Petrarch, in the fourteenth century, explained that a poem—that is, a poem like his epic *Africa*—was "history enlivened by imagination." Note he said history—truth, not fiction. It is also almost certain that behind Petrarch's generalization was hidden the idea of the perfect prince (Scipio Africanus in the *Africa*) to inspire the emulation of contemporary monarchs.[2] These aims and purposes looked forward to the new age, but the vehicle was outmoded. Ancient history and the Latin language had been the vehicle of Virgil and Lucan; from neither could their imitator escape, but all that could be created with their aid was an imitation.

Out of this pitfall there were two ways of escape. More than anything else it was Latin that locked a poet into the tradition. One key to his release, therefore, was the vernacular, but to turn the key required the courage of considerable conviction, for the vulgar tongue was vulgar in every sense. If indeed Romance speech had been seen for what it was, a modification of Latin, it is certain that the modification would have been counted degeneration and proof positive of vulgarity. As it was, the linguistic science of the age, which is represented for us by Dante's *De Vulgari Eloquentia*, failed to make the connection and so was free to ascribe nobility to the vernacular, the primary form of speech, as opposed to Latin, a secondary and acquired mode of communication.[3] This worthy medium, however, came with its own conventions of poetical form—rhyme and stanza—which owed nothing to the conventions of Latin. The poet who adopted it, not for the courtly lyric or romance of the Middle Ages but for a long and serious work, had no literary guide. Not surprisingly, the *Divina Commedia* is sui generis. It is a *commedia*, Dante explained, not because it has dramatic form but because it begins in woe and ends in happiness. It has the vision and function of an epic poem in that it expresses in canonical form the medieval idea of the destiny of the human race, and in that sense it is an epic. It is, however, innocent of the form of an epic poem in the classical tradition; it has no hero, that is, a central figure by or to whom deeds are done, nor is it heroic in any sense. It is doubtful if it is even a story. For the student of literary forms the *Divina Commedia* echoes the problem of Apollonius' *Argonautica*. The *Argonautica* is certainly epic in form but hardly so in spirit; Dante's poem is epic in everything except form. A tour of the underworld had been part of the furniture of the epic since Homer had put it in the *Odyssey*, but it was the sort of thing Aristotle had brushed aside as an episode, an interlude that refreshed and delighted the reader but arrested the progress of the plot. But Dante knew Aristotle only as a logician and a philosopher, not as a critic. Nothing either in the theory of the epic, of which he was fortunately ignorant, or in the practice of Virgil and Lucan, which he had discarded with their language, prevented Dante from making an interlude into the substance of the whole. What he owed to the ancients was something much more intangible than the events and characters he freely appropriated to illustrate the crimes of mankind; it was a sense that a great poem was a serious poem. That intuition was perceptive and original in an age when the great sagas of the classical epic had degenerated into the *Romance of Troy*, the *Romance of Aeneas*, and the *Romance of Thebes*.

The romances were written to amuse the medieval world; the

purpose of the *Divina Commedia* is no more definable in a word than those of Homer and Virgil. Renaissance critics contrasted pleasure with utility and identified utility with reproof or edification. But these are low ideas with which to tackle the heights of the great epics. The *Divina Commedia* is quintessentially medieval, just as the *Aeneid* is quintessentially Roman. That is why both are still read and translated, whereas the *Africa* is neither. The weakness of the *Africa* —it would be unjust to name it except as the finest example of its class—is not that it is unoriginal in form but that it is not imbued with the true spirit of its age. Significantly, its author did not publish the poem, and its nine books, three short of the canonical twelve, suggest that Petrarch abandoned his ambition. The same fate awaited those whose imitation of their models was so slavish that it amounted to transposition. For it was possible to use the vernacular while repudiating the liberty it bestowed. Virgil had sung of the Trojan ancestry of the Romans and won everlasting fame. Could not the charm work a second time? Ronsard renamed Astyanax, Hector's son, Francion, rescued him from Troy, caused him to love a Cretan princess, and brought him to Gaul, where he founded a city named after his brother Paris. It is as if languages were different metals and the *Aeneid* a mold into which they could be poured to produce replicas in whatever idiom was desired. Lead, however, is more easily cast than gold, and Ronsard's unfinished *Franciad* has sunk without trace.

What broke the mold was the rediscovery of Aristotle's *Poetics*. A Latin translation was published by Valla in 1498 and the Greek text by Aldus Manutius in 1508. The Italian critics and humanists—Trissino, Minturno, Cinthio, Manzoni, and Castelvetro—rushed to impose its thoughts on the Renaissance literatures, creating by a synthesis of Aristotle, Virgil, and some remnants of medieval thinking the idea of the new epic. The culmination of this criticism is Tasso's *Discorsi del poema eroico* (Discourses on the heroic poem), revised and finally published in 1594.[4] Note, after a long eclipse, the reappearance of heroism as a defining feature of the epic. For was it not laid down in the opening sentences of the *Poetics* that poetry was about action? Not any action, of course, but the sort that reflected the glory of ancestors and delineated the ideal man. That view was not so much Aristotle's, who had carefully stated that the action of the higher genres should be serious, as Aristotle's commentators'

(Horace's in particular), who forced themselves to justify poetry by its utility while practicing the art for its own sake. As is the way with smoke screens, it blew back in their faces when in the end the pretended didacticism became a deliberate, conscious element in the idea of the epic poem.

The romances of medieval chivalry, a blend of adventure, fantasy, and love, were the true narrative poetry of the late Middle Ages. They had flowered to perfection in Ariosto's *Orlando Furioso*. The Roland who died at Roncevalles would not have recognized his transformation into the witless lover of the great khan of Cathay's daughter, even if he had admitted in principle the existence of sorcerers and voyages to the moon. Ariosto's *Orlando* was a huge popular success. But was it serious? Was the humor that found a natural home for the goddess Discord in a convent of holy friars acceptable to the post-Tridentine church? Was the pleasure that its readers took in the dalliance of Alcina and Ruggiero conducive to their Christian edification? Tasso could not help contrasting the discreet veil that Virgil had drawn over the intimacies of Dido and Aeneas. He might have added that in the classical epic love, unless it is implicitly homosexual, is a feminine passion, an accident that aids or hinders the hero's pursuit of duty or glory. If Tasso did not do so, it was because he saw no reason why an epic hero should not, temporarily at least, be enamored or bewitched. His audience expected it. And though an epic poet, by telling in the loftiest style an action that is noble, great and perfect, aimed to give profit, he had to do so by giving pleasure as well and therefore had to borrow some of the romantic color of an Ariosto. Tasso had before him the grim example of Trissino's epic of the emperor Justinian's conquest of the Goths, a blend of patriotism, religion, and heroism that seemed to be perfect according to all the canonical rules of art except one—no one derived any pleasure from reading it. A competent, if conventional, critic, Trissino was a dull poet. A great and noble action was uselessly sung if it was unread.

Fortunately, the bridge between the austerity of the epic and the romantic richness of Ariosto was to be found in a footnote to Aristotle (*Poetics* 24.1460a): the epic could relate what tragedy could not depict, the impossible. Aristotle did not like impossibilities in literature. But he was honest enough as a critic to recognize that there was an emotional gain in the telling of some impossibilities:

they aroused wonder. In Tasso's idea of the epic the footnote has become a cardinal part of the doctrine: it is by moving the mind to wonder that the epic poet achieves his aims. Much flowed from this concession to the romance. It restored the concrete visualization of the supernatural world as Homer and Virgil had depicted it, for Tasso had little time for Lucan's abstractions. But to be morally stimulating, the supernatural had also to be credible.

At this point the Italian poet parted company with Camões, his Portuguese contemporary. More concerned with glory and less with the salvation of souls, Camões saw nothing repugnant to sense in ornamenting the voyage of Vasco da Gama with the Olympian gods of the classical epic. What had been good enough for Virgil was good enough for him. Such gods were convenient, for what use are gods if they cannot foresee the future and extend the vision of the epic? But in a serious poem founded on real events how much disbelief must be suspended to make such ornaments credible? Even Petrarch two hundred years before had treated the classical gods with circumspection, and that in a Latin epic. No councils on Olympus encumber the *Africa*, but Scipio could be given a soul like that of a medieval man, a soul that could fly off to heaven to converse with Jupiter. There in embryo was the answer Tasso sought. The classical supernatural was heathen fantasy, much the same as was Astolfo's flight to the moon in *Orlando Furioso*. It had to be replaced by a Christian supernatural. Angels would intervene to defend the righteous cause of the crusaders, and the forces of evil would be aided by the black arts of witchcraft and by devils out of hell. Not perhaps since the epics of Homer had the divine world had such an awesome reality.

Truth, or that verisimilitude that in poetry passes for truth, was essential to the epic. Whimsical fantasies, like the stoppered bottles of men's wits with which Ariosto strewed the moon, had no place in the real world—Tasso meant the world of his patrons, the dukes of Ferrara, for anything was possible in Norway or America. Truth meant history, but what sort of history? Tasso grappled with some old problems and one new one. A Christian poet might easily be drawn to sacred history.[5] But Tasso was wary: theology was best left to priests, and sacred history could not be embroidered without impiety. Secular history, then, would have to serve. But it would have both to give the poet a certain freedom to improve and modify, a liberty Lucan had wrongly eschewed, and to engage the reader's commitment. Ancient history conferred the former but not the latter, contemporary history the latter but not the former. What lay between, by a happy chance, was the same stories as filled the romances of chivalry, the crusades of Christendom against the infidel. Here was the noble action, great and perfect, that clothed in classical form would give profit through delight.

Whether Tasso conceived *Gerusalemme Liberata* according to the theory or the theory according to *Gerusalemme Liberata* matters little.[6] The practice and the theory between them defined the most important idea of the epic for the Renaissance and the whole neoclassical period in literature. Such a sense of form can be very strong. Even Milton first conceived the epic according to Renaissance ideas. Not that he turned to the crusades for inspiration; crusades were not calculated to stir the hearts of seventeenth-century English men and women of the Protestant persuasion. The Arthurian legend, mystical, mythologized, and potent, was the English equivalent. "What king or knight before the conquest might be chosen in whom to lay the pattern of a christian *Heroe*": that sentence from Milton is pure Tasso.[7]

Form is indispensable to all sentimental genres. It signals to readers what it is that they hold in their hands.[8] Epic poets who wished to be known as such invoked the Muse or her Christian equivalent; they found a role for God or gods; they were generous with marvels, similes, and funeral games; and they divided the poem into books. The poetical story would begin near the end of the natural course of events and compress its narrative within a short span of time. So precisely was the recipe conceived that it could be achieved—and on the whole more successfully—in prose, as in Fénelon's *Télémaque*. Not every poem incorporates all the details hallowed by Homer and Virgil, but the more the formal characteristics are dispensed with, the harder it is to call a poem an epic. What, for example, should we call so long a poem as *The Faerie Queene?* Spenser knew that an epic should be edifying and patriotic and that it should begin in the middle, and he was careful to proclaim his allegiance to Virgil and Lucretius, but the *The Faerie Queene* remains for most of its readers a medieval allegory, not a late descendant of the *Odyssey*. Remove the form altogether and to call a work an epic becomes a way of saying that its author has a mind like Homer's—a vague (if extravagant) compliment. It expresses admiration for scale, or for the breadth of view and ambition of the author, or for the author's insights into great matters, or for the moral qualities enshrined in the work, or for all of these. Yet these are virtues that are not confined by some necessity to one form or medium.

After Milton

> . . . that Epick form whereof the two poems of
> *Homer,* and those other two of *Virgil* and *Tasso* are
> a diffuse, and the book of *Job* a brief model.
>
> Milton

Milton's tracing of his own literary odyssey (in the unlikely context of *The Reason of Church Government*) offers a neat summary of the history of the epic and a remarkable testimony to the neoclassical equation of idea with form. It lacks only a comment on the gestation of the form within the womb of heroic poetry and (of course) any obituary on its demise or notice of its afterlife. No doubt Milton could have turned even the story of some worthy knight before the Norman Conquest into poetry if public duty had not engrossed all his talents. Yet in the later seventeenth century royal courts, whose ideas of life were centered on kings, battle, and courtesy, were ceasing to be the focus of literature. *Paradise Lost* was addressed to a new audience, the devout bourgeoisie.[1] They had no use for conventional heroism, an idea that only enters *Paradise Lost* in the person of Satan, by the wrong route. Despite the Latinizing style, the *Odyssey*-like narrative of Raphael, the rhetoric of Satan, and the obvious employment of Homeric and Virgilian devices, a doubt lurked in the minds of some contemporaries whether the poem was really an epic.[2] They expected a biblical epic to have a heroic theme, like Abraham Cowley's *Davideis;* they were unprepared for an epic where thought and argument were as important as action. Milton's view of the destiny of the human race, which makes the visions of Tasso, Camões, or even Virgil himself seem contracted, is what in combination with its form raises *Paradise Lost* to epic status and thereby shows better than any theoretical discussion what makes a long verse narrative an epic poem. It did not matter that it broke the mold Tasso had fabricated. No form by itself can be a recipe for success; epic successes have a curious way of being unrepeatable, as if an original genius must express itself by being untraditional in some important respect. Epics that were conventional in idea as well as form have enjoyed only a temporary acclaim, however skillful their execution. Each one of the major epics in the classical tradition was in some significant respect an innovation and was made worthwhile by the very way in which it was unconventional. The *Iliad* itself broke out of a tradition of heroic and folkloric narrative poetry to set up the idea of a tragic epic; the poet of the *Odyssey* reacted against the *Iliad* with the epic of heroic adventure, and Apollonius with the epic of romance. Ennius then made a hero out of a nation. Virgil made the Muse a philosopher, not describing so much as explaining the course of history. Lucan took a lower road and made the epic a political manifesto. Among all of them, however, there was a clear filiation. Confronted with such a variety of aim behind a superficial similarity, the Renaissance sought the essence of the epic in the accidents that Aristotle had extracted from the Homeric exemplars, that is, in its form. Such a prescription might seem to reveal the secret of composing a great poem; it certainly encouraged many unwise attempts.

Yet Homer was an epic poet, not a historian or a dramatist, because heroic poetry was the natural medium of his age. When the age changed, it would have been reasonable to expect the genre to have faded away, as did the choral lyric form of Pindar in its turn or the mystery play of the Middle Ages, and to have been supplanted by other forms. But the epic did not make excessive demands on the cultural resources of its audience. It required hardly more than a reciter and an occasion or, later, the apparatus of books and readers. It was therefore a relatively easy matter to revive it and to transpose it into other languages and cultures, at the same time retaining more or less the form in which Homer had cast it. The litany of Homer, Virgil, and Tasso tells its own story: the classical epic, apart from its two Homeric progenitors, was a sentimental genre, a conscious preservation or re-creation in a literary environment of a form that had once emerged in a natural way. The neoclassical epic of the Renaissance was doubly sentimental; it re-created Virgil as Virgil had re-created Homer.

The finest examples of epic poetry explore some theme, as the *Iliad* explores the idea of heroism and the *Aeneid* that of empire. If an epic does not evaluate the world it describes, we feel in some degree deceived. We enjoy the preposterous stories of Ovid's *Metamorphoses* provided we do not think it is an epic poem, and we enjoy the witty games the author plays with us, his readers. A reading of Apollonius' or Statius' elegant and solemn retelling of myths that have lost their potency is an amusement of a different order. We are asked to admire the poets' skill in re-creating a perished world and insinuating themselves as they reproduce the manner of a classical model. We admire, but we must not ask what it is all about. Reading the *Argonautica* or the *Thebaid* is a literary and aesthetic experience, not a moral one. It would be absurdly pedantic to refuse those and similar works the title of epic; their lineage, their *form*, demands inclusion. Yet without their form are these poems epics? And what would happen if the form lost its authority?

The rise and fall of literary forms is harder to understand than the rise and fall of empires. Milton's epics, even when their content had been made exclusively Christian, were given to an unappreciative public and were the last great poems of their kind.[3] Before the end of his century the war between the admirers of the ancient and modern literatures—the Battle of the Books—had been bravely fought by the ancients—and lost. The defeat sapped the authority of the classical poets; their works were less respected as exemplars and more regarded as poems. In the preface to his translation of the *Iliad* Pope had much to say about Homer's quality as a poet but not a word about his role as model; and before that he had composed mock epics, *The Rape of the Lock* and *The Dunciad*, satires, among other things, of the epic form. When we read about the footrace of the London booksellers Curl and Lintott, we realize that as a form the epic had collapsed and that we are reading its epitaph. The French, who had failed to produce a neoclassical epic masterpiece, were quicker off the mark and had already burlesqued Virgil in the middle of the seventeenth century.[4]

The message of these parodies is that in the new literary world the formal characteristics of the epic were too obviously unnatural. But if they were discarded, what would be left? Without its epic form heroic epic such as Homer's would revert again to its antecedent heroic lays. Remove all the elements of form from *Paradise Lost* and what is left is theology; but no theology, in whatever is the natural form of that science, would be called epic. Without their form the *Bellum Civile* becomes political history and the *Argonautica* a romantic novel. What else could a historical epic or a romantic epic

become? Vernacular forms that were native growths, not trans-
planted aliens, in due time replaced the epic in giving expression to
philosophy and fantasy. Only rarely are such things, with epic
breadth and depth, now attempted in verse: prose can do it better.[5]

It is time that the term *heroic* reentered the discussion. The
national and other themes that the epic has served are cumulations
on a heroic base. Taken together, the corpus of heroic poems created
by a people may give those with the patience to read them an insight
into part of that people's view of the world, into the myths that
sustain their morale and justify their aspirations. At its best, heroic
poetry could be "an art of blending anachronisms, of successfully
exploiting their historical, moral and dramatic tensions and possibilities, within a highly stylized convention which creates the illusion
of a unified reality."[6] Such a body of poetry is to an epic what parish
churches are to a cathedral: the ideas are the same, but the cathedral
expresses them with a sense of finality and achievement. Churches
(but not many cathedrals) are still built; yet when the circumstances
of the neoclassical epic (which included a special kind of literary
education) fell away, there were no underlying minor forms, no
heroic poetry, to which the genre could revert.[7] What the epic once
had done had now to be done, for those who still required to see the
world through the parables of heroic action, not by heroic poetry but
by some generically unrelated equivalent.

Heroism, empire, destiny, and faith are all necessary myths that
have been sustained and sometimes created by art. The art was that
of heroic poetry at the beginning of literature, when heroic poetry
reached society as a whole. In those times society *listened;* in the
twentieth century society *views.* In its capacity to create myths while
entertaining and to reach whole peoples, the modern heroic medium
is film, and not necessarily the productions that are held in highest
critical regard. The western, in its violence and unreality, is not
much different from Bellerophon's battles with Amazons. The naive
heroization of one's own side in the war movie echoes Nestor's
complacent tale of his raid on Elis. Sometimes one film or tale rises
above the rest and shows a wider vision than the myth that it
perpetuates. Bellerophon's is a tale of virtue rewarded, of faith in the
ultimate justice of the gods. John Ford's cavalry trilogy, *Fort Apache,
Yellow Ribbon,* and *Rio Grande,* has a vividness that does not evade
the pain and danger of frontier life and the demands it made of

those, on both sides, who made their lives there. Kurosawa's *Seven Samurai* did the same for another culture. Eisenstein's *Potemkin* and *Ivan the Terrible* are more conscious (and much more ambitious) mythmakers.

The analogy may be pressed a little further. Can the cinema create an epic? Some films have indeed been miscalled epics in acknowledgement of the directors' pretensions or the unwieldiness of their crowd scenes; this is the vulgar sense of the word *epic* and means hardly more than "astounding." But a true visual epic? The cinema film, and the television film more easily, can surmount the problem of length by serialization, a modern version of the classical book divisions. Such productions, however, are usually thought of as pictorial novels and in fact are often adapted from novels. Naturally, they share the same preoccupations and like the novel can only be called epic in a secondary sense of the term.

In our modern vocabulary the proper secondary use of *epic* expresses admiration for more than scale. (An epic, considering the depth of thought or the breadth of vision that it can express, is relatively economical.) We commend grandeur of subject, vision, and moral force—in a word, depth and breadth. Goethe's *Faust* consciously aims at epic depth in an ostensibly dramatic form. Later, Thomas Hardy's *Dynasts* uses the same means to a similar end. But when an epic quality can be seen in Wagnerian opera it is clear that this sense of epic does not imply any formal or generic links with Homer's line.

Is then the term too vague to be useful? When Henry Fielding suggested, half-seriously, that his novel *Joseph Andrews* was a "comic epic poem in prose," one may wonder whether he was making a claim to more than literary achievement.[8] He certainly did not mean that his work bore any significant relation to the classical epic. Still less would, or could, historians like Gibbon and Macaulay, the novelists and philosophers of the nineteenth century, or the great classical composers make such a claim.

If we see something heroic in the work of these people, it is because there is something heroic about the people themselves—not least about Edward Gibbon himself, a diminutive, maimed figure but an indefatigable mind. However, the heroic stature of the person and the heroic quality of the work are not the same thing. It is for that reason that the middle-class novelists of the nineteenth century are hard to place on the heroic scale. Their stature as men and women may inspire in the sculptor's métier such works as Rodin's *Balzac*, especially the nude *Balzac* of 1892 with his squared shoulders, folded arms, and arrogant paunch. But the question arises whether a middle-class hero or heroine can really be heroic. It is the totality of the novelist's work, the energy that his or her life displayed, not any of the separate pieces, that in a previous age would have qualified that artist to become an epic poet.

Such a generalization cries out for counterexamples. The well-known exception that puts this rule to the test sprang from a society where middle-class preoccupations had taken shallow root, Tolstoy's Russia. He celebrated the natural human in *The Cossacks* at the expense of the overcivilized European. He was (as he was not ashamed to say before he came to devote himself to the welfare of the peasants) an aristocrat, who wrote in *War and Peace* "only about princes, counts, ministers, senators, and their children," as Homer had ostensibly sung only of the great heroes. But when Tolstoy pretends not to understand the minds of policemen, merchants, and theology students, we know that he is being disingenuous. Like Homer (of whom many readers were reminded) his view is comprehensive, and his scale matches his view. Scale and breadth are possible against any social background, and they would not make that part of *War and Peace* that is a family chronicle an epic in any sense if the climactic historical setting had not been 1812 and if the novel had ended with the scene in Vilnius at the ball, the symbol of cultured elegance, when the news comes that the French have crossed the Neman.[9] Napoleon was to Russia what Xerxes had been to Greece, but Tolstoy achieved (among much else) what the feeble genius of Choerilus could only attempt, an artistic expression of the survival myth of a nation.

Let those words stand as a succinct description of epic quality in literature. Whatever the outer form in which that quality is found, we should not bestow the title on something that is merely grandiose or ostentatious or astounding. We look for something like that which the old verse epic of Homer distilled from the fragments of its ancestral heroic poetry—ideas that stood at the center of its audience's view of themselves and the world.

Notes

Chapter 1: *What Is an Epic?*

1. The quotations are taken from Aristotle, *Poetics* 23.1459a; Torquato Tasso, *Discourses on the Heroic Poem* (1594), book 1, trans. M. Cavalchini and I. Samuel (Oxford: Oxford University Press, 1973), p. 14; and C. M. Bowra, *From Virgil to Milton* (London: Macmillan, 1945), p. 1.

2. For a brief account of these controversies, with select bibliography, see H. Clarke, *Homer's Readers* (Newark, Del.: University of Delaware Press, 1981), pp. 106–55.

3. Essays, designed for comparative study, have been published on these traditions of heroic poetry by F. J. Oinas, ed., *Heroic Epic and Saga* (Bloomington, Ind.: Indiana University Press, 1978), and A. T. Hatto and J. B. Hainsworth, eds., *Traditions of Heroic and Epic Poetry*, 2 vols. (London: Modern Humanities Research Association, 1980, 1989). C. M. Bowra, *Heroic Poetry* (London: Macmillan, 1952), covers much of the ground, but by topic (the hero, the bard, etc.). For fine detail the three volumes of H. M. Chadwick and N. K. Chadwick, *Growth of Literature* (Cambridge: Cambridge University Press, 1932, 1936, 1940) remain indispensable.

4. M. A. Bernstein, *The Tale of the Tribe: Ezra Pound and the Modern*

Verse Epic (Princeton: Princeton University Press, 1980), pp. 11–14, provides further suggestive discussion of the problems of definition. His own description, that epic poetry is an expression of a society's cultural heritage and therefore is public, anonymous, and didactic, though appropriate for his purposes, seems to focus on incidental or secondary properties; the poet sets out primarily to celebrate an event, and the grander the concept, the more likely it is to express a personal viewpoint.

5. The emergence of heroic/epic poetry is not a verifiable part of literary history. N. Frye, *Anatomy of Criticism* (1957; repr. Princeton: Princeton University Press, 1971) argued for a logical development: myth-romance-epic; and G. R. Levy, *The Sword from the Rock* (London: Faber, 1953), asserted an actual development of epic from myth, when heroes took over roles once discharged by gods. Historically, of course, romance may succeed epic, as in medieval Europe, and Levy's view seems to be affected by the absence of a major divine epic in archaic Greece (a *Titanomachia* is reported, but the poet failed to rise to the occasion). For the warrior's boasts as one of the roots of heroic poetry see J. Opland, *Xhosa Oral Poetry: Aspects of a Black South African Tradition* (Cambridge: Cambridge University Press, 1983). The transition from eulogy to narrative is illustrated by *Gododdin*, the earliest Scottish heroic poem, which breaks down into a string of eulogies of those who fought at the battle of Catterick.

6. Cf. Bowra, *Heroic Poetry*, pp. 91–131. The crucial point is whether the divine ancestry, divine horses, and divinely forged weapons and armor, which compliment the hero, confer on him any practical advantage.

7. For literal audience participation see D. Biebuyck and K. Mateane, *The Mwindo Epic from the Banyanga* (Berkeley and Los Angeles: University of California Press, 1969), pp. 12–13. (The Mwindo epic comes from Zaire.) Most collectors of modern heroic poetry, who for long had to work by dictation, have noted that the stimulus of an audience, at the very least, is essential for competent performance; see A. B. Lord, *Serbo-Croatian Heroic Songs* (Cambridge, Mass.: Harvard University Press, 1954), p. 8.

8. What E. A. Havelock, *Preface to Plato* (Oxford: Oxford University Press, 1963), pp. 36–96, has argued with reference to the Homeric poems should be applied to heroic poetry generally; cf. Bernstein's description of the epic, *Tale of the Tribe*, pp. 11–14.

9. E. M. Forster, *Aspects of the Novel* (London: Arnold, 1927), p. 41.

10. Demail Zogić, an illiterate Bosnian singer, in conversation with M. Parry in 1934, in Lord, *Serbo-Croatian Heroic Songs*, 1:241.

11. There is, however, a difference between, on the one hand, the "high seriousness" demanded by Matthew Arnold and erected by some critics into almost a defining feature of epic (cf. T. M. Greene, *The Descent from Heaven: A Study in Epic Continuity* [New Haven: Yale University Press, 1963], pp. 8–25; A. S. Cook, *The Classic Line: A Study in Epic Poetry* [Bloomington, Ind.: Indiana University Press, 1966], pp. 3–48; and Frye, *Anatomy of Criticism*, pp. 33–67), and, on the other hand, the "high mimetic mode" in which the epic is often, but by no means invariably, expressed. Much of the *Odyssey*, for example, is in a low mode; see G. F. Lord, *Heroic Mockery: Variations on Epic Themes from Homer to Joyce* (Newark, Del.: University of Delaware Press, 1979).

12. A sentimental work, as the term is used by Frye (*Anatomy of Criticism*, p. 35) with derogatory intent, refers to the resuscitation of an earlier form. Romanticism is a sentimental response to the medieval romance, and the modern fairy tale to the ancient folktale.

Chapter 2: Greek Primary Epic

THE HEROIC AGE AND HEROIC POETRY

1. The phrase "famous deeds of men" is Homeric (*Il.* ix 189, 524; *Od.* viii 73; with variants at *Hom. Hymn* xxxii 18 and Hesiod *Theogony* 100). If expanded, the phrase becomes "deeds of men and gods" (*Od.* i 338; Hesiod *Theog.* 100). Gods are ever-present in the Greek heroic tradition, and among early heroic poems was a *Titanomachia*, a tale of the wars in heaven.

2. Judicious remarks on these calculations are made by A. M. Snodgrass, *The Dark Age of Greece* (Edinburgh: University of Edinburgh Press, 1971), pp. 10–16. The best popular account of the site of Troy is in C. W. Blegen, *Troy and the Trojans* (London: Thames and Hudson, 1963). The identification of the pottery styles is controversial: some sherds may belong to a later phase than that recognized by Blegen in his reexamination of the site in the 1930s. If so, the date of the sack of Troy VII A must be lowered or Homer's city identified with Troy VI.

3. Thus Arminius, the hero of their victory over the Romans in A.D. 9, was celebrated by the Germans before Tacitus composed *Annales* ii 88, 4. Many modern instances are cited by the Chadwicks (*Growth of Literature*): see also J. A. Notopoulos, "The Genesis of an Oral Poem," *Greek, Roman and Byzantine Studies* 3 (1960): 135–44 (on the exploits of Cretans in World War II).

4. The standard commentary on Mycenaean texts is M. Ventris and J. Chadwick, *Documents in Mycenaean Greek,* 2d ed. (Cambridge: Cambridge University Press, 1973). For an excellent popular account see J. Chadwick, *The Mycenaean World* (Cambridge: Cambridge University Press, 1976).

5. The fresco was first published by Blegen, "The Palace of Nestor Excavations of 1955," *American Journal of Archaeology* 60 (1956), pl. 41. The figure is that of the divine patron of song according to T. B. L. Webster, *From Mycenae to Homer,* 2d ed. (London: Methuen, 1964), p. 47.

6. The best account of heroic ages is that in the pioneering work by H. M. Chadwick, *The Heroic Age* (Cambridge: Cambridge University Press, 1912). For the nostalgic element see also C. M. Bowra, *The Meaning of an Heroic Age,* Earl Grey Memorial Lecture (Newcastle-upon-Tyne, 1957).

7. This is the same area as is minutely described in the Homeric gazetteer of heroic Greece, the so-called catalog of ships (*Il.* ii 484–759). The coincidence of legendary and archaeological data is the theme of M. P. Nilsson, *The Mycenaean Origin of Greek Mythology* (1932; repr. Berkeley and Los Angeles: University of California Press, 1972). The Athenians make a poor showing in Homer.

8. On the relation of the Mycenaean Age (= LH I–III) and the Heroic Age see G. S. Kirk, *Homer and the Oral Tradition* (Cambridge: Cambridge University Press, 1978), pp. 1–18.

9. The fullest argument for the existence of a Mycenaean heroic poetry is Webster, *From Mycenae to Homer,* pp. 91–135, but the main development of the tradition reflected in the Homeric poems probably belongs to the Dark Age; cf. Kirk, *Homer and the Oral Tradition,* pp. 19–39.

10. The daggers, now in the National Museum in Athens, are illustrated in E. Vermeule, *Greece in the Bronze Age* (Chicago: University of Chicago Press, 1964), pl. 12. For subtle traces of the tower shield in Homeric diction see the analysis of W. Whallon, *Formula,*

Character and Context (Washington, D.C.: Center for Hellenic Studies, 1969), pp. 34–54.

11. The best example is *Il.* v 519; the plural *Aiantes* at *Il.* vii 164 has a similar sense. For the exciting vistas of an Indo-European heroic diction see R. Schmitt, ed., *Indogermanische Dichtersprache* (Darmstadt: Wissenschaftliche Buchgesellschaft, 1968).

12. Lord, *Singer of Tales,* pp. 13–29, is still the best attempt by a modern scholar to understand the mind of an oral poet. See also J. M. Foley, *The Theory of Oral Composition* (Bloomington, Ind.: Indiana University Press, 1988).

13. These brief comments on the Homeric epithet are intended to make a point that translations often obscure. The use of epithets is complex and still a matter of dispute; see, for example, R. Sacks, *The Traditional Phrase in Homer* (Leiden: Brill, 1987). The basic work on Homeric noun + epithet diction was published in the papers of M. Parry from 1928 to 1935; see *The Making of Homeric Verse: The Collected Papers of M. Parry,* ed. A. Parry (Oxford: Clarendon Press, 1971).

14. On this aspect of Homeric language one must still have recourse to the papers of K. Witte in *Glotta* 1–5 (1909–14) or to K. Meister, *Die Homerische Kunstsprache* (Leipzig, 1921; repr. Stuttgart: Teubner, 1966). *Kunstsprache* is often used as a technical expression for the mélange of dialectal and other forms that makes up the so-called Homeric dialect.

15. Lord, *Singer of Tales,* p. 92. The choice of the term "theme" is not altogether fortunate, since in criticism "theme" (as in "the theme of the *Iliad* is pride") has quite another sense. Lord's themes are clusters of motifs, themselves traditional, making up scenes of council, journey, battle, etc. The Homeric technique of themes in an area where the material for analysis is plentiful has been explained by B. Fenik, *Typical Battle Scenes in the Iliad* (Wiesbaden: Steiner, 1968); see also C. A. Sowa, *Traditional Themes and the Homeric Hymns* (New York: Bolchazy, 1984).

16. Other fragments of heroic tales are the tale of Meleager (*Il.* ix 524–99), which lacks its introduction (the hunting of the Calydonian boar), and an exploit of Nestor (*Il.* vii 133–57), from an uncertain context. Odysseus' lying tales (*Od.* xiv 245–86, xvii 424–44) are almost certainly ad hoc inventions.

17. Much attention, not to be ignored by the student of verse stories, has been paid by linguists and psychologists to the ways in

which stories are comprehended—and so indirectly to their composition and criticism. The bibliography is now extensive; see R. A. de Beaugrande and W. Dressler, *Introduction to Text Linguistics* (New York: Longman, 1981), and G. Prince, *A Dictionary of Narratology* (Lincoln, Nebr.: University of Nebraska Press, 1987), pp. 106–18.

18. G. Nagy writes, "The social context of Panhellenism implies an audience that is in the end considerably different from the local folk listening to after-dinner songs performed by the singer of tales" ("An Evolutionary Model for the Text Fixation of Homeric Epos," in J. M. Foley, ed., *Oral Traditional Literature: A Festschrift for Albert Bates Lord,* [1981; repr. Columbus, Ohio: Slavica, 1983], p. 392). On the Panhellenic aspect of the Homeric poems (they came into existence at the same time as renewed intercity intercourse, colonization, and such Panhellenic institutions as the Olympic Games and the Delphic oracle) see Nagy, *The Best of the Achaeans* (Baltimore: Johns Hopkins University Press, 1979), pp. 7–10.

HOMERIC EPIC

1. The prehistory of the Trojan saga is a matter for pure speculation, much of it baseless. For some sensible guesswork see M. P. Nilsson, *Homer and Mycenae* (London: Methuen, 1933), pp. 248–66. The typology of the saga is discussed by J. B. Hainsworth, "The Fallibility of an Oral Heroic Tradition," in L. Foxhall and J. K. Davies, eds., *The Trojan War: Its Historicity and Context* (Bristol: Bristol Classical Press, 1985), pp. 111–35. The ultimate archetype of the theme is seen in such episodes as the sack of Lyrnessus taken "with much toil" by Achilles (*Il.* ii 690) and plundered (*Il.* xx 191–94) or the pillage of Ismarus (*Od.* ix 39–61).

2. Note the unobtrusive way in which Hector is introduced in the *Iliad* (i 242). The space devoted to Thersites (*Il.* ii 212–23), however, suggests that he was an unexpected intrusion, borrowed from the *Aethiopis* story, in which he was killed for his insolence by Achilles; likewise the fortification of the Achaean camp (*Il.* vii 436–41), a notorious crux, leads to the assault scene (*Il.* xii 88–471) but intermittently disappears from view.

3. See the summary of Demodocus' song, above, p. 21.

4. On the Argonauts see below, pp. 70–71.

5. Hence the digressions in the *Aethiopis* (the murder of Thersites) and especially in *Beowulf* (the lays of Sigemund and Finn, the episodes

of Offa and the Heathobard-Danish feud) pose problems unless their essential subordination to the main structure is recognized: see A. Bonjour, *The Digressions in Beowulf* (Oxford: Blackwell, 1950).

6. The literary historian may speak of the poet Homer with a clear conscience. The Greeks believed in his existence and genius, criticizing his work and allowing it to influence their own on that assumption.

7. That the time intervals of Book i—one, nine, one, and twelve days—are exactly mirrored in Book xxiv has been taken as evidence for an externally imposed articulation of events; see C. H. Whitman, *Homer and the Heroic Tradition* (Cambridge, Mass.: Harvard University Press, 1958), pp. 249–84.

8. The point is stressed by Aristotle *Poetics* 23.1459a and Horace *Ars Poetica* 136–52: it follows from the value that the Aristotelian school placed on unity of action. As a narrative principle its value is easily overestimated; see p. 71 with reference to the *Argonautica*.

9. The fastest sustained pace is probably attained in the battle scene at *Il.* xvi 306–50: for a leisurely equivalent see *Il.* v 37–84.

10. H. T. Wade-Gery, *The Poet of the Iliad* (Cambridge: Cambridge University Press, 1952), pp. 49–50, rendering the similes before the catalog of ships (*Il.* ii 455–79), introduced each with the exclamation "See them!"—an imaginative and truthful touch.

11. The similes have been rather overdiscussed: the most recent account is that of C. Moulton, *Similes in the Homeric Poems* (Göttingen: Vandenhoeck und Rupprecht, 1977), which gives a proper emphasis to their literary function. It is a pity that Longinus' account of the simile (*On the Sublime* 32) has been lost in a lacuna.

12. The chapters on the "epic illusion" are one of the best parts of S. E. Bassett's Sather Lectures, *The Poetry of Homer* (Berkeley and Los Angeles: University of California Press, 1938), pp. 26–80.

13. An interesting comment on the effect of reading the *Iliad* on an unusually perceptive schoolboy in chapter 4 of A. Kinglake's *Eothen* (1844):

The beautiful episode of the sixth book: the way to feel this is not to go casting about, and learning from pastors and masters how best to admire it. The impatient child is not grubbing for beauties, but pushing the siege; the women vex him with their delays and their talking—the mention of the nurse is personal, and little sympathy has he for the child that is young enough to be frightened at the nodding plume of a helmet; but all the while that he thus chafes at the pausing of the action, the strong vertical light of Homer's poetry is blazing so full upon the people and things of the *Iliad,* that soon to the eyes of the child they grow familiar as his mother's shawl. Yet of this great gain he is unconscious, and on he goes, vengefully thirsting for the best blood of Troy, and never remitting his fierceness till almost suddenly it is changed for sorrow—the new and generous sorrow that he learns to feel—when the noblest of his foes lies sadly dying at the Scaean gate.

The tragedy of Hector is the main topic of J. M. Redfield, *Nature and Culture in the Iliad* (Chicago: University of Chicago Press, 1975); on Homeric pathos generally see J. Griffin, *Homer on Life and Death* (Oxford: Clarendon Press, 1980), and S. L. Schein, *The Mortal Hero* (Berkeley and Los Angeles: University of California Press, 1984), pp. 67ff.

14. Cf. the "pity and fear" of Aristotle's tragic audience (*Poetics* 6.1449b) and the reactions of Ion the rhapsode's audience (see p. 40).

15. Less than a third of Lucan's epic, for example, consists of direct speech, against more than half of the *Iliad.* In very inferior work the proportion could drop to as low as 12 percent (as in the so-called *Orphic Argonautica*). Equally inimical to the dramatic effect is the later tendency to make speeches into declamations requiring no response rather than conversations. What effect, if any, the use of the first person in *Od.* ix–xii (where a "narrator," a speaker presented by the author, takes over from the poet) has had is one of the few unexplored areas of Homeric criticism.

16. The styles are described, with exemplifications, in [Cicero], *Ad Herennium* iv 11–16. The purists, of course, demanded that the language as well as the syntax of the plain style should conform to common speech.

17. The simplicity of the Homeric style admits exceptions: Homer has a natural rhetoric, exemplified in the long discourses of *Il.* ix; he uses hyperbole in the description of the battle between Achilles and the river Scamander in *Il.* xxi (supernatural conflicts are by nature hyperbolical; cf. Hesiod on the war of Zeus and the Titans, *Theog.* 666–728.), and can occasionally be dark and mysterious, e.g. in Theoclymenus' peculiar vision of Penelope's suitors, *Od.* xx 345–57. The fundamental introduction to the Homeric style is E. Auerbach, *Mimesis,* trans. W. Trask (Princeton, Princeton University Press,

1953), chap. 1, and the comments of Kirk, *Homer and the Oral Tradition*, pp. 99–112. A good Greek example—in the epic poetical speech—of Auerbach's dark allusive style is the proemium to Parmenides' poem (frag. 1 Diels), translated in G. S. Kirk and J. E. Raven, *The Presocratic Philosophers* (Cambridge: Cambridge University Press, 1957), pp. 266–68.

18. This important aspect of the Homeric style is discussed by Griffin, *Homer on Life and Death*, pp. 1–49, and M. N. Nagler, *Spontaneity and Tradition: A Study in the Oral Art of Homer* (Berkeley and Los Angeles: University of California Press, 1974), esp. pp. 44–63. Nagler considers the technique to be in principle characteristic of all oral heroic poetry. The whole subject has been put on a theoretical footing by I. J. F. de Jong, *Narrators and Focalizers: The Presentation of the Story in the Iliad* (Amsterdam: Grüner, 1987).

19. The best parallel, also heavily heroized, is the Turkic epic tale of Alpamysh (described in N. K. Chadwick and V. M. Zhirmunsky, *Oral Epics of Central Asia* [Cambridge: Cambridge University Press, 1969], pp. 292–95).

20. Some of these episodes are well discussed by D. L. Page, *Folktales in Homer's Odyssey* (Cambridge, Mass.: Harvard University Press, 1973).

21. For a lively account of the effect of retelling the *Odyssey* in the form of a linear narrative, see H. D. F. Kitto, *Poiesis: Structure and Thought* (Berkeley and Los Angeles: University of California Press, 1966), pp. 122–31. In brief, the effect is to turn an epic into a romance.

22. Note the programmatic speech assigned to Zeus at *Od.* i 32–43: human beings, like Agamemnon's murderer Aegisthus, bring grief upon themselves beyond what is allotted them by fate.

23. It is clear that the present arrangement of episodes in the *Odyssey*, so transparently artificial, is secondary; yet any attempt to write its prehistory must be speculative. Such research has long been the peculiar province of German scholarship, of which there is an excellent review in H. Eisenberger, *Studien zur Odyssee* (Wiesbaden: Steiner, 1973).

24. Observe (in addition to the obvious examples of Virgil and Milton) the use of the Odyssean structure in the novella *Aethiopica* of Heliodorus (third century A.D.), who "seems hell-bent on complicating matters to an impossible degree" (G. Anderson, *Ancient*

Fiction: The Novel in the Graeco-Roman World [Totowa, N. J.: Barnes and Noble, 1984], p. 125). Most ancient novellas kept to a chronological plan.

25. Cf. Charles Dickens, *Nicholas Nickleby*, chap. 22: " 'Size!' repeated Mr. Crummles; 'why it's the essence of the combat that there should be a foot or two between them. How are you to get up the sympathies of the audience in a legitimate manner, if there isn't a little man contending against a big one—unless there's at least five to one.' " Achilles had no equal antagonist at Troy until the arrival of the Amazon Penthesileia.

26. The two speeches are vital for an appreciation of the Homeric world view; see C. W. Macleod's commentary in *Homer, Iliad, Book xxiv* (Cambridge: Cambridge University Press, 1982), 131–32.

27. Aeschylus composed a trilogy, *Myrmidons* (on the death of Patroclus), *Nereids* (the sisters of Achilles' mother Thetis), and *Phrygians* (on the ransoming of Hector). Only fragments survive. The *Myrmidons* is interesting as containing the first attested homosexual interpretation of the Achilles-Patroclus friendship.

28. This view seriously affects the moral language of the Homeric poems: see the discussion in A. W. H. Adkins, *Merit and Responsibility* (Oxford: Clarendon Press, 1960), pp. 1–60.

29. The quotation is from the Chadwicks' summary of a nineteenth-century Montenegrin heroic poem (*Growth of Literature*, 2:415). The hero, it is useful to note, was, like Hector, an enemy. Hostility, or even detestation of wickedness, is not incompatible with admiration of courage: Hagen in the *Nibelungenlied* treacherously murdered Siegfried but became the hero of the last fight.

30. On this difference between epic and tragedy see Bowra, *Heroic Poetry*, pp. 75–77.

31. The whole exchange is illuminating; see *Correspondence between Schiller and Goethe*, trans. L. Dora Schmitz (London: Bell, 1914), 1:305–25.

32. The literary study of Homer has been overshadowed by the technical problems presented by the poems. In addition to Redfield, *Nature and Culture*, Griffin, *Homer on Life and Death*, Schein, *Mortal Hero*, Nagler, *Spontaneity and Tradition*, and de Jong, *Narrators and Focalizers*, see also M. Mueller, *The Iliad* (London: Allen and Unwin, 1984), M. W. Edwards, *Homer: Poet of the Iliad* (Baltimore: Johns Hopkins University Press, 1987), M. Lynn-George, *Epos: Word, Nar-*

rative and the Iliad (London: Macmillan, 1988), I. C. Johnston, *The Ironies of War* (Lanham, Md.: University Press of America, 1988), and, more briefly, the two excellent introductions to the poems published by the Cambridge University Press in the Landmarks of World Literature series: M. S. Silk, Introduction to *Homer: The Iliad* (1986), and J. Griffin, Introduction to *Homer: The Odyssey* (1987).

AFTER HOMER

1. For an account of the poems that completed the saga of Troy see M. Davies, *The Epic Cycle* (Bristol: Bristol Classical Press, 1989).

2. The epigram (*Greek Anthology* xii 43 lines 1–2) expresses a distaste for what another writer of epigrams (*Gk. Anth.* xi 130) called "these cyclic poets, these people who say 'But thereupon...,' " citing one of the commonest epic connective formulas. Callimachus detested sloppy writing.

3. For the romanticism of the cyclic epics see the definitive paper of J. Griffin, "The Epic Cycle and the Uniqueness of Homer," *Journal of Hellenic Studies* 97 (1977): 39–53.

4. For Hesiod's *Works and Days* as a specimen of "wisdom literature" and for parallels to his *Theogony* see the introductions to the Oxford editions of Hesiod by M. L. West, *Works and Days* (1966) and *Theogony* (1978).

5. There is a good account of this literary undergrowth in G. L. Huxley, *Greek Epic Poetry from Eumelus to Panyassis* (London: Faber, 1969).

Chapter 3: *Hellenistic Epic*

THE THEORY

1. Cf. G. M. A. Grube, *The Greek and Roman Critics* (London: Methuen, 1965), pp. 207–230, on the critical methods of Dionysius of Halicarnassus. Of the ancients only the author of *On the Sublime* writes like a modern critic.

2. The vase is illustrated, for example, in J. Boardman, *Athenian Red Figure Vases: The Archaic Period* (London: Thames and Hudson, 1975), no. 289.

3. For the Homeric epic as the expression of its society's ethos, hence didactic in effect if not in intention, see Havelock, *Preface to*

Plato, pp. 61–96. For Bernstein, *Tale of the Tribe,* this aspect of the epic is an essential part of the genre.

4. The argument is implicit from the beginning of the fifth century B.C. in the fragmentary works of Xenophanes (fr. 11) and in general terms in his contemporary Heraclitus (frr. 42, 56, 57). The poet's defenders began the tradition of allegorical exegesis.

5. In addition to the Platonic passages cited in n. 6, see the remarkable essay in praise of poetry by the sophist Gorgias, fr. 11 (the *Helen*), 8–14.

6. The principal Platonic passages concerned with art are *Gorgias* 501d–502d (the social purpose of art), *Ion* passim (poetry as the inspired and universal source of knowledge), *Republic* 377b–392c (poetry as teacher of falsehood), 392c–401d with 602c–608b (the effects of mimesis). Plato himself, of course, is not above pandering, by irony and satire, to the feelings of an intelligent and sophisticated readership. In *Republic* 595c–602b he presents a metaphysical argument against mimesis: the poet imperfectly represents what is itself an imperfect copy of the metaphysical Forms, the true reality. There is no hint of this in the other passages. For a concise account of Plato's literary views see Grube, *Greek and Roman Critics,* pp. 46–65, together with Havelock, *Preface to Plato,* pp. 20–35.

7. Aristotle's views on the epic are found in chaps. 23–26 of the *Poetics,* with anticipatory remarks in chap. 2 (the characters of epic are morally superior), and chaps. 3 and 5 (the length of epic). The literature, mostly on the Aristotelian view of tragedy, is voluminous; recent contributions include S. Halliwell, *Aristotle's "Poetics"* (London: Duckworth, 1986), and his commentary, *The "Poetics" of Aristotle* (London: Duckworth, 1987). The emphasis on plot in the Aristotelian approach is peculiarly repugnant to the students of heroic poetry; see the papers of J. A. Notopoulos, "Parataxis in Homer: A New Approach to Homeric Literary Criticism," *TAPhA* 80 (1949): 1–23; "Towards a Poetics of Early Greek Oral Poetry," *HSPh* 68 (1964): 45–65; and Alfred B. Lord, "Homer as Oral Poet," *HSPh* 72 (1968): 1–46.

8. For discussion of the *Iliad* as a drama, indeed as the prototype of Attic tragedy, see Rhys Carpenter, *Folktale, Fiction, and Saga in the Homeric Epics* (Berkeley and Los Angeles: University of California Press, 1946), pp. 78–85. Aristotle's statement that Homer alone used the mixed narrative-dramatic mode (*Poetics* 4.1448b) cannot be verified; it would be remarkable if it were not an exaggeration.

9. G. F. Else, *Aristotle's "Poetics": The Argument* (Cambridge, Mass.: Harvard University Press, 1957), p. 39.

10. For Neoptolemus see the discussion in C. O. Brink, *Horace on Poetry* (Cambridge: Cambridge University Press, 1963), pp. 43–74. It is possible he was reacting against the forthright view of the great polymath Eratosthenes that poetry was a matter of *psychagogia*, "pleasure," and nothing else.

11. Observe, for example, the excellent use made of suggestive points in the scholia in the chapter "Symbolic Scenes and Significant Objects" in Griffin, *Homer on Life and Death*, pp. 1–49.

12. On Greek blame poetry see Nagy, *The Best of the Achaeans*, pp. 213–64. Folktale, the student of the *Odyssey* soon becomes aware, is much more hospitable to the low mimetic mode than heroic poetry.

13. Even the Roman Statius avoided direct mention of the cannibalism (*Thebaid* viii 751–66). Dante's audience had stronger stomachs; cf. *Inferno* xxxii 125ff., where Ugolino gnaws at his enemy's skull.

14. The basic discussion of Homeric expurgations is still that of G. Murray, *The Rise of the Greek Epic*, 4th ed. (Oxford: Oxford University Press, 1934), pp. 120–45. C. Segal, *The Theme of the Mutilation of the Corpse in the Iliad* (Leiden: Brill, 1971), has shown that brutality in general, not just specific manifestations of it, is recognized as atrocious; therefore Segal can plot the accelerating crescendo of ferocity in the later Iliadic books, culminating in book xxii. There is an interesting ancient discussion of the tone of *Il.* xxii 395–411 (the dragging of Hector) compared with a tasteless passage in the orator Hegesias on the same theme in Dionysius of Halicarnassus, *De Compositione Verborum* 18.

15. Cf. Longinus, *On the Sublime* ix 7: "But although these things [the battle of the gods, *Il.* xx 54–74] are awe-inspiring, yet from another point of view, if they be not taken allegorically, they are altogether impious, and violate our sense of what is fitting"—a good instance of sense impeded by morality.

16. The lines are actually omitted from the medieval manuscripts but are preserved by Plutarch (*Moralia* 26f–27a).

17. For the way Homer was read by the Neoplatonist school and its influence consult R. Lamberton, *Homer the Theologian: Neoplatonist Allegorical Reading and the Growth of the Epic Tradition* (Berkeley and Los Angeles: University of California Press, 1986).

18. See Strato fr. 3 = Athenaeus 382c. The first line of Antima-chus' *Thebaid* (c. 400 B.C.) has been preserved: *ennepete Kronidao Dios megaloio thugatres* ... ("Declare, daughters of great Jove, son of Cronus ..."). The first and second words are linguistic fossils, the terminations of the second and fourth are archaisms, and the last has an artificially reduced stem; only the third coincides with the classi-cal vernacular. Neither Apollonius (c. 275 B.C.) nor Nonnus (c. A.D. 400) felt any need to update his language.

19. E. Schwyzer, *Dialectorum Graecarum Exempla Potiora* (Leipzig: Hirzel, 1923), no. 190; Cicero, *Pro Archia*; Petronius, *Satyricon* 59, 68.

20. Such is the implication of Callimachus' difficult epigram on the didactic poet Aratus, *Gk. Anth.* ix 507. Aratus did not try to rival Homer but followed the example of Hesiod; his style was refined (*leptós*, "refined"), the product of much lost sleep. Unqualified approval is not to be expected from Callimachus; he thought Aratus' work smelled of the lamp. For Dionysius of Halicarnassus, Hesiod exemplified the "smooth" style, Antimachus (whom Callimachus detested) the "austere," that is, a more rugged manner that affected nature rather than artifice (*De Compositione Verborum* 22–23).

21. The most important texts for Callimachus' criticism are his *Aitia* fr. 1 with the scholia, *Hymn to Apollo* 105–13 (see the com-mentary of F. Williams [Oxford: Clarendon Press, 1978], pp. 85–89), *Iamb.* 13, and frr. 398, 465. Besides *Pakhús* the principal slogans are *katharós*, "pure," *leptós*, "refined," and *tékhnē*, "craftsmanship"; the poet is a bee or cicada that sips at a clear spring and seeks "untrod-den paths."

22. The fragments of the *Hecale* are collected in R. Pfeiffer, ed., *Callimachus* (Oxford: Clarendon Press, 1949), vol. 1, frr. 230–377. There are good accounts in G. O. Hutchinson, *Hellenistic Poetry* (Oxford: Clarendon Press, 1988), pp. 56–63, and A. S. Hollis, *Callimachus: "Hecale"* (Oxford: Clarendon Press, 1990).

23. Few would have shared the enthusiasm of the Younger Pliny: "This year [A.D. 97] has proved extremely fertile in poetical produc-tions; during the whole month of April scarce a day has passed in which we have not been entertained with a recitation of some poem, although... there seems to be little disposition in the public to attend" (*Epistulae* i 13). The passage should be read in conjunction with the opening lines of Juvenal's first satire and the satirical bathos of *Satires* iii 9 (where recitations are called the worst of Rome's horrors).

PRACTICE: CHOERILUS, RHIANUS, AND APOLLONIUS

1. An excellent commentary on the remains of Antimachus is B. Wyss, *Antimachi Colophonii Reliquiae* (1935; repr. Hildesheim: Weidmannsche Verlagsbücherhandlung, 1974). The best collection of the scanty fragments and testimonia of Choerilus is that of P. Radice Colace, *Choerili Samii Reliquiae* (Rome: Bretschneider, 1979), with remarks on the novelty of the historical epic.

2. The epigrammatist, Antipater of Sidon, may be suspected of a certain irony, but he goes on to rank Antimachus as an epicist second only to Homer. Antimachus' best claim to fame in Hellenistic times, however, was his elegiac poem *Lyde*.

3. Aristotle's assessment of Antimachus is unknown, for the *Poetics* pays scant attention to writers who from its author's viewpoint could be thought of as postclassical. Antimachus, however, gained a place in Proclus' canon of ancient epicists—Homer, Hesiod, Pisander, Panyassis, and Antimachus, a list that shows how inchoate an idea of the epic the ancients had formed.

4. That there is a certain epic quality about the range and vision of the *History* of Herodotus has often been noted since Dionysius of Halicarnassus (c. 25 B.C.) called him an emulator of Homer; for a modern evaluation see E. M. W. Tillyard, *The English Epic and Its Background* (London: Chatto and Windus, 1954), pp. 41–51.

5. The *Suda* (a Byzantine encyclopedia) reports that "it was decreed [by the Athenians?] that Choerilus' poem [here called *The Athenian Victory over Xerxes*] should be recited with those of Homer," but that practice seems to reflect the excellence of the subject, not its execution.

6. Cf. Tasso's considered view that the epic poem should be a blend of truth (*sc.* historical truth) and the miraculous: "The history of an age or nation distant from us appears a subject well suited for a heroic poem, because, since those things are so buried in antiquity that there scarcely remains a weak memory of them, the poet is able to change them and tell of them as he pleases" (*Discorsi* ii 15). Space could replace time: Tasso cites with approval the epics of Camões and Ercilla, set respectively in the East Indies and South America. Such devices, however, are useless if the reader is too coldly rational to share the illusion; cf. Gibbon's sarcasm on the fantastic stories surrounding the origins of the Goths, "this wonderful expedition of Odin, which, by deducing the enmity of the Goths and Romans

from so memorable a cause, might supply the noble groundwork of an epic poem" (*Decline and Fall of the Roman Empire,* chap. 10 [Everyman's Library, 1980], 1:236).

7. Pausanias iv 16–21. Some of Aristomenes' exploits reappear in the military writer Polyaenus (*Strategemata* ii 31). Rhianus also composed poems on Achaea, Elis, and Thessaly, as if his ambition were to complete a panorama of what we may call the Dorian Heroic Age as opposed to the Achaean Heroic Age of Homer. A good discussion of Rhianus as a source for Messenian history is in L. Pearson, "The Pseudo-History of Messenia and Its Authors," *Historia* 11 (1962): 397–426.

8. The best study of Hellenistic historical epic is K. Ziegler, *Das Hellenistische Epos,* 2d ed. (Leipzig: Teubner, 1934, 1966), which should, however, be read with the critique of B. Otis, *Virgil: A Study in Civilized Poetry* (Oxford: Clarendon Press, 1964), pp. 396–98.

9. Tillyard, *English Epic,* p. 61. For Tillyard the *Argonautica* is no epic at all but an elegant romance. It is interesting that Longinus should seize on one of the "prettiest" pictures in the *Iliad,* Poseidon's chariot at xiii 18–29, and not, for example, the great epic moment when Hector bursts the gates at xii 457–66.

10. G. Zanker, *Realism in Alexandrian Poetry: A Literature and Its Audience* (London: Croom Helm, 1987), pp. 195–209, examines realism in the *Argonautica* and its impact on Apollonius' conception of the epic.

11. E.g. *Arg.* i 648 (apology for a digression), ii 844 (apology for neglect of ritual), iv 984 (apology for an unsavory story), and iv 445 (a curse on Love for inspiring the murder of Apsyrtus).

12. For this aspect of the narrator's presence in the narrative see the suggestive pages of C. R. Beye, *Epic and Romance in the Argonautica of Apollonius* (Carbondale, Ill.: Southern Illinois University Press, 1982), pp. 10–38.

13. For the idea of unity as used by classical critics see M. F. Heath, *Unity in Greek Poetics* (Oxford: Clarendon Press, 1989).

14. This is grandeur in a different sense from that intended by J. Garner: "The greatness of [the *Argonautica*] is that, in deconstructing the grand old myths, it seems true and, like those myths, gives us a sense of the grandeur of human life" (Beye, *Epic and Romance,* p. xi), like the pessimism that infects great historians.

15. A. M. Dale, introduction to *Euripides, Helen* (Oxford: Clarendon Press, 1967), p. ix.

16. Beye, *Epic and Romance,* pp. 169–75, has an account both of the lukewarm traditional assessments of Apollonius and more sympathetic views, to which add Hutchinson, *Hellenistic Poetry,* pp. 85–142.

Chapter 4: *Roman Historical Epic*

1. The best edition of *Annales,* with introduction and definitive commentary, is that by O. Skutsch (Oxford, Clarendon Press, 1985). Fragments of approximately 560 lines are extant.

2. Cicero, *Pro Flacco* 9, a startling instance of ethnic prejudice; cf. Virgil, *Aeneid* vi 847–53, and Juvenal, *Satires* iii 58–125, vi 185–99.

3. Quintilian, *Institutio Oratoria* x 1, 93. A better choice would have been the love elegy of Ovid and his predecessors.

4. Horace, *Odes* iii 30, 13 (Alcaeus and Sappho), *Epistulae* i 19, 23 (Archilochus); Propertius, ii 34, 66 (Callimachus), iv 1, 64; Virgil, *Eclogues* vi 1 (Theocritus), *Georgics* ii 174 (Hesiod).

5. O. Skutsch, *Studia Enniana* (London: Athlone Press, 1968), pp. 7–10.

6. *Altivolans,* "high-flying," 76; *induperator* for *imperator,* "commander," 78; and *propritim* for *propriatim,* "properly," 90. The rest would not be out of place in Augustan prose writing.

7. A commentator remarks of the "epics" of Claudian (c. A.D. 400), "It is hardly an exaggeration to say that all Claudian's major poems, epics no less than panegyrics and invectives, consist of little but a succession of speeches and descriptions." (A. Cameron, *Claudian: Poetry and Propaganda at the Court of Honorius* [Oxford: Clarendon Press, 1970], p. 262). Claudian's epics are recognizable by their "war" titles, *De Bello Gildonico, De Bello Getico,* etc.

8. The Ennian tradition of Latin verse, however, did produce one of literature's miracles, a genuinely didactic *poem,* Lucretius' *De Rerum Natura.* Epic in scale and epic in its earnest concern for its message, *De Rerum Natura* showed that Latin verse could be a successful vehicle for sustained exposition. The example can only have encouraged Virgil, who knew the poem intimately; see P. Hardie, *Virgil's Aeneid: Cosmos and Imperium* (Oxford, Clarendon Press, 1986), pp. 157–240.

9. Catullus' remarks on the *Annales* of Volusius (nos. 36 and 95) are not repeatable. He does not mention Varro.

Chapter 5: *Virgil*

THE LONG ROAD TO THE *AENEID*

1. Augustus, *Res Gestae* 1, 25, and 33. Augustus undercuts his protestations by his emphasis on imperialism and lavish expenditures.

2. Cassius Dio, *History* liii 17, 1. Dio's view is jaundiced by the eventual failure of the Augustan constitution and its degeneration into autocracy.

3. The point of the name Augustus is explained by Suetonius "on the ground that this was not only a new title but a more honorable one [than Romulus] because sacred places and anything consecrated by augural rites are called august" (*Divus Augustus* 7). Significantly Suetonius cites the Ennian line *Augusto augurio postquam incluta condita Roma est* (*Ann.* 155).

4. On buildings see *Ars Amatoria* i 67–90; on Romulus and the Sabine women see *ibid.* i 101–34, esp. 131–32; on games see *ibid.* i 213–28; on a golden age of Rome see *ibid.* iii 113–28. Nor can Ovid easily forget that the mother of Aeneas, and therefore ancestress of the Julii Caesares, was the goddess of love. For the social significance of his attitude see *Amores* i 15.

5. Lucretius ejected only as much of the poetical apparatus as his faith required; see Hardie, *Cosmos and Imperium*, pp. 169, 193–99. He wrote of the philosopher Epicurus where conventional poets invoked Apollo or the Muses.

6. Silenus' song (which I take to describe a single poem) is anticipated in the song of Orpheus in Apollonius, *Arg.* i 496–511, which moves from the creation to the birth of Zeus. For more discussion of the relation of the sixth *Eclogue* to the contemporary literary scene see D. O. Ross, *Backgrounds to Augustan Poetry* (Cambridge University Press, 1975), pp. 18–38.

7. A bibliography by N. Horsfall of work on the role of patronage in ancient literature is in *Classical Review* 38 (1988): 268. The important point is that literary protégés are not a special class but fulfill many of the normal duties of clients.

8. Varius Rufus wrote a panegyric on Augustus, thus taking the pressure off Horace, who responded with high praise (*Satires* i 10, 43; *Odes* i 6). Yet Virgil trusted Varius' taste well enough to make him a literary executor.

9. The literary world so decoded Virgil's language. Before 23 B.C. Propertius was announcing the birth of something "greater than the *Iliad*" (ii 34, 61–66) while still assuming that Augustus' victories would balance the mythological element.

THE *AENEID*

1. Translation based on that of H. R. Fairclough (Loeb Classical Library). The lines defy rendering into language as monumental as the Latin. In *Aen.* vi the contrast is drawn between Roman and Greek, but the same idea has already been expressed at *Aen.* i 263–64—Aeneas will crush the arrogant peoples of Latium and impose on them order and civic life—with an implied contrast between Roman and barbarian.

2. Livy's moral and religious preoccupations are analyzed by P. G. Walsh, *Livy: His Historical Aims and Methods* (Cambridge: Cambridge University Press, 1961), pp. 46–81. They coincide remarkably with those of Virgil.

3. It goes without saying that Virgil was well aware of the symbolism of Hercules; by a number of discreet and ingenious allusions, carefully examined by G. K. Galinsky, *The Hercules Theme* (Oxford: Blackwell, 1972), pp. 131–49, he usurps Hercules' symbolism for the benefit of his own hero. Aeneas' inner struggle, however, is Virgil's contribution to the theme.

4. The only account of Aeneas' wanderings besides that of Virgil is in the *Roman Antiquities* of Dionysius of Halicarnassus (i 49–53, 55–60, 64–65), which omits the detour to Carthage.

5. Strictly speaking the sack of Troy (*Aen.* ii) is not Homeric either, being derived from the cyclic epic *Iliupersis;* but that work was Homeric in character, if not in quality. Stesichorus' lyric version of the story would also have been known to Virgil. The cycle (viz. *Aethiopis*) also provided him with an Amazon, Camilla (*Aen.* xi 498–835).

6. The denseness of Virgil's use of Homeric elements is not easily apprehended without the help of an apparatus such as the appendixes to G. N. Knauer, *Die Aeneis und Homer* (Göttingen: Vandenhoeck und Rupprecht, 1964); for *Aen.* i 1–250 Knauer cites 261 parallels ranging from half-lines to whole scenes.

7. F. Cairns, *Virgil's Augustan Epic* (Cambridge, Cambridge University Press, 1989), argues that the *Aeneid* is a Romanized *Odyssey* with

Iliadic insertions. Note, however, the second proemium (vii 37–44), which clearly marks a new start and a new theme (*horrida bella*).

8. This is the thesis of R. R. Schlunk, *The Homeric Scholia and the Aeneid* (Ann Arbor: University of Michigan Press, 1974).

9. For the evolution of ethics (i.e. Greek ethics) from the competitive Homeric code to the relatively civilized attitudes of the late classical and Hellenistic periods see A. W. H. Adkins, *Merit and Responsibility* (Oxford: Clarendon Press, 1960). It was not easy for the poetry of action to keep up with these developments.

10. Lucretius' proemium (*De Rerum Natura* i 1–43) is an outstanding instance of an unbeliever demythologizing the traditional poetical apparatus—and mythologizing it again to suit his own purposes. Virgil's situation, though it may not be so readily apprehended, is not much different from that of the Catholic Camões in the sixteenth century; in the Portuguese epic the Olympians are turned into symbols of the attributes of God.

11. Sir James Frazer took the horrid ritual of the Rex Nemorensis at Aricia as the starting point of his research into classical anthropology in *The Golden Bough* (1890). Virgil omits the primitive, aboriginal elements of the cult—the priest was murdered by his successor—in favor of a Hellenizing fable. A primitive feature, the exclusion of women, is likewise cut out of Virgil's account of the Ara Maxima (*Aen.* viii 102–279).

12. *Magne Cato* at *Aen.* vi 841, to judge by his epithet and the company he keeps in the passage, refers to the elder Cato (Cato the Censor, 234–149 B.C.), not to the republican hero who, however, receives a mention at viii 670.

13. The resonances of the poet's diction can hardly ever be reproduced in translation, even when the second language has a recognized poetical style. In its context the plain and ordinary character of Juno's Latin at *Aen.* vii 293–322 gives a distinct impression of spite. See also R. O. A. M. Lyne, *Words and the Poet* (Oxford: Clarendon Press, 1989).

14. The rendering is that of John Dryden (1697). Dryden's translation of Virgil does not enjoy the fame of Pope's translations of Homer, but like the latter it is done in a legitimate, vital heroic style that gives it a conviction modern versions seem (to me, at least) to lack. On this important aspect of translation consult H. A. Mason, *To Homer through Pope* (London: Chatto and Windus, 1972). Virgil's

lines should be compared with Statius' description of Tisiphone at *Thebaid* i 88–113, where all the horrors are made explicit.

15. Otis, *Virgil*, pp. 41–96.

16. On the third book and other unrevised sections see Otis,*Virgil*, pp. 415–20, and Gordon Williams, *Technique and Ideas in the Aeneid* (New Haven: Yale University Press, 1983), pp. 262–78.

17. One may compare the fatuity of Cicero's proposed introduction of the god Apollo into his self-laudatory epic *De Temporibus Meis* to prophesy Cn. Piso's humiliating return from his province (*Ad Quintum Fratrem* iii 1).

18. Thus it was the thesis of V. Pöschl (*The Art of Virgil*, transl. G. Seligson [Ann Arbor: University of Michigan Press, 1962], p. 153) that Turnus is, and is intended to be, a sympathetic character. Like Hector, Turnus has an honorable cause; like Lucan's Caesar or Milton's Satan, he may have fascinated his creator. But in fact Turnus' war is wrong, and Virgil has said so (*Aen.* vii 583–84); cf. the impression made on Tibullus, *barbare Turne* (ii 5, 48).

19. It is worth noting that Augustus' aims and legislation are unoriginal. Cicero (who always swam with the tide) had outlined the program of regeneration to Julius Caesar twenty years before Augustus took it up; see Cicero, *Pro Marcello* 23.

20. This is the theme of W. R. Johnson, *Darkness Visible: A Study of Vergil's Aeneid* (Berkeley and Los Angeles: University of California Press, 1976), esp. pp. 135–54. It is a tribute to the *Aeneid* that few works on the poem are received with general acclaim. The relatively old book of Otis, *Virgil*, remains one of the most interesting. A. J. Boyle, *The Chaonian Dove: Studies in the Eclogues, Georgics, and Aeneid of Virgil*, Mnemosyne Supplement 94 (Leiden: Brill, 1986), is a good expression of the "conservative" position. Hardie, *Cosmos and Imperium*, and Cairns, *Virgil's Augustan Epic*, are indispensable for the study of the poet's "ideology" and public voice. For the private voice see R. O. A. M. Lyne, *Further Voices in Vergil's Aeneid* (Oxford: Clarendon Press, 1987), and Susan F. Wiltshire, *Public and Private in Vergil's Aeneid* (Amherst: University of Massachusetts Press, 1989). Quinn, *Virgil's Aeneid*, and Williams, *Technique and Ideas*, give an excellent overview of the poem. Good criticism will also be found in two volumes of essays, R. A. Cardwell and J. Hamilton, eds., *Virgil in a Cultural Tradition: Essays to Celebrate the Bimillennium* (Nottingham: University of Nottingham, 1986), and J.

D. Bernard, ed., *Virgil at 2000: Commemorative Essays on the Poet and His Influence* (New York: A. M. S. Press, 1986).

AFTER VIRGIL

1. Cicero's worst fears (see above, p. 86) were confirmed: see T. P. Wiseman, *Catullus and His World* (Cambridge: Cambridge University Press, 1985), pp. 15–19, or J. Griffin, *Latin Poets and Roman Life* (London: Duckworth, 1985), pp. 1–31.

2. Ovid, *Amores* i 15. The joke is that poets (by the usual confusion of literary and real personas) were thought ipso facto to be *desidiosi,* "indolent dropouts."

3. For the view that Antony lived out the fantasies of literature see Griffin, *Latin Poets,* pp. 32–47.

4. The prime reference is Propertius iii 5: he will abandon love poetry and the way of life supposed to go with it and at the appropriate time attempt the composition of a didactic poem in the manner of Lucretius' *De Rerum Natura.*

5. Notwithstanding his appearance in Apollonius and Virgil, Cupid is an unheroic god; moreover, he is the god of elegy, who forbad Ovid to compose epic hexameters in *Amores* i 1. His prominence is a symbol of Ovid's mingling of the genres.

6. A lapidary discussion of the effect of Ovidian and Virgilian metrics is in B. Otis, *Ovid as an Epic Poet,* 2d ed. (Cambridge: Cambridge University Press, 1970), pp. 74–77: for details consult G. E. Duckworth, *Vergil and Classical Hexameter Poetry* (Ann Arbor: University of Michigan Press, 1969).

7. The best discussion of Ovid's gods is still L. P. Wilkinson, *Ovid Recalled* (Cambridge: Cambridge University Press, 1956), pp. 190–203; more briefly see Otis, *Ovid as an Epic Poet* pp. 56–58.

8. It is instructive to compare the speech of Jupiter here (*Met.* i 182–98) with the parody of Augustus in Seneca, *Apocolocyntosis* 10.

9. This is the thesis argued, for example, by R. Coleman, "Structure and Intention in the *Metamorphoses,*" *CQ* 21 (1971): 461–77; but see the discussion by G. K. Galinsky, *Ovid's "Metamorphoses"* (Oxford: Blackwell, 1975), pp. 14–25. Galinsky rightly protests at the tendency to categorize the poem as necessarily either epic or antiepic.

10. Ovid's "Aeneid" (*Met.* xiii 623–xiv 608) cannot avoid touching on the major episodes of Virgil's *Aeneid,* but refuses to treat them

on the same scale; Dido's story is told in eight lines (xiv 74–81) and Aeneas' descent to the underworld in twenty-one (xiv 101–21).

11. See C. P. Segal, "Myth and Philosophy in the *Metamorphoses*," *AJPh* 90 (1969): 278–89, for a full discussion of Pythagoras' discourse.

12. Otis, *Ovid as an Epic Poet*, pp. 93, 129, 168, 278, endeavours to set out the major structures, but his groupings often override the book divisions, which at this period are surely significant. Ovid groups stories according to various principles—family, region, contrast—anything that will allow his onward momentum; cf. J. S. Solodow, *The World of Ovid's "Metamorphoses"* (Chapel Hill: University of North Carolina Press, 1988), pp. 9–36.

13. According to Otis, Ovid moves through the theme of the gods as comic figures to that of the gods as avengers, thence to the pathos of love and the destiny of Rome. Insofar as parts of the poem have topics (rather than themes) in common, that is the result of the chronological arrangement.

14. For the notorious ambiguity of the Roman episodes (Books xiv–xv), whether they are pro-Augustan, anti-Augustan, or (as is likely) neither, see Otis, *Ovid as an Epic Poet*, pp. xiii, 351, and Galinsky, *Ovid's "Metamorphoses,"* pp. 210–17.

15. Most criticism of the *Metamorphoses* has been concerned (as this chapter necessarily has been) with its relation to the epic form and idea. For a brief study of the poem as the realization, in a hugely expanded way, of a Hellenistic minor genre, the catalog poem based on a cosmogony (see above, p. 92), see P. E. Knox, *Ovid's "Metamorphoses" and the Tradition of Augustan Poetry* (Cambridge: Cambridge Philological Society, 1986).

Chapter 6: *Lucan and Flavian Epic*

THE BELLUM CIVILE

1. Ovid lists Marsus, Rabirius, Macer, Pedo, Carus, Severus, the two Prisci, Montanus, Sabinus, Largus, Camerinus, Tuscus, Marius, Trinacrius, Lupus, and Tuticanus. Cornelius Severus was held in some regard by Quintilian (*Institutio Oratoria* x 1, 89); a fragment (Seneca, *Suasoriae* 6, 26) on the death of Cicero would not be unworthy of Lucan: Pedo was not without gifts; the rest are unknown to history, or deserve to be.

2. That verse was synonymous with a boring rehash of mythology was the constant complaint of the satirists: Persius i 34, 69–75, 92–106; Martial x 4; Juvenal i 1, vii 53–92.

3. The younger Helvidius Priscus was executed by Domitian c. A.D. 93 for supposedly satirizing the emperor's divorce through the myth of Paris' desertion of Oenone (Suetonius, *Domitianus* 10). Statius, who has much to say about Eteocles, was careful to avoid any allusion to the famous lines from Euripides' tragedy on the sons of Oedipus: "If crime must be, then were it best to sin / To gain a throne, and let the rest be clean" (*Phoenissae* 524–25). The general intellectual atmosphere of the Silver Age and Lucan's response to it is well discussed by G. Williams, *Change and Decline* (Berkeley and Los Angeles: University of California Press, 1978), esp. pp. 161–92.

4. By A.D. 64 Nero's regime was on the defensive. But Lucan was a prolific writer, and his immediate offense may well have been his declamation on the great fire of Rome (an act of imperial arson, it was alleged): see F. M. Ahl, *Lucan: An Introduction* (Ithaca: Cornell University Press, 1976), pp. 333–53. But Nero was sensitive to literary affronts: he exiled Cornutus for criticizing his artistic projects (Dio lxii 29, 2).

5. The ancient scholiasts were willing to believe that "shining aslant" was a comment on Nero's defective eyesight, and Ahl, *Lucan,* p. 30, supposes that the axis-toppling weight of the deified Nero (weight was a normal attribute of divinities) was an insulting allusion to the emperor's corpulence.

6. Tacitus, *Annales* i 13, 7. Haterius was admittedly of a servile nature (cf. *Annales* iii 57, 3) and Tiberius disliked such demonstrations (Suetonius, *Tiberius* 27). Literary groveling was not unknown under Augustus: see Propertius iv 6 and Ovid, *Tristia* ii.

7. Observe also the ostentatiously topical allusions in the *Bellum Civile:* Caledonios Britannos, vi 68; the Stoic cataclysm, i 72–80; and the ice-bound Euxine, v 436–41.

8. Fronto, *Epistulae* 189 (2:105 in the Loeb edition). Fronto represents the chaste antiquarian taste of the second century A.D. Seneca was sometimes blamed for the corruption of style in the Neronian period, a manner that was already condemned by Quintilian (*Institutio Oratoria* xii 10, 73–80): he preferred the bland style of Valerius Flaccus.

9. Lucan's similes are listed by W. E. Heitland in C. E. Haskins' edition of the *Bellum Civile,* entitled M. *Annaei Lucani Pharsalia* (London: Bell, 1887), pp. lxxxiv–xc. Heitland's essay represents the conventional, and hostile, assessment of Lucan's achievement.

10. Note the opposite situation in the work of Statius. There the gods are overworked and the role of Fortune minimized.

11. Lucan (*Bell. Civ.* viii 858, 872) avers that Pompey's tomb will eclipse the shrines of Jupiter—and, of course, the altars of the deified Caesar.

12. Caesar's own account of the battle may be read in his *Bellum Civile* iii 88–99. He alleges that the Pompeians were overconfident of victory and too fond of their comfort; as for his address to the troops, they were entertained with protests of innocence and a detailed account of his negotiations to preserve the peace (iii 90).

13. Hardly less overdrawn is Lucan's depiction of virtue. The characterization of Cato as the joyless Stoic sage (*Bell. Civ.* ii 380–91) cannot be read without a smile.

14. The genre of the *Bellum Civile* perplexed even Lucan's contemporaries. Martial (xiv 194) seems to imply that the work is poetry only because it is verse. In medieval curricula Lucan is usually classed as a historian; Joseph Scaliger called him a rhetorician. Commentators who had read Aristotle and Tasso, such as P. Burmann in his edition of 1740, diagnosed the trouble as the choice of a subject too close to the poet's own time. For a modern assessment see M. P. O. Morford, *The Poet Lucan* (Oxford: Blackwell, 1967). Morford attempts to rehabilitate Lucan by relating his work to the poetical and rhetorical conventions of his time.

AFTER LUCAN

1. The references are to Quintilian, *Institutio Oratoria* xii 10, 11–12 (the orators), x 1, 87–92 (the epicists), x 1, 90 (Lucan).

2. For this judgment see Pliny, *Epistulae* iii 7. German scholarship has been kinder to Silius; see J. Küpper, *Tantarum Causas Irarum: Untersuchungen zur einleitenden Bücherdyade der "Punica" des Silius Italicus* (Berlin: de Gruyter, 1986). Silius and the other Flavian epic poets used their Virgil as Virgil had used his Homer, to enrich their style and mark their allegiance.

3. This violent verdict on Statius' *Thebaid* was passed by Greene, *Descent from Heaven*, p. 101: for a more considered assessment see D. Vessey, *Statius and the Thebaid* (Cambridge: Cambridge University Press, 1973).

4. Claudian is well served by Cameron, *Claudian*. Neither Quintus Smyrnaeus nor Nonnus has been thought worthy of extensive literary study in English. What might be done for Quintus is

shown by R. Schmiel's brief study, "The Amazon Queen: Quintus of Smyrna Book I," *Phoenix* 40 (1986): 185–94.

5. Nonnus' language is the verbal equivalent of the preciosity of contemporary plastic art. It is the quantity of his virtuosity that impedes its appreciation; cf. M. Roberts, *The Jeweled Style: Poetry and Poetics in Late Antiquity* (Ithaca: Cornell University Press, 1989).

6. Criticism of Prudentius has tended to concentrate on his hymns rather than on his epic/didactic poem, the *Psychomachia* (Battle for the soul). Even in the hymns, however, he relied on models in mythology, as shown by M. A. Malamud, *A Poetics of Transformations: Prudentius and Classical Mythology* (Ithaca: Cornell University Press, 1989). Some of the stylistic problems he confronted are explored in A.-M. Palmer, *Prudentius and the Martyrs in the "Peristephanon"* (Oxford: Clarendon Press, 1988).

7. The efforts of the Carolingian renaissance were hampered by the collapse of the narrative style in late Latin literature and the blending of epic with panegyric; see P. Godman, *Poets and Emperors: Frankish Politics and Carolingian Poetry* (Oxford: Clarendon Press, 1987), especially 12–37. Contemporary pious paraphrases of Scripture (on which see M. Roberts, *Biblical Epic and Rhetorical Paraphrases in Late Antiquity* [Liverpool: Cairns, 1985], pp. 61–106) do not transmit the classical tradition.

8. For classical influences on *Beowulf* see T. M. Andersson, *Early Epic Scenery: Homer, Virgil and the Medieval Legacy* (Ithaca: Cornell University Press, 1976), pp. 145–59.

9. The Latin *Waltharius* (c. A.D. 930) in Leonine hexameters is related to the Old English *Waldere* fragments, but this marriage of Latin and the vernacular heroic lay was unproductive.

Chapter 7: *The Form of Epic*

RE-FORMING THE EPIC

1. The determination of the Renaissance to reflect on its inheritance is the subject of three indispensable books: G. Highet, *The Classical Tradition: Greek and Roman Influences on Western Literature* (Oxford: Clarendon Press, 1949); E. R. Curtius, *European Literature and the Latin Middle Ages*, trans. W. R. Trask (London: Routledge, 1953); and R. R. Bolgar, *The Classical Heritage and Its Beneficiaries* (Cambridge: Cambridge University Press, 1954).

2. *Africa* ix 92–98. Important citations from Petrarch are given by Tillyard, *English Epic*, pp. 186–92.

3. Dante's linguistic theory is described by W. D. Elcock, *The Romance Languages* (London: Faber, 1960), pp. 455–58. Adam conversed with Eve in Hebrew, of course, but the linguistic unity of their descendants was shattered at the Tower of Babel. The result of Babel, according to Dante, was the three European linguistic groups, and the Romance group fragmented in Italy into fourteen dialects. It is astonishing that having got so far, and having recognized that languages evolve, Dante did not perceive the ancestral status of Latin in the Romance area.

4. For the Italian critics see Tillyard, *English Epic*, pp. 222–33. Translated selections from these critics are in A. H. Gilbert, *Literary Criticism: Plato to Dryden* (1940; repr. Detroit: Wayne State University Press, 1962). Criticism elsewhere in Europe was largely dependent on the Italians, even in France, where the passion for rules was greatest. A good brief account of the development of French epic theory is in R. A. Sayce, *The French Biblical Epic in the Seventeenth Century* (Oxford: Clarendon Press, 1955), pp. 6–26.

5. Biblical epic might almost qualify as a subclass of the genre. It is best known, if it is known at all, from the four books of Abraham Cowley's unfinished *Davideis* (1656); there is a handy critique of this dull work in Greene, *Descent*, pp. 366–70. The home of the biblical epic was seventeenth-century France, where it shared the literary honors with poetical histories of the wars of Alaric and Clovis; see Sayce, *French Biblical Epic*.

6. After working on the *Discorsi* Tasso revised *Gerusalemme Liberata*, lengthening it to twenty-four cantos and omitting some romantic episodes (Olindo and Sofronia, Erminia among the shepherds). Despite Tasso's claims the revision, *Gerusalemme Conquista*, was not a great success.

7. *The Reason of Church Government*, Book ii, in *The Complete Prose Works of John Milton*, ed. D. M. Wolfe (New Haven: Yale University Press, 1953), 1:813. The more bloodthirsty parts of the Old Testament crossed the minds of others; cf. Cowley's unfinished *Davideis*. The Wars of the Roses provided minor English poets with heroics yet more Homeric in style.

8. Hence the Miltonic verse of some modern epyllia, such as Keats' *Hyperion*, Tennyson's *Idylls of the King*, and the "epics" of

Swinburne. An extreme example is the marginal commentary that Coleridge supplied to the *Ancient Mariner* to assimilate his poem to the edited versions of genuine narrative ballads.

AFTER MILTON

1. For this aspect of *Paradise Lost* see D. H. Burden, *The Logical Epic: A Study of the Argument of Paradise Lost* (London: Routledge and Kegan Paul, 1967).

2. There are many studies of Milton's Latinized diction and the other ways in which he recasts English into the likeness of Virgil's diction. One of the clearest brief statements is still that of C. Day Lewis, *Introduction to Paradise Lost* (Oxford: Oxford University Press, 1942). For Milton's originality see C. Martindale, *John Milton and the Transformation of Ancient Epic* (London: Routledge and Kegan Paul, 1986).

3. That avid book buyer, diarist, and man-about-town, Samuel Pepys, quite fails to mention the first publication of *Paradise Lost* in 1667.

4. The poet and wit Paul Scarron practically invented the burlesque style. His *Virgile Travesti* was published between 1648 and 1658.

5. Cf. Bernstein, *Tale of the Tribe.*

6. S. Koljević, *Epic in the Making* (Oxford: Clarendon Press, 1980), p. 24. Koljević is characterizing specifically the Kosovo cycle of South Slavic heroic poetry, but the same could be said of any well-developed tradition.

7. Sentimental heroic verse, e.g. Tennyson's *Revenge* or Browning's *Hervé Riel* or *Ride to Aix,* has no significant connection with neoclassical epic. Apart from the content the outer form, essential to any sentimental genre, is distinct.

8. Author's preface to *Joseph Andrews.* Fielding's purpose was to distance his work from vulgar romances, "which contain very little instruction or entertainment."

9. Cf. R. F. Christian, *Tolstoy's "War and Peace": A Study* (Oxford: Oxford University Press, 1962).

General Index

Index Locorum

Compositor: Metro Typography
Text: 10/12 Goudy Old Style
Display: Goudy Old Style
Printer: Braun-Brumfield, Inc.
Binder: Braun-Brumfield, Inc.